The Heyday of Muncie, Indiana

The Heyday of Muncie, Indiana

Joy Charlene Henley

Copyright © 2020 Joy Charlene Henley

All rights reserved. Created in the United States of America. No part of this book may be reproduced or transmitted in any form without the written permission of the author.

ISBN: 978-0-578-72089-0

Dedication

For the victims and families, entertainers and crew and everyone affected by the stage collapse at the Indiana State Fair in Indianapolis, Indiana, on August 13, 2011.

The frenzy and horror that ensued would demonstrate the utmost humanity. Onlookers risked their own lives- running toward the stage to help others- instead of running from it.

The world witnessed love, courage, strength, and compassion beyond measure. This is the true Hoosier Spirit... there is no finer example.

Table of Contents

Dedication	ii
Preface	vi
Acknowledgments	x
Chapter 1- No Holding Back, I Am Going Home	1
Chapter 2- Driving Into the Past	7
Chapter 3- The Telling Moment	16
Chapter 4- Through a Child's Eyes of Wonder	24
Chapter 5- Seems Like Yesterday	42
Chapter 6- Anthony	60
Chapter 7- We Lived to Tell About It	72
Chapter 8- Feminine Wiles	85
Chapter 9- Near-Death	94
Chapter 10- Groovy Things	117
Chapter 11- Superstars!	127
Chapter 12 -The Boob Tube with Rabbit Ears and Rooftop Antennas	144
Chapter 13- Actress Kathy Garver Dishes on the Hit CBS Show, Family Affair	171
Chapter 14- Magic in the Air	175
Chapter 15- What was Happening Out at WERK Radio?	191
Chapter 16- Our Betty Harris	207
Chapter 17- The Secret Ingredient in the Ball Stores Chocolate Cake	213
Chapter 18- It is About More Than Cornfields	233
Chapter 19- 50 Things to Love and Do in Muncie	244
Chapter 20- 50 Ways to Help "Create" a Heyday for the Child(ren) You Love	253
Chapter 21- God Gave Us Memory so That We Might Have Roses in December	262
Picture Index	279

Preface

The very word, "heyday" is an oldie but goodie. It has been around since at least the year 1590, and today is considered an outdated word. So, welcome back to the word, the era, feelings, and memories.

The heyday in one's life was the ultimate time! Life was in its prime or at the height of power or influence. It seemed at its peak with great success, popularity, and vigor. A heyday can refer to the spirit of a city, the ideas, and beliefs of the day. Indeed, there was "something in the air!" It was most likely when jobs were plentiful, family units were more intact, and children basked in creative play. Wherever your heyday occurred, life seemed to be in sync and flowed.

When you awakened, it was instantly a bright morning! Pictures you colored as a child had the sun in the upper corner. The birds sang a bit louder. Your bike leaned by the front door next to the milk box with some colored chalk scribblings on the cracked sidewalk. The world was yours, and every day, you could not wait to get outside and tackle it! The American Dream lingered out on the horizon.

Hometowns, each of us has one. Whether you are familiar with my hometown of Muncie, Indiana, or you have never been there in your life, you are in for a treat! Perhaps you grew up in the approximate 1960s era and will see yourself within these pages. Or you are curious about the period in which your parents or grandparents lived. It was a once-in-a-lifetime season. We probably could not recreate the social behaviors, coming-of-age scenarios, and the sometimes-startling way of life if we tried.

What is it about my hometown of Muncie, Indiana, that is so special? What is it about yours? Have you ever thought about what makes you smile when you look back? What do you remember years or decades later? Why do you remember it, and how has it impacted your life today?

In the heyday, many recall a dynamic music scene that seemed to have an undercurrent all its own. In my hometown, it seemed every teenager was either in a rock band or following one. WERK-AM 990 radio on-air personalities Larry McCabe, Bill Shirk, and a relatively unknown, Ball State University college student named David Letterman, reached celebrity status and reigned supreme as they spun the hits.

Muncie was alive and booming in the 1960s. Often referred to as "Middletown," it was described as an average or typical, small American city. Muncie was a factory manufacturing land where families thrived, and communities were strong.

Why reminisce? It can make us feel stable, laugh, cry, and combat feelings of depression and loneliness. In other words, it can be uplifting to our emotional happiness. A look back at the yesteryear priorities and values instilled in us can provide a sense of well-being of who we are today.

Jerry M. Burger, Ph.D., is a Professor of Psychology at Santa Clara University. He interviewed people who made trips "home," and their stories are presented in his book, *Returning Home: Reconnecting with Our Childhoods* (Rowman & Littlefield). His comments appeared in a *Psychology Today* article titled "You Can Go Home Again, and Maybe You Should."

He has concluded, "My surveys tell me that roughly one-third of all American adults over the age of 30 have made such a trip. These individuals aren't necessarily interested in seeing the people from their past. Rather, they visit the houses, apartments, playgrounds, schools, neighborhoods, parks, and other places that once made up the landscape of their childhood. The majority of people who make a trip to see a former home select a place they lived in during their elementary school years (ages 5 to 12)." Dr. Burger and his team learned to have a box of tissues handy as one in five people cried when talking about their childhood homes.

Many of the people interviewed brought photographs of their homes to share, much like parents showing off pictures of their children. The most common reason people return to a childhood home is to re-establish a psychological link between the child in the black-and-white photographs and the person they are today.

People placed in the second category used the visit to help them deal with personal issues they were facing at the time.

People in the third category visited a childhood home to take care of unfinished business. Most of the people in the latter group did not have happy childhoods.

If you have been thinking about visiting your childhood home, Dr. Burger, who has made the journey, suggests you just do it.

I created this book for six primary reasons:

To demonstrate the power of faith

To encourage you to pursue your dreams

To support businesses that may bring jobs to my hometown, which will feed families

To promote the benefits and effects of nostalgia and the belief, it can have a similar effect as an escape or "anti-depressant"

To share the importance of closure and peace that comes from returning "home" just one more time

To bring a smile to our faces in a too hectic, struggling world

This journey is intentionally described in a rather simple way. You see, life was simple back in the day. So many of the chapters and times of our lives did not contain stress and drama. This, my friend, is the appeal. We did not require extravagances, and we were content with elemental blessings.

Just like in the heyday, black and white pictures are part of the story. Had they been featured in color in the printed version of this book, the printing price could significantly increase the cost of the book. There were efforts to keep the cost low.

How awesome are we? Well, we survived without high-tech gadgets, and we could not possibly imagine a thing called Google. Our way to dig deep for information for that dreaded class assignment was to head to the library. Believe it or not, the ho-hum of facing a day of boredom and the anticipation of going outside to "go play" as mom and dad ordered us to do, always had its rewards. Fresh air, sunshine, exercise, meeting new friends, and being sociable were significant parts of our lives. The simplicity was so grand that many of us have spent our entire adult lives trying to recapture it. Through these pages, you will better understand why. For many, childhood was a happy time in life. It is not to say or assume every person had a wonderful childhood, and family situations were ideal. For some, it can be difficult or downright painful to look back, and it is vital to acknowledge and respect this. Heydays often happen before the despair of disappointment, unrequited love, family turmoil- with problems and outcomes that were unimaginable, divorce, and the sorrow of tragedy and loss. In other words, before life blew our innocent world to smithereens. It is profound that nostalgia is usually associated with positive emotions- even when the trigger for recalling a memory is negative. Some people leap from childhood to adulthood sooner than others- depending on life experiences, circumstances, and coping skills. Many of us retreated to the shadows of young dreams – eventually wrapped in layers of life experience.

Whenever we decided to take the plunge into adulthood, we were eager to cross the bridge to a greener pasture. It is a rare person who will not look back. Like a precious child who visits and often leaves a doll or other adored possession behind, it can be comforting to leave pieces of our heart in cherished places.

So, kick off your shoes, grab a Cream Soda, put your feet up on that hassock and come on a journey with me! You see, Muncie is calling this child's name.

She was a curious, playful girl who would skip and run against the wind one moment and admire the most colorful tulips on the planet, the next! Once upon a time, she had big dreams of becoming a social worker or a writer, well, maybe a nurse or singer...actually a ballerina!

Welcome to my subjective stroll into yesteryear. What would happen on my journey would be unexpected and life-changing, as I would soon discover.

Acknowledgments

Jim Willhight for being a Production and Publishing Extraordinaire

Rod McClure for making the initial cover idea of polka dots and innocence come alive

Roger Overbey for creatively telling so many stories through the camera lens and sharing his legendary expertise

Nora Mullins for her contagious enthusiasm and positive thinking when needed most

Carol Towle for her generosity in too many ways to count

1 The beautiful White River in Muncie, Indiana

I will get old.

You will get old.

But I will still look in your eyes the way I looked

at them when we were young.

Author Unknown

Chapter 1

No Holding Back, I Am Going Home

"What's for dinner, mom?" It was such a common question for a heyday youngster. Sometimes we lucked out with cheeseburgers, delicious frozen TV dinners or soup, and sandwiches. Or occasionally, we had breakfast for dinner. Scrambled eggs with ketchup and sizzling bacon at 6:00 p.m. on a weeknight, at first, seemed odd but quickly became the occasional norm. We fetched the TV trays, the family moseyed into the living room, said grace, dined, and watched some *I Love Lucy*.

Other times luck was not on our side when mom adjusted her frilly apron and announced we were having her Ham and Banana Surprise. When those bananas wrapped in thin, ham slices with Hollandaise sauce were on the menu, I usually would not be setting an extra place at the table for a friend. Who wanted *this*?

Sometimes, mom would mix three cans of Spaghetti-Os with plain gelatin in a round mold to create her Macaroni and Cheese Gelatin Cake Ring. The tops of Vienna Sausages were glazed with ketchup.

Children knew the rules – either eat or be hungry. We were famished from after-school play. There was no saving mom's hideous Mixed Vegetable, and Celery flavored JELL-O, though. Those taste buds could sure take a beating at times.

Saturday mornings made up for it, though. A familiar ritual involved scurrying to the TV in pajamas and turning on cartoons. Whether we climbed up on the kitchen counter to get our sugared cereal, mom waited with Pop-Tarts or a piping bowl of Cream of Wheat topped with a scoop of ice cream; the fun was about to begin!

Whether you call it the good old days, back in the day or yesteryear, certain scenes, emotions, and even flavors still linger from that time. So often throughout my life, I have mumbled, "If we could only go back." It was usually a passing, somewhat negative thought as if to imply it would be impossible to do. What is it that prevents us from taking it a step further and returning to where our heyday occurred? Of course, I can never again sit as a teen with my grandmother on a Saturday night and watch her *Perry Mason* or *Mannix* episodes. I still, though, yearn for the time when life moved a bit slower. Or when I could laugh at a corny joke, and it was so hysterical, I could not stop.

I anticipated returning to the Hoosier State throughout my adult life. I attended the original Muncie Central High School at 311 South High Street, through my sophomore year in 1970, then graduated from high school and college in a Seattle suburb.

I yearned to see the childhood home my parents built, sit on the playground of my elementary school, and aimlessly wander downtown. I could go anywhere in the world, but "Hoosier" always flowed through my veins.

Life somehow swept me away through a whirlwind of years, which plunged me into a world of single parenting, challenges, and struggles. We know life has a way of doing this.

Still, I kept in contact with many Muncie friends, looked at pictures of the city on the Internet, and frequently read the local newspaper online.

I knew one day I would return. I just did not plan on circumstances such as the economy and personal issues forcing me to do so.

There are many reasons why one would leave their Pacific Northwest home after 39 years and go on such an adventure; for closure, to confront unresolved childhood issues, visit family and friends, a high school reunion, to care for an ill relative, or to get back in touch with one's self.

In October of 2008, a Friday before lunchtime, I was notified at work to clean out my desk. Due to the economy, layoffs were necessary. It was time to take a closer look at my circumstances. For several years, I had felt a "nudge" or luring to return to Muncie. It was more than a mere "nudge" now. I had to do *something*! Living in a high cost of living state was just no longer feasible. In the spur of the moment, I pondered, why not go where the cost of living is much less?

Immediately after the layoff, I searched for cities with low costs of living. The search included my hometown. Unfortunately, I kept delaying action, hoping things would turn around, and I could get back on my feet. You do this when you believe in miracles. You also do it when you do not want to leave your family. It was humbling to need help and even more humbling to be forced to ask for it. As a social worker for many years, I was the one desperate people often came to see for resources, assistance, and hope. I was the one who usually sat on the giving side of the desk.

The Heyday of Muncie, Indiana

So, I spent the summer of 2009 trying to stay financially afloat, wallowing in crisis, having a bit of a "pity party" and faking smiles to friends. Trust me, it is not emotionally healthy. It was unlike me to not have goals and approaches to reach them. I laughed at the irony that it had not always been financially possible to return to my hometown, yet I was in a financial crunch contemplating going there.

I reasoned, perhaps the current time was a perfect time. It was the end of summer so I could stay in Muncie until the following spring, and then if things did not work out, I could return to Seattle.

My son Justin grew up hearing about Muncie and had also searched info online about it. He slowly began to grow interested in my Muncie hype. Justin was 21 at the time and agreed to go with me. An added plus was that he could share the driving. He had never resided anywhere but the Pacific Northwest.

Muncie was a world away from the glitz and glamour of dazzling lights in Seattle. A nagging thought hit me like a ton of bricks... *Is 55 too old to do this?* Friends lovingly added to my hesitancy by saying they would be scared to death even to consider such a trip. Of course, they emphasized they were telling me this because they care. Thank you, I think. I reasoned I was a woman of middle-aged wisdom (or so I liked to believe), I was a planner, a risk-taker and I was daring, so these traits entered into the fantasy to just drive off into the sunset.

Most of us have confronted challenges, and it can be stressful. It can be easy to procrastinate even when we know we need to make a change. They say a crisis can be a positive or a turning point. Crisis or not, it can be downright challenging to step out of our comfort zone in any circumstance. To do so can require tremendous courage, planning, and energy. Sometimes we must dig deep to find our strengths, especially if we have been beaten up by life, and the emotional reserves are approaching empty.

Some people adapt to change better than others, which is also a factor. Having been a single parent for many years, I was familiar with working two jobs and a 60-hour week. I could usually handle sleep deprivation and go with the flow. I knew, deep down inside, that we could do the 2200+ mile drive.

Throughout my life, people have asked me if I felt extraordinary growing up in such a famous place as Muncie. After all, Muncie – the county seat of Delaware County, was labeled a typical American city in the United States. *The Middletown Studies* were sociological case studies of residents of the City of Muncie, conducted by Robert Staughton Lynd and Helen Merrell Lynd, husband and wife. Their studies were the focus of *Middletown: A Study*

Joy Charlene Henley

in Modern American Culture, published in 1929 and *Middletown in Transition: A Study in Cultural Conflicts*, published in 1937.

The word "Middletown" suggests the average or typical American small city. The Lynds were followed by numerous other sociologists and agencies, making Muncie one of the most studied communities in the world.

The County derived its name from the Delaware Indians, an Eastern tribe that was slowly pushed into Ohio and finally settled in east-central Indiana during the 1770s. The Delaware Indians established several towns along the White River, among these Munseetown or Muncey Town, because so many Delaware Indians of the Munsee clan lived there.

It was from this town that the present-day Muncie was named. Munseetown, as it was initially known, incorporated in 1865. By 1900, the population had grown to nearly 50,000 people- 20,000 of whom resided in Muncie. Muncie had earned its nickname the "Magic City" because the city grew like magic. Looking back, I never really saw Muncie as extraordinary. I just believed every child lived in such splendor. Muncie superbly captured the zeitgeist of the 1960s.

My Indiana hometown is approximately 60 miles northeast of the State Capital, Indianapolis. Some nearby cities are Anderson, Chesterfield, Cowan, Daleville, Eaton, Elwood, Farmland, Fairmount, Fishers, Frankton, Gaston, Hartford City, Kokomo, Marion, Middletown, New Castle, Royerton, Selma, Winchester, and Yorktown.

Muncie is best known as the home of Ball State University and the birthplace of the Ball Corporation (Ball Canning Jars). The city population has approximately 70,000 residents and is located off of the I-69 corridor between Indianapolis and Fort Wayne.

On the countdown to Muncie, Justin studied our route from online maps, and the first distinct task was to have the car inspected by a mechanic. The mechanic said it would be wise to take along a case of motor oil while assuring me we would be fine. Seriously? That much, huh? Well, you have to admit traveling across the country in a 10-year-old, small five-speed hatchback, 3-cylinder Chevrolet Metro would require some earnest prayers. We had them! If ever there were a time to believe in miracles, this would be it, right?

I did a mental preparation of sorts, to remind myself that Muncie would be different. I knew I would not see a Dog n Suds, Burger Chef, Mister Fifteen (yes, the hamburgers were 15 cents), or Frisch's Big Boy. Neither could I visit the downtown Five and Dime stores – the Woolworths with its creaking floors, S. S. Kresge (or Kresge's as we called it) with the tasty sub sandwiches, the majestic, elegant Ball Stores at Walnut and Charles streets and Stillman's clothing store. I remembered the old courthouse in the heart of downtown where John F. Kennedy stood on the steps greeting his supporters at his 1960 rally.

Still, I remained logical. Why should we expect things to be the same? After all, we are not the same. I tried hard to embrace the anticipated changes, although I felt a twinge of sadness. In my heart of hearts, I just wanted Muncie to be like I remembered. For decades, I dreamed of making the big turn on to downtown Walnut Street and feeling like I was home.

Yes, I had significant plans when I returned to my hometown. Friends joked that I could campaign for a Muncie City Council seat. The late, Erwin Davis (or Ervin as some knew him) of Muncie, also played a role in encouraging me. We emailed for several years about the Muncie community and political issues after meeting through a website he created about the city. Ervin was an ideal, caring citizen, who was on a mission to keep Muncie safe with Block Watches and Cop Shops. If needed, he would patrol streets in the middle of the night to ensure safety for the citizens. He was a recipient of the Key to The City.

We joked about a campaign slogan of bringing "Joy" to the City Council. Who would not want "joy" there? It could not help but be a happy group! Seriously, a few heyday friends have considered returning to Muncie and sharing or merging their "expertise" (since they were there during the heyday) of some retro ideas for the city. It is all in fun, and wouldn't that be an excellent discussion?

Before leaving Seattle and its beauty, my dear friend Ruthie had some profound words. She assured me that God would not have us go on this journey without having something wonderful waiting on the other end.

2 Des Moines, WA marina (near Seattle) on a summer's eve

Joy Charlene Henley

On August 23, 2009, an overcast, Sunday morning, Justin and I departed Seattle for our cross-country road trip to Muncie. My talking Sister Belle doll was along for the ride. Sister Belle was a gift from Santa at Christmas in 1962, so in a sense, she was going "home," too. I slid into the driver's seat and got comfy as things around the seat tumbled onto me. I got out, moved the seat forward, and rearranged everything. Eventually, with Justin and I packed in tight, I took my place behind the steering wheel. As we pulled out, I reminded Justin, "We'll be just fine as long as we don't move and breathe."

Mother and son on the road! Yes, we were about to be renowned travelers on our quest for excitement! Just how much zest for travel would we have on about two hours of sleep? Well, the thought did cross my mind. The Adrenaline raged for both of us throughout the night and took its toll. Why wasn't that Adrenaline kicking in now, as we approached eastern Washington?

We made it as far as Spokane, approximately 280 miles later. At this rate, Muncie was going to be a more extended trip than we imagined. And I thought I could handle sleep deprivation.

We arrived in Spokane and made our way to a hotel room, turned on the air conditioning, I went out for some food and brought it back to the room, we ate until we were too full and crashed. The following morning, we were raring to go!

As we headed east on I-90, we discussed no longer being a short, two, and a half-hour drive to the Pacific Ocean. Ocean Shores was a favorite destination, and we would bring home Saltwater Taffy from a quaint shop there. We would miss the beauty of Mount Rainier and picturesque Alki Beach, and we cherished the fun times at the Seattle Mariners games at Safeco Field.

I thought of the Kingdome when it stood in Seattle and attending The Rolling Stones concert there. I glanced over at Justin and vowed to be sensitive that this was my journey- not my son's. Most of the things that would excite me or bring tears to my eyes would probably have little- if any, impact on him. He did not share my secure emotional connection to the heyday. I hoped he would not be too bored on my trip down Memory Lane.

It seems like yesterday, when, like so many of my high school friends, I could not wait to leave Muncie. Now, I could not wait to return. I wondered about our rental place. I committed to it without seeing it, after answering an ad in the local Muncie newspaper, *The Star Press*. Our soon-to-be landlady, Shirley, had a small space in an upscale neighborhood, and I clung to her every descriptive word about our temporary home. It seemed perfect for us, and I trusted her. Sometimes, you just embrace your faith.

Chapter 2

Driving into the Past

On the road, Justin and I talked about what we would see when we finally arrived in Muncie. At the top of the list was seeing my childhood home on Rosewood Avenue. Our family home came to be when I was six years old and is by Ball State University. I grew up in the shadows of Ball State Teacher's College and watched in awe, its eventual expansion to a university in 1965.

I wondered, has Rosewood Avenue changed? Is that small bike shop still around the corner of the house? Is the Duck Pond, where my friends and I used to ice skate, still at Ball State? How many stores are at the Northwest Plaza today? Is McCulloch Park as I remember? Does Pizza King still serve its Beef Boat sandwiches? I remembered the field trips to near-by Christy Woods.

As a student of the Eleanor Cole Dance Studio, I danced on stage at Emens Auditorium on the Ball State University campus. In about 1967, I began performing throughout Muncie, in the choreographed, singing group "Up with People." Why did I yearn to stand in the exact spots where I did in the 1960s? I reasoned I would better understand when I arrive.

We would drive through nine states: Washington, Idaho, Montana, a short distance of Wyoming, South Dakota, Minnesota, Iowa, Illinois, and finally arrive in Indiana.

As with any long-distance trip, there can be what feels like endless miles of boredom. We never know what awaits us around the bend. Perhaps a rainbow of bold colors announcing God's Promise, to meeting a friendly clerk in a convenience store in the Northern Cheyenne Indian Reservation vicinity to spotting twelve Hell's Angels bikers approaching in the rear-view mirror.

On a "Big Sky Country" road in a land of the unknown, I began not only to wonder if Montana would ever end, but what were the odds of finding a restroom in the middle of nowhere?

I waited another half hour until seeing a rest area and sped into a parking space. I prepared to leap out of the car. Then, I saw it and froze.

3 Rattlesnakes in Montana

Well, on second thought, I tried convincing myself that this Mother Nature call could wait. Maybe not. After a few minutes of procrastination, I leaped across the lawn and heard hissing. Did something touch my ankle? Was that a snake that tugged at my foot? I entered the cold, dark restroom. I heard someone in the stall next to me but could not see anything but what appeared to be a dark fog or haze. As I sat down on the coldest throne I have ever graced, I imagined a snake in the toilet. Yikes! My mind went into overdrive, and my heart decided to pump a little faster as I imagined every traumatic scenario. My hands reached for the sink only to touch a broken faucet.

I could not get out of there fast enough, ran across the lawn, and we were on our way. We drove a short distance, and I noticed "Sapphire Mountain" etched high atop the rugged peak in front of us. What a dazzling name! Being on the flat road as "Sapphire Mountain" looked down upon us was a nice change from the many hills. Traveling in such a small, packed-to-the-brim car certainly made going up the hills a challenge. I prayed as we crawled up them at about 40 mph, with the accelerator pressed to the floor. As we approached the top of each hill, we could not escape the nagging feeling that we would coast backward, down from whence we came.

South Dakota, home of Mount Rushmore, was worth the trip up that hill! Now, that was one slow climb, and I thought Montana hills were challenging. Once, while flooring the accelerator up a mountain, we began to roll backward. It was a fleeting thought that the car could break down. Being a risktaker, I figured it would be fine. It probably just needed some oil again. I looked at the traffic coming down the hill from across the road and knew it would be better over there.

4 The majestic Mount Rushmore

Small town, South Dakota, and what a night! It was a challenge to find a motel with a vacancy. It was loud with blasting Oldies music, bright red pillars, and it gave off some strange vibes. A little before midnight, we slowly made our way down the long driveway. As we parked and got out of the car, I wished I had a set of earplugs. Cheap oldies were playing, ones certainly not for my ears. Give me the original artists or a solid cover band that will knock my socks off!

A friendly, black cat wandered over to greet us at our car door and snuggled up against my leg. The sound of loud crickets enveloped us. As I entered the dim motel office, a man who looked eerie rose from a desk. He said he would show me the available rooms. I waited on him to lead the way. He had a Dracula or Eddie Munster appearance of sorts with his eyeliner, black hair, bulging eyes, and black attire.

He stared a hole through me as he instructed me to look on the back of the door. I took a few steps back toward the front door, and he coaxed me to go ahead and shut it. I hesitated until he explained the laminated pictures of each room were on the back of the door.

The décor was somewhat out of style with the maroons, velvets, and outdated furniture. The rooms looked like something from the disco days. As the fake oldies blasted, the man announced, "You can have my last two rooms for the price of one." I was a bit suspicious of why he would offer this. Wondering what was wrong with the rooms, I declined, merely telling him my son and I could just share one room with double beds. He was adamant, "I just want to get rid of them for the night." Well, at least the price was right at two rooms for $60.00.

I parked the car and feeling weary, approached the unlocked outside door. It gave access to a small seating area in the middle of three rooms and a shared restroom between the rooms. I did a double-take and looked back at the entry. Why did this feel unsafe? Was I overreacting? We headed to our accommodations. Our side-by-side rooms were small. Justin went his way, and I went mine. I immediately locked my door. Although it was late, I attempted to call the front desk about getting a bite to eat. There was no dial tone.

We eventually decided to walk over to the refreshment area. We petted our new cat friend who scampered behind us. As I glanced over at the motel entrance, it had a "horror movie-like" image. Instead of the "Vacancy" sign changed to "No Vacancy," it was turned off. The place looked unusually dark. I wondered if motels actually "close." The distant profile of a lone older woman could be seen through a picture window in the motel, doing something at a table. Perhaps she was crocheting or something similar with her hands. A purple-colored light highlighted her presence. It looked like a scene out of a thriller movie. I reasoned my intuition was in overdrive due to exhaustion.

We picked up a snack from a vending machine and headed back to our rooms. I turned on David Letterman and told him, "I'm coming to Muncie, Dave," as I walked across the lop-sided floor to a ragged chair. I tried to get into the show to escape my unsettling surroundings but did not have much luck. I heard the outside door slowly open and faint footsteps. Then silence. Someone slowly entered the room next to mine. I shuddered, thinking about sharing the tiny restroom with this stranger. It was sure slim pickings in this small town.

I sat still in the wobbly chair for probably an hour or so. I tried laying down but wondered how long it had been since that maroon bedspread went through a washing machine. Then, out of the corner of my eye, I thought I saw something. I concluded I really needed sleep. Suddenly, I knew I was not alone in the room. I slowly looked over and saw them. Several of them wandered in and out of the baseboard heater. My heart skipped a few beats. Roaches?

The room started getting smaller as I imagined the bugs crawling on the bed. There was only one thing to do, so I visited Justin next door. I laid down on the edge of the extra bed. I pulled the covers up around me and tossed and turned. After a while, we shared small talk as my Adrenaline soared off the charts. Finally, as it approached 4:30 a.m., we decided to travel on down the road. First, we peeked into the dining area. Breakfast items were not available until 6:00 a.m. We quietly grabbed some fruit and bagels that were set on the counter while an employee left the area. We had paid for our room, so we assumed it was ok to take a few items. I still felt a little like a bandit in the night. We went across the street, filled up the gas tank, and left town with a second wind.

To this day, when I mention the creepy motel in the boonies, Justin asks, "You mean the Five Star Hotel?" It does have a Five Star rating! Go figure.

5 A current tribute of celebration for Native American heritage in South Dakota

While in Iowa, we traveled through several construction areas. One area, in particular, was so scenic it made the crawling, stop-and-go traffic more bearable. We may have only been moving at a snail's pace, but I could sure bask in the calm surroundings on the narrow road.

6 Rest Area at the Iowa-Illinois Border, a peaceful site today

Wind turbines bordered the road and stretched as far as the eyes could see, moving in slow, dreamlike motion. The sky was a canvas of bright purple, orange, and red hues. That had to be a first: feeling peaceful while sitting in backed up traffic, surrounded by heavy-duty trucks, gravel, and dust flying everywhere. On our final day Thursday, we drove fourteen hours from Rapid City, South Dakota, to Muncie. When we crossed the Indiana State Line, rain, odd-looking cell phone towers, and license plates that said, "In God We Trust" greeted us.

7 We made it!

A quick call to Shirley, our landlady, and we arranged to meet her the following morning. On Interstate 69, we took the Indiana 32 exit to Muncie, and I thanked God for our safe trip. As we entered Muncie, we drove by some boarded-up homes. Justin was silent and looked concerned. We exchanged a few awkward glances. Although it was nearly midnight, the late hour was not the reason the area seemed so abandoned and dead.

We discussed how parts of Muncie – like many other areas in the country, were economically and financially devastated by the closing of factories. Some areas of the city had suffered more than others. Justin questioned why there was so much difference between the south and northwest regions of town. Good question.

This girl still knew her way around Muncie, even in the dark. I wanted to show Justin the hill behind my former family home where my friends and I sledded in the winter. I planned to cruise McGalliard Road, where I used to have an "Awful Awful" sandwich at John's Awful- Awful Drive-In. Why yes, it was "awful awful" good! I could still see myself standing in Woolworths at the Northwest Plaza, buying penny candy or a cheap chain to hold my boyfriend's ring around my neck. I yearned to visit the Muncie Airport (Muncie Aviation Corporation), where my dad and I watched planes arrive and depart through a worn fence.

Justin glanced over at me and asked where I wanted to go first. He guessed it. Off we went to see the house on Rosewood Avenue that my parents built-in 1959. We headed out West Jackson Street and drove by Burkie's Drive-In. Back in the day, if you wanted a tasty, giant tenderloin sandwich, or cheeseburgers and fries with curb service, this was the place to go.

We made a quick trip through McDonald's on Tillotson Avenue, then headed out Tillotson to Bethel Avenue. I slowly veered off of Bethel onto Rosewood, turned off the headlights, and pulled to the curb. I was 16 the last time I saw my family home in 1970. Decades later, at age 55, through tears and under bright stars, I strained to see a remnant that resembled the home I remembered.

A flurry of memories returned that I had not thought of in ages. I flashed on many birthday parties and how my childhood friends lined up to play the game, drop the clothespin in the milk bottle.

I wanted to just once more, see my dad's reaction when I told him he had a call, and he answered the phone saying, "Hello? Hello? Is anyone there?" My little friends and I would become hysterical on those April Fools' Days! Well, dad did not find it quite as amusing as he rolled his eyes. We somehow knew a telephone company four-digit test number to call and make the phone ring. I believe I still remember it and have to wonder why.

Joy Charlene Henley

If, just one more time, I could lay my eyes on mom's alluring mink stole hanging in the bedroom closet, dad's worn bowling bag by the front door and hear some Lenny Welch or Johnny Mathis on the familiar Hi-Fi. I remembered the excitement of pulling the aluminum Christmas tree in its box, out of the hall closet each year to decorate and plugging in the revolving color wheel.

There was my bedroom window, where my record player endlessly spun The Beatles while my girlfriends and I practiced the latest dance steps. I could still hear the giggles of boy-crazy teen divas who lip-synched and taped their bangs.

I thought of my white "Hollywood" bed that was situated by the window and the pink Princess Phone with the light-up dial. Of course, I remember my phone number from back then. It was probably in the "Little Black Book" of innocent 13-year-old boys everywhere. And we *were* innocent.

As Muncie slept, I aimlessly cruised the area in a daze. My dream had come true. It was a long journey, but I was finally home!

We headed toward an area by the university that used to be cornfields. It was a hub of activity with several hotels/motels, restaurants, stores, and other businesses. I grabbed my Sister Belle doll as we prepared to go into a motel.

Later, as I laid in the dark, I thought of my life since the last time I was in Muncie. I lapsed into a self-evaluation of sorts. Questions played in my mind. I did ok, didn't I? Have I accomplished essential things? Did I make a difference in this world? At that moment, I strangely felt as if the years I had lived away from Muncie, now somehow required the city's validation. I returned to where my dreams originated, so did I pass the mustard? I flashed on standing in front of my 8th-grade class when it was my turn to share a career I planned to pursue. I said I wanted to help people and gave a vague description because it was difficult to explain. The teacher approached me curiously, asking, "like a Psychiatric Social Worker?" Well, she made it sound intense, so I did not know about that. The simple way to tell it was to say I wanted to save the world. I may not have managed to do this, but I believe my 30+ years in the Social Work profession were worthwhile.

So, why the sprinkled tears on my pillow? The thought that I have more years behind me than lie ahead suddenly gnawed at me. I wondered what my life would have been like had I stayed in Muncie. Would I have attended Ball State? Would I have married my middle school/high school sweetheart? I wished I would have returned several years earlier before Sheila; my childhood friend passed, then I could visit her the following day. Through years of telephone conversations, I repeatedly told Sheila I would be there. Decades later, I made it. Too late.

The Heyday of Muncie, Indiana

The years are gone. What did I miss? I laid in the small motel room feeling sad, and yet, feeling like I was supposed to be celebrating *something*. The journey was not just a trip with a destination. It was a sentimental journey back to the curiosity of what might have been had I stayed.

As I looked back at my life that first night in Muncie, I concluded this blonde-haired, blue-eyed girl who arrived in life prematurely at Ball Memorial Hospital, did ok. I grew up embracing my naivety that life would be as perfect as those colorful tulips I passed each day to and from elementary school. I returned wiser, as one should be when they have taken risks, made choices (not always perfect ones), and lived life.

I am perfectly flawed.

There are so many blessings in the world to count...so I decided to try counting them instead of sheep.

8 Sister Belle

Goodnight, Sister Belle.

Chapter 3

The Telling Moment

The following morning, we met our landlady, Shirley. She warmly greeted and welcomed us. My first impression was that she was a genuinely kind person who would be important in our lives. You know how you meet someone; you just click and feel you will always be friends? It is a great feeling! When Shirley gave us the key, and we went around the side of her sprawling home to see our rental, we knew that leap of faith paid off. Appearing as what was once a large garage area, the space appeared converted into a sort of "guest house" or mother-in-law space. What are the odds of finding such a beautiful home in such a nice area, sight unseen? There was a kitchen window, and I immediately imagined gazing at the snowfall. Yes, I do that, even in August! It took a few days to get settled into our small, cozy place.

The "cottage," as I immediately called it, would meet our needs just fine. I could pay an entire month's living expenses in Indiana for what my rent alone would have cost in Seattle. When I phoned my car insurance agent, and she gave me such a low quote, I asked why. She simply responded, "Because you are in Indiana now." As for Shirley, I never doubted that our connection was a God-thing! You just know.

Our first day in Muncie, I drove over to see my childhood home again on Rosewood Avenue. It felt different in daylight. Students now reside in the houses, and the neighborhood is considered "on campus." Handwritten "For Rent" signs welcomed visitors at front doors, and old bicycles sat against the doors and windows. Three and four cars sat in driveways. Gone was the small rose bush under the bedroom window of my childhood home (yes, this kooky girl hoped it would miraculously still be there), and the sidewalk looked much narrower.

I smiled as I remembered when we ran up and down the street in our bathing and sunsuits. Mom would fix grilled cheese sandwiches oozing with Velveeta. I giggled, thinking of the time a large appliance (a refrigerator, perhaps) was delivered, and my friends and I grabbed the box. We must have played in it in the front yard for a week. One of us would get in it, a friend would seal it, and we would be rolled all over the yard! As I confronted my first 16 years of life, I wanted to march up to the door of my childhood home and ask if I could come inside. I reasoned if I mentioned my parents had built the house, perhaps it would happen. Or, the occupants would call the police thinking I was strange. I remember mom and dad taking me to the property when I was about six. It was rather amusing that day with the anticipation of going to see my new home, arriving, and seeing a pile of dirt!

Once the house was underway, I browsed through design swatches with mom to choose the perfect pattern for the countertops. I saw door designs and selected the one I liked with three small windows at the top of the door. I am not sure why a child would be interested in this, but I must have had a good design sense. I chose the door. Perhaps I missed my calling as an interior decorator! As a child, I marveled at the speckled living room walls and ceiling. Although my little fingers found the stuccoed walls to be especially rough, I was captivated by the sparkle.

Before heading downtown, I stopped at a local gas mart and told the cashier I needed plenty of change for the downtown parking meters. She flashed me an odd look as she counted the coins.

The day finally arrived! Downtown, here I come! As I approached Walnut Street and made the turn, I yelled, "H-e-l-l-o Muncie!" I drove perhaps a couple of blocks and abruptly pulled over. My first thought was, *what happened to Muncie?* A few more negative thoughts followed: *I came all this distance for this? I do not even know this place.* I mumbled to myself, "What are you doing here?" I mentally scolded myself because I knew this was going to look different. I believed I was ready for this. I wanted to have the same feelings I had the last time I was in town. I was not angry with Muncie; I was mad at myself. Muncie certainly looked different, but I was not ready for how it would feel. I kept looking out the car window and wondered if I was trying to celebrate a place that no longer existed. I observed if my car were any closer to the curb, I would be on a sidewalk. Downtown was a place where I once knew the names of all the stores. I was not used to being the new kid on the block as people dined outside and greeted one another. Didn't anything remain the same? I just wanted to go home. Wait, I was home, right?

It was like wearing blinders. I could only see yesterday's Muncie. The result of vanished decades, significant change, and distance greeted me that day on Walnut Street. I blinked through a few tears of raw emotion as it suddenly became real just how long I was away. My thoughts felt jumbled and scattered as I questioned what I was thinking, returning to a place I did not even recognize. I looked up and remembered the Christmas decorations that, once upon a time, lined the streets above me. Alvin and the Chipmunks sang "The Christmas Song" on the radio. I glanced over where B & B Loan once stood, where I could drop in and say hi to Andy. I thought of friends and the many milestones I missed in their lives.

Joy Charlene Henley

I impatiently searched for a familiar sign or landmark. Then I saw it! The Pazol's Jewelers sign looked the same as I remembered! I glanced around the corner to a familiar public bus stop where I caught a city transit bus ride to and from high school each day. I searched the faces of people as if I would recognize someone. To my surprise, I happened to see a free parking lot! Now, this was a real plus to someone who fed starving parking meters in Seattle. Oh, my Seattle friends would be so jealous! No wonder the gal at the gas station flashed me a weird look when I wanted a purse full of change. I found a parking place and began to explore.

I glanced over where Sears was once open. Dandelions Flowers and Gifts appeared inviting. Then, I glanced at Vera Mae's Bistro, which looked fun, as people dined outdoors. Seeing where the classy Ball Stores once stood was bittersweet as Muncie could not possibly be the same in its absence. Ball Stores was the crème de la crème of an upscale, high-end merchandise department store. It was a tradition to see the elegant, animated Christmas window displays setting downtown aglow with holiday cheer. I smiled at the memories of Ball Stores that danced in my mind: the perfume and glitter, the mezzanine, the cafeteria, and the elevator operator sitting on the tiny stool announcing floors as we ventured up and down. Mom and I felt like royalty at Ball Stores!

Driving around the block, I promised myself I would not be an emotional wreck when I arrived at 224 South Mulberry Street. I just had to see where the grand Rivoli Theatre once stood, where I saw *Toby Tyler*, *Pippi Longstocking*, *The Shaggy Dog*, and *The Moon-Spinners*. Inside the Rivoli Theatre and toward the back corner of the lobby, there was an ice cream machine. It had three compartments where Creamsicles, Fudgesicles, and assorted ice cream bars awaited hungry movie watchers. The third one on the right produced a Creamsicle!

A Muncie kid could spend a large part of a Saturday at the Rivoli Theatre. Some children were dropped off for the day by their parents. Once upon a time, mom was safe giving her child a quarter on Saturday- 10 cents for bus fare and 15 cents (or 6 Pepsi caps) for three movies, movie-shorts, and cartoons. Movies at the Rivoli Theatre later increased to 35 cents for children and 50 cents for adults. Eventually, admission jumped to 50 cents for children and 75 cents for adults. At the Rivoli Theatre, the ticket-taker at the window could be a bit lax at times when checking ages. For example, it was easy peasy for young, curious teens to sneak in and see an adult film like *Fanny Hill*.

As a teen, I screamed with all the other crazed, frenzied girls watching The Beatles in *A Hard Day's Night* and *Help*. The balcony was closed off in later years, which probably put a crimp in the love lives of teens who went up there to make-out. Many teens were given their first hickeys in the throes of passion up there. Oh, if those balcony walls could have only talked! A Muncie heydayer said for years; he grew up believing "theatre" was the correct spelling (and not "theater") because of the Rivoli's listing in the phone book. He used to call to hear the recorded message of upcoming movies.

The Rivoli Theatre has such a glorious history. The theatre, with 1803 seats, opened in 1927, with vaudeville and motion pictures. The Y & W theater circuit in Indianapolis sold the theatre to an independent operator in the early 1980s. In the mid-late 1980s, the Ball Brothers Foundation purchased the Rivoli Theatre, then razed it, to make way for its new headquarters. Had I been in Muncie at the time of the demolition, I probably would have been one of those die-hard protesters who refused to leave, who chained herself to the fence in despair or who laid down on the concrete. My address would have been the city jail where I would have cried. Watching your local movie palace implode would be emotional for anyone.

Today, when you drive by the location, you will notice the light-colored squares that were carefully removed from the exterior of the Rivoli Theatre and incorporated into the Ball Brothers Foundation building.

9 The Rivoli Theatre in all its glory- Photo Credit: John Disher

The Strand Theater at 115 East Jackson Street was another favorite place. Then, there was the Wysor Grand Opera House, an older, more majestic theater. It had Opera Boxes or three-tier balconies, and young moviegoers could catch three movies- some popular ones being westerns, horrors, World War II movies, or various combinations. Older classic films dating back to the 1950s were sometimes shown, including *Ivanhoe* and *Knights of the Round Table*, and the blockbuster movies were frequently held over for a second week. The Wysor usually had a double-bill and cartoon previews. The theater delighted children with Black Cows (similar to Root Beer Floats) and Slo Pokes or suckers. The Wysor closed in 1961 and was later demolished in 1963. Also, Heekin Park, on Muncie's southside, often hosted free movies.

The Carnegie Library or "main library" as we used to call it, at 301 East Jackson Street, was another familiar sight.

At home at the cottage that evening, I had to admit Muncie did not feel like the city I remembered. What was I to do with this? Maybe take a step back and consider I could be overreacting? Grieve? In an odd, unexplainable way, I was sad that Muncie continued without me. Muncie and I always shared such a strong bond, and I was struggling to feel it. My most profound thought was that I did not return to see a "new" Muncie, I came to see *my* Muncie. I eventually began to wonder if the problem was not Muncie at all. Perhaps I was the problem, and my expectations were unrealistic. I believed that the challenge would be to embrace my homeland today.

I thought of the razed Chevrolet Plant over on West Eighth Street that closed its doors in 2006. It was a day of tears. Ditto for Acme-Lees, Delco Remy, Indiana Steel & Wire, and Warner Gear/Borg Warner, who all closed doors in the 2000s as well. The Marhoefer Meat Packing Plant on Granville Avenue is another employer long gone. The company was considered one of the 12 largest meatpacking companies in the country. It occupied 45 acres, with 12 building complexes and 380,000 feet of floor space. It was undoubtedly an essential part of the local economy during its 33 years of business. When you mention Marhoefer, people recall that not-so-pleasant aroma when driving by. In its heyday, the Ball Brothers Glass Manufacturing Company at 1401 East Memorial Drive in Muncie produced 30 jars a minute, along with lids and the cardboard boxes to ship them. The Muncie headquarters employed as many as 2,500 workers as early as 1936. People still remember other companies back in the day, such as Maxon Premix Burner Company, Owens-Illinois Consumer & Technical Products Division, Delaware Machinery & Tool Company., Inc., and Shepherd Manufacturing Corporation of Muncie.

Kudos to the factories and workers! In the 1960s, the factories and jobs our fathers and grandfathers held enabled Muncie area families in their quest to achieve the American Dream. We did not just dream it; it was achievable to have the whole kit and caboodle! It was possible to live the American Dream on a factory worker's wages, with mom being a full-time homemaker! Life was that grand. It is profound that we earned less and had more.

The Heyday of Muncie, Indiana

10 A familiar spot

The following day, I headed to the house where I resided before age six. The home sits on West Main Street in the Historic District. To my surprise, I pulled up, and the familiar play area by the black fence greeted me. Whether the original or a perfect replica, I thought of how I used to play with my Dennis the Menace doll in that spot.

I peeked through the fragile structure, from the front door to the back. I figured it looked like it had about all of the life it could handle. But what memories! I remembered the Christmas in the front room when Santa brought the large, walking doll and tea set. Mom and I would occasionally sit in the dark and watch TV until dad came home late from work. On paydays, I would be ready in my pajamas, and we would head out in the dark to South Madison Street to Carter's Restaurant to bring sandwiches home. I looked at the cracked sidewalk that led to downtown. I could see this little girl in her frilly slip or "crinoline" (as some moms called it) and dress, walking up Main Street toward town, clutching mommy's hand, to "window shop." It required no money to gaze in the store windows at the lavish displays and just dream. Occasionally, we would stop in the Davis Restaurant over on Mulberry Street (before it opened on South High Street) for a Beef Manhattan.

On a Friday at noon at the cottage, the Tornado Test Alarm reminded me that I was no longer in Seattle. It was startling. I had no idea what it was, and a friend on the phone tried to calm me down while hysterical with laughter. While growing up in Muncie, there was a legend that tornadoes would not occur there because of a bend in the White River. Although it proved to be untrue, it thankfully helped to alleviate some of our fears at the time. At a young age, I recall sitting by the black and white TV, hearing names of counties under tornado warnings and seeing and fearing the blackest skies and clouds I would ever encounter in my lifetime.

As days passed, I grew rather fond of the sound of the hoot owl somewhere in the yard, and I loved to hear the train. The cost of living was cheap. So, we settled into our temporary home, where we planned to live until at least spring. In the coming months, we drove pointlessly around Muncie and vicinity, and on one, especially adventurous day, we ended up in Chicago! You could say it took Justin to new heights! I cannot resist a corny joke, well, people loved a good one back in the day!

11 Justin at the top of the 110- story Willis Tower (formerly Sears Tower), overlooking Chicago. Mom kept her feet firmly planted on the ground in a nearby McDonald's.

Before I became too comfortable, I had to get another car. I was not surprised when my beloved hatchback croaked. Not even a case of oil could fix it. The journey was just too much for the old girl.

So, I returned to downtown several times in the coming weeks in my new car. I began to accept that sometimes, we need to mourn the loss of once, familiar surroundings so we can move forward. It felt comforting that my "new" hometown was growing on me.

12 A glowing Indiana sunset on the way back to Muncie

13 Gifts ready to be placed under the tree

Chapter 4

Through a Child's Eyes of Wonder

There is a quote by Author, Larry Wilde: "Never worry about the size of your Christmas tree. In the eyes of children, they are 30 feet tall." Christmas trees were humongous in the heyday. In the 1960s at holiday time, the instrumentals "Sleigh Ride" and Bing Crosby's "White Christmas" were playing on the car radio. A drive to the winter wonderland of downtown Muncie was enchanting. Ask any child who sat in the backseat of the 1963 Chevy, while gazing in awe at the shoppers. There was something in the air, and it was contagious! It was called the spirit of Christmas, and Muncie took it seriously.

The Christmas tree, in the picture window of the living room, was such a focal point. My friends and I would kneel there for what seemed like hours, watching the color wheel spin 'round and 'round as it illuminated the tinsel. It was easy to spot a house with children because there were candy canes, trees, bells, and other holiday art projects on the windows.

Scotch Tape was our best friend as we secured our masterpieces, usually made from colored construction paper. Downtown was, of course, bustling during the Christmas season. As Christmas approached, people simply stopped shopping when they ran out of money, as in cold cash. What a concept!

On Christmas Eve, after completion of shopping, some families had traditions such as attending church or opening one gift. At night, the snowy sky was brighter, the ground appeared covered in diamond dust, and all was serene. Once, when leaving my aunt's house, I remember her looking up at the roof and declaring, "Listen!" She told a detailed story of hearing Santa's sleigh! As coincidence would have it, at that exact moment, the song, "Up On The Housetop" played on the radio. You could not orchestrate this so perfectly! My cousins scurried indoors, and mom and I quickly hurried home because Santa was on his way!

The 1960s was a golden era for toys. There was a huge selection compared to previous decades, and if possible, parents were exceptionally generous purchasing them.

Some children helped curb the Christmas budget by being given a choice of Santa bringing a significant gift or two and only a few small surprises or receiving many small presents. In some homes, it was a treat to find an orange in the Christmas stocking!

Many of the toys stood the test of time. It is common for heydayers to have these toys still 50+ years later! Boys played war, and girls enjoyed kitchen sets. We had a gift called imagination, and a stick could be anything!

Joy Charlene Henley

Toys on Santa's Sleigh in the 1960s

Action Toys

Action Figures/Action Man
Farm Animals
Jack-in-the-Box
Klackers

14 Jacks

15 *Did you play marbles?*

Marvel the Mustang

Pedal Cars/Tractors

Playmobile – a steering wheel with a full dashboard of a working car with moving windshield wipers, turn signal indicator and ignition

Satellite Jumping Shoes

See 'n Say

Slinky Dog

16 *Slinky*

Smoking Monkey – blows smoke rings

Space Hopper

Spinning Tops

Super Balls

Tabletop Pinball Machine

Wacky Wind-Ups

Whee-Lo (a handheld toy that spins up and down on metal rails)

Wind-Up Toys - especially boats

Wonder Rocking Horses

Yo-Yos

17 A Kid's Favorite Ride

Bicycles, Tricycles, and Accessories

Banana Style Bicycle Seat

Baskets for the front and/or back of the bicycle

Bicycle Bell to put on handlebars

Bicycle Light Kit with Generator

Bicycle Streamers and reflectors

Bicycle Tire Repair Kit

Bicycles 16, 20, 24, 26 inches in various colors

Big Wheel Trike

Custom handlebars for bike

18 Red Wagon

Scooters – red Radio Flyer ones were popular

Training Wheels for the first bicycle

Construction

Airplanes of all kinds, models and paper ones were popular

Cardboard Building Bricks of all colors

Erector sets

19 Lego Building Set

Lincoln Logs

Model Cars and Trucks

Model Navy Ships and Tanks

Molded Plastic Play Sets

Remco Showboat

Stickle Bricks

Tinker Toys

Tool Sets – Handy Andy was a favorite, made of plastic

Clothing (Santa included among toys)

Boots

Hats, Mittens, Gloves, Ear Muffs, Scarves, Sweaters

Nightgowns

Getting Creative

Colorforms

Flubber

Lite-Brite

Play-Doh

Pop Bead Necklaces

Puzzles

Silly Foam

Silly Putty

Silly Sand

Toon-A-Vision – makes 65,688 faces

For the Artist

Chalk and Blackboard set

Coloring Books and Crayons

Magic Slate

Paint Sets

Paint-by-Number Kits

Spirograph

Stencils

Vehicles

Cars – Hot Wheels and Matchbox with Carrying Cases

Die-Cast Model Cars

Johnny Speed Race Car

Matchbox Cars and Carrying Case

Tonka Trucks – dump, fire, garbage, tanker, tow

Ready, Set…Learn

Baseball and Football Cards

Books – "Hardy Boys" and "Nancy Drew"

Chemistry set

Crystal Radio Kit

Dictionary

Doctor Kits

Dr. Seuss Books and Toys

Math, Alphabet and Spelling Flash Cards

Microscope Lab Kits

Monster Card Collections

Pegboard Desk

Science Kits

World Almanac

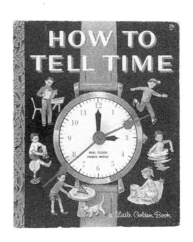

20 Little Golden Books

Dolls and Accessories

- Baby Boo
- Baby Cheryl
- Baby Dear
- Baby First Step
- Baby Fun Doll
- Baby Go Bye-Bye
- Baby Pattaburp
- Baby Secret
- Baby Small Talk
- Baby Tender Love
- Baby Whisper
- Barbie
- Barbie Doll Case
- Barbie's Dream House
- Beautiful Crissy
- Betsy McCall
- Betsy Wetsy
- Blabby Baby
- Bozo the Clown Talking Doll
- Buffy Paper Doll
- Captain Action and Action Boy
- Captain America
- Casey
- Chatty Cathy
- Cheerful Tearful
- Dancerina
- Dee
- Doll Cribs
- Doll Houses
- Easy-Bake Oven
- Dottie
- Drowsy
- Francie
- Franny
- G.I. Joe Action Figure
- Giggles
- Ginger
- Girl Scout
- Gumby and Pokey
- Ken
- Kissy Doll
- Little Kiddles
- Little Lulu
- Little Miss Echo
- Little Miss No Name
- Matty Mattel
- Midge
- Monster Figurines, some battery-operated
- Paper Dolls
- Patti-Play-Pal Walking Doll
- Pebbles Inflatable Doll
- Pepper
- Perthie
- Puppets – hand and push-button
- Raggedy Ann
- Randi Reader
- Sister Belle
- Skipper
- Sleepy Eyes
- Snuggles
- Suzy Smart doll with desk and chalkboard
- Swingy
- Tammy
- That Kid
- Tickles
- Tiny Tears
- Toodles
- Tressy
- Troll Dolls
- Tutti and Todd
- Western Figures

Dolls from TV Shows or Movies

Batman

Casper the Friendly Ghost – he talks!

Dennis the Menace

Flintstones

Herman Munster

Major Matt Mason – he lived on the moon!

Mickey Mouse

Mrs. Beasley

Popeye toys

Shirley Temple

Thumbelina

Games

Ants In The Pants

Barrel of Monkeys

Button, Button, Who's Got The Button? 101 button games

Cold Feet

Cootie

Eye Guess

Green Ghost

KerPlunk

King of the Hill

The Last Straw

Magic Eight Ball

Magilla Gorilla

Mentor

Milton The Monster

Miss Popularity

Molded Plastic Playsets (Army Men, Cowboys & Indians, Civil War, Farm, etc.)

Toy Soldiers

Trouble

Yahtzee

Activity Games

Action Baseball (Game by Roger Maris)

Blockhead

Bucket of Fun

Cat and Mouse Game

Crazy Clock

Donkey Party

Don't Break the Ice

Don't Spill the Beans

Drop-In the Bucket

Dynamite Shack

Electric Football and other sports games

Feeley Meeley

Hot Wheels – Hazard Hill Race Set

Lie Detector

Marble Race

Mouse Trap

Mr. and Mrs. Potato Head

Pick-Up Sticks

Pie Face

Pinball games – handheld

Shooter Arcade games

Skill Ball Marble Game

Smack-a-Roo

Table Tennis

Tiddly Winks

Tip It

Toss Across

Twister

Board Games

Aggravation

American Heritage: The War Games of the 1960s

Battle Cry

Battleship

Bingo

Booby Trap

Candy Land

Chutes and Ladders

Checkers

Chinese Checkers

Civil War

Clue

Game of Life

Game of The States

Go to The Head of The Class

Hands Down

Hands Up Harry/Showdown at the Circle

Haunted House Game

Hi! Ho! Cherry-O

Kreskin's ESP

Mystery Date

Operation

Ouija Board

Parcheesi

Perfection

Risk

Scrabble

Sorry

Spill and Spell

Spy Detector

Stratego

The Beatles

The Ten Commandments Bible Game

Tickle Bee

Tiger Island

Uncle Wiggily

World's Fair

Games based on TV/Movies

Art Linkletter's House Party
Barnabas Collins Dark Shadows
Batman
Beat the Clock
Ben Casey, M.D.
Bonanza
Buck Rogers
Captain Kangaroo
Casper The Friendly Ghost
Combat
Concentration
Dennis The Menace Board Game
Deputy Dawg
Dr. Kildare
Dracula Mystery Game
F Troop
Fascination
GI Joe
Gidget
Gunsmoke
Hogan's Heroes
Honey West
I Spy
Jeopardy
Lone Ranger and Tonto

Lost in Space
Mary Poppins
McHale's Navy
Mickey Mouse Treasure Hunt Game
Mission Impossible
Mod Squad
Monkey's Uncle
My Favorite Martian
NBC-TV News Game- Chet Huntley
Outer Limits
Password
Patty Duke
Perry Mason
Petticoat Junction
Quick Draw McGraw
Route 66 Travel Game
Sea Hunt
77 Sunset Strip
Shenanigans
Spiderman
Star Trek
Stump the Stars
The Addams Family
The Archie Game

The Beatles

The Beverly Hillbillies

The Detectives

The Dick Van Dyke Game

The Flintstones

The Flying Nun

The Great Escape

The Jetsons

The Man from U.N.C.L.E.

The Match Game

The Monkees

The Munsters

The Price is Right

The Waltons

Thunderball

Tom and Jerry

You Don't Say?

Card Games

Batman

Casper

Crazy Eights

Cribbage Board

Fish

Flintstones

Old Maid

Popeye

Rack-O

Slapjack

War with a standard deck of playing cards

Toy Guns

Agent Zero

Army men/plastic soldiers and tanks

BB

Bat Masterson Derringer Belt gun

Cap Pistols

Cowboy Outfits

Hubley Atomic Disintegrator James Bond 007

Johnny 7 OMA

Lost in Space

Roto Jet Gun

Lunar Launcher Toy Gun

Pistols

Rifles

Secret Agent Toys – radios and cameras that turned into guns

Shootin' Shell Guns

Spy Kits with all you need to go undercover

Squirt

Star Trek Tracer Gun

21 Boys will be boys!

Getting Domestic

Big Burger Grill

Cash Registers

Cola Dispensers

Creepy Crawlers with real molding oven

Dishes and Tea Sets

Frosty Sno Man Sno Cone Machine

Incredible Edibles

Ironing Boards

Play Lighter and Candy Cigarettes

Potholder Loom Kit

Suzy Homemaker

Tea Party China

Outdoor Toys and Play

Badminton

Balls for Elimination and Four Square

Baseball Mitts

Batons

Blowing Bubbles

Bop Bag

Bowling Pins

Bozo the Clown Punching Bag

Cup Ball - the player, holds the cup by the handle and lets the ball hang freely. The player then tosses the ball upward by jerking the arm holding the toy, attempting to catch the ball in the cup.

Darts

Horseshoe Set

Hula Hoops

Ice Skates

Jump Rope

Kites

Paddle Balls

Punching Bags

Roller Skates

Skateboards

Skip-It/Ball Hop Set - Place one ankle in the ring and swing the ball. Jump with the other foot as the ball swings around on the floor. Great exercise and excellent for developing coordination.

Sleds

Tether Ball

Waterfall Ring Toss

Yard Darts

Joy Charlene Henley

Having Fun with Tech

Dick Tracy Two-Way Wrist Radio

Electric Train Set and Accessories

Etch-A-Sketch

Mr. Machine

Music Boxes

Musical Instruments

Race Cars/Slot Cars of all kinds

Record Player – Close -n-Play was popular

Records

Remote Control models

Road Racing tracks and cars

Rock 'Em Sock 'Em Robots

Rockets

Slot Cars

Spaceships

Trains – Lionel sets were popular

Transistor Radio

Walkie Talkies

Watches

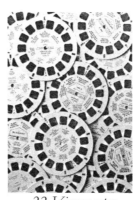

22 Viewmaster

23 Tinsel for the tree

Do you believe in Santa? Back in the heyday, parents went to great lengths to keep Santa alive. It was considered a significant highlight of Christmas and a healthy, acceptable thing to do. It was rare to meet a child who did not believe in Santa. On Christmas morning, there could be two long lines in the snow in the front or backyard, and it was apparent Santa had parked his sleigh there. Around the Santa sleigh marks, glitter was visible, which of course, was the magic dust that made the sleigh fly through the sky. Real snow, spray snow…it's all good!

A wise child once said, "Love is what you hear at Christmas when you stop opening presents and listen." While secluded in our homes due to snowfall and snug in our jammies on Christmas morning, tranquility prevailed.

Children loved leaving traditional cookies and milk for Santa, but in my home, Dr. Pepper awaited Santa. My parents somehow had an "in" with Santa and personally knew that Dr. Pepper was his favorite. Mom had something in common with Santa since this happened to be her favorite drink too!

In the heyday, people knew not to underestimate children on Christmas Eve. They were tuned in to every noise and determined to not only hear Santa but catch him in the act! Would you believe many children never caught the guy?

24 Alphabet Blocks

Chapter 5

Seems Like Yesterday

Don't you just love how thinking of your hometown ignites the senses? How could you forget the faint fragrance of grandmother's Cashmere Bouquet as she served homemade Apple Pie a la Mode on her rose petal china? How about those warm cinnamon rolls on Sunday mornings before church?

Did you ever sneak into mom's closet and prance around in her high heels? Add a splash of her Evening in Paris perfume? The cobalt blue bottle had a prominent place on her vanity table. Remember mom's fury when she came into the room and demanded to know, "What's that smell?" As if she did not know. If ever there were a time to play dumb, this was it! You knew mom could answer her own question. Do not even try to slip anything by her.

It may have been a half-century ago, but I can still remember that small, bridal shop on the southside and that tiny soda fountain downtown with the thick, fresh strawberry milkshakes.

The courteous, uniformed, milkman came to our homes- often in the wee hours of the morning, to deliver fresh, bottled milk. Most homes had a milk box outside by the front door where the empty glass bottles were left. The route driver would replace them with full half gallons of the essential household beverage, milk, and at the request of mom, would leave other dairy products such as cream and butter.

Dad had a strong work ethic, and mom kept an immaculate house. The Bible had a special place on the coffee table.

We Remember!

Air was free for your tires

The aroma of mom's kitchen

Asking mom and dad to be excused from the table after a meal and being a member of the "Clean Plate Club"

Avoiding stepping on a sidewalk crack, step on one and you will break your mother's back

Babies getting baths in the kitchen sink

Baby Chicks at Welles Department Store – some were dyed colors

Badminton in the backyard after supper

Ballerina figurines on birthday cakes

Believing Fairy Tales do come true

Bicycles – girls putting streamers on the spokes or handlebars and boys putting a playing card in the spokes to make the sound of a motorcycle

Bird Drawings

25 Does this look familiar?

Joy Charlene Henley

Birthday Parties and playing the following games:

Hot Potato- yes, the potato was hot from the oven!

Musical Chairs

Pin the Tail on the Donkey

Birthstone rings

Black Patent Leather shoes

Blanket Forts

Blood Tests before getting married

Blowing dandelion fluff

Bobbing for apples at Halloween parties

Bonfires

Book Fairs

Bookmobiles

Borden's Elsie, the Cow

Bosco Chocolate Syrup

Bottle Caps

Bowling Alley pins manually set

Bowling scores totaled in pencil

Bread bags worn inside your boots in the snow

Bread slices – used for a sandwich, hot dog, hamburger buns and garlic bread

Breaking off an icicle and eating it

Bright stars on a clear night

Brush hair curlers and pins

"Bubble gum" pink liquid Amoxicillin

Bubble gum cigars

Bubble gum packs - The Beatles pictures in wrappers

Buster Brown shoes

The Heyday of Muncie, Indiana

Buying goldfish, hamsters, mice, and turtles at the small pet section of Woolworths

Cakes being decorated downtown in the bakery window in front of an audience

Calamine Lotion

Calling "Collect" when making a long-distance call - the person you called paid for the cost of the phone call and told the Operator they would accept the charges before you talked. Dialing 0 was required to make a long-distance call.

Campbell's Soup Kids

Candy Stripers

Canneries – where seasonal employees canned tomatoes, picked apples, and other foods at orchards

Canopy beds

Car door ashtrays

Car key left in the car ignition or above the visor

Cars – dimmer/bright switch for the headlights was on the floor, and the stick shifts were on the columns

Cartoons and the occasional violence in them

Cash - was the usual method of payment, although there was a "Revolving Card" that could be used at Sears and Roebuck in 1911, years before the credit card industry itself was born.

Cashiers – no protective gloves

Cassette Tapes

Cereal loaded with sugar and the prize at the bottom of the box

Charles Chips

Cheerwine

Chenille bedspreads at grandma's

The Children's Clinic

Dr. Henderson, a local Pediatrician, calling girls "princess" and telling them they would grow up to be Miss America! He made every child feel special!

Dr. Henderson's fish tank

Dr. Henderson's nurse, Alice, Dr. McCoy, and Dr. Gibson

Joy Charlene Henley

Choir robes – slipping into one in a room at the Muncie Fieldhouse before the Annual Christmas Sing

Choo Choo Bags - train case purse

Christmas trees were left at the curb for the garbageman after the holiday as recycling was not widespread until the late 1960s

Cigarettes advertised during prime-time cartoons

Climbing trees

Clothes on the clothesline with wooden clothespins; Mom would prop the pole, and dresses would blow in the breeze. Did you ever find frozen clothes on the line on a frigid winter day?

Colonial Bakery- driving by and smelling the warm bread

Colored toilet paper – some with pink flower designs

Coloring Easter Eggs

Comic Books

Convertibles

Conveyor belts bringing your groceries outside the store for your pick-up

Cooking with heaping tablespoons of Crisco or Lard

Cornfields as far as the eye can see

Cotillion

Cracker Jacks

Crayola Crayons – the smell of a new box of them and the many colors

Croquet in the backyard

Cubed flashbulbs for the camera

Dance lessons

Darned socks

Day of the Week underwear (girls, I KNOW you remember these!)

26 Ballerina

The Heyday of Muncie, Indiana

Debating if Paul, John, George, and Ringo wore wigs - surely, that could not be their real hair

Defrosting the freezer

Dentists/Hygienists - no masks

"Dick and Jane" readers

Di-Gel mint tablets

Dixie Cups in the bathroom

Doilies on the end tables in the living/family room

Door to Door salespeople who would come into the home during the day and visit

Doors left unlocked when leaving home

Double Cola

Double dog dares

Double Ferris Wheels

Dress-up – boys playing in Union and Confederate outfits

Dressing up to go downtown – nylons with seams, high heels, gloves, hats

Drinking Choc-Ola

Drive-In Movies – children, going in their pajamas with mom and dad

Easter bonnets – a necessity for church on Easter Sunday

Eating the lunch special at Woolworths for 95 cents, which included turkey, savory dressing, whipped potatoes, gravy, garden vegetable, and cranberry sauce

Eating your morning cereal while you read the back of the cereal box

Family vacations

Farmhouses

First kiss on the elementary school grounds

Fizzies

FlashCards

Flashing your headlights for curb service

Flintstones jelly glasses

Flintstones television commercials with Fred and Barney smoking Winston cigarettes

Flintstones vitamins

Flying Kites

Freeze Tag

Fritos Corn Chips in a can

Fuller Brush Man

Furniture covered in plastic slipcovers

Fuzzy Wuzzy Soap that grew "fur"

Girdles

Goff's French Fries

Goldfish – winning them at school carnivals and fairs

Goulash

Grandma cutting the mold off of the block of cheese and saying it was good

Grandma's collection of cute little soaps

Grandma's crocheted dress toilet paper roll, dish soap bottle dolls

Grandma's ink-stained hands from using carbon copy paper at her secretarial job

Grease jar by the stove

27 *Greyhound Bus*

Gum wrappers woven into rings

The Heyday of Muncie, Indiana

Hand turkey drawings – began by tracing your hand

"Hardy Boys" books

Helping mom put S & H Green Stamps or Top Value stamps in the saver book

Home Economics class

Home Entertainment Centers with a television, record player and liquor cabinet all in one

Homework completion happened before supper

Hot Dr. Pepper

House calls by the Pediatrician

Hymn Directory page numbers on the church wall during service

Ice Cream boys on pedal carts

Ice Cream Cake Roll

Ice Cream stands in the country

Ice on humid days – big bowls of it, placed by the fan to create cold air

Immunizations

Inner Tubes for swimming

28 Ice Trays- made of metal and aluminum with a pull lever

Ironing Boards – made of wood and the old pop bottle with holes in the bottle top "sprinkled" clothes with water before ironing

Jewelry Boxes – a ballerina spins in the center

Jiffy Pop and watching the foil on it fully expand

Jingle Bells in shoelaces so we "jingled" as we walked at Christmas time

Jukeboxes – tableside in diners

Jumping Rope - "Cinderella dressed in yellow, went upstairs to kiss her fellow, how many kisses did she get…"

Keys – two of them needed for a car

Kickball

Kitchen Hand Crank Can Opener

Knock, Door, Run - A childhood game where you knock on someone's door and then run away and hide, watch them open it, see no one is there and laugh at their annoyance and confusion

Joy Charlene Henley

Kool-Aid

Ladies nylons in two pieces

Lawn Mowers – push ones were trendy

Lemonade Stands

Licking the beaters- or dipping a finger in the frosting

Lightning Bugs (Fireflies) – catching them, putting them in a jar with poked holes in the lid

"Little Iodine" Dell Comics, 10 cents

Little white gloves are worn to church

Mom telling you to not jump around because she had a cake in the oven

Mom using a round drinking glass sprinkled with flour on the sides, like a rolling pin for dough

29 Mom's vibrating exercise belt, when exercising meant standing still while the belt did the work

The Heyday of Muncie, Indiana

Monkey Bars

Mouseketeer Certificate that said you were a Mouseketeer in good standing

Mouseketeer Ears

Mouseketeers - Annette was such a sweetheart!

"Nancy Drew" Mysteries

Nehi Soda

Neighbors knowing and helping one another

Nestle Quik – using a knife or spoon to pry open the lid

Nik-L-Nip – paraffin bottles with colored, sugar water

No helmets while riding the bike

Office supplies such as a typewriter, Dictaphone, and Rolodex

One potato, two potato, three potato, four…

PF Flyers - the PF stood for the "Posture Foundation" insole

Paper Boy collecting at the door

Paper Dresses sold in 1966 for $1.25 (a promotion by the Scott Paper Company)

Passing notes during class

Patrol Boys at school

Pay toilets in stores – remember the sign that said you were not permitted to share or crawl under stalls?

Pea Shooters – specialized "peas" for guns and target practice

Pedal Pushers

Peeling glue off of your fingers

Penny Loafers

Pet turtles

Piano lessons

Pillow fights

Pink bathrooms

Pinwheels – watching them go 'round with the wind

Playing 123 Red Light

Joy Charlene Henley

Playing Hangman

Playing Jacks

Playing on the drive-in movie playground before the movie started

Playing outside, unsupervised all-day

Playing tag in the dark

Pole lamps in the living room

Pontoons

Pop Rocks

Popsicles with two sticks

Porch Swings – face-to-face Porch Gliders

Prayer before the game at the Muncie Fieldhouse

Prayers after brushing teeth at night

Public Transportation- when it cost a dime to ride the bus

Pulling a bottle of soda out of the pop machine and that sound

Railroad Train in McCulloch Park with the real steam engine

Record player needle required perfect positioning on each line to play records

Red rubber rain boots

Riding the horse outside the supermarket

Rock collecting – choosing sparkle rocks that glistened in the sunlight, cleaning then displaying them in empty egg cartons

Roller skates with steel blades and keys

Rotary dial phones

Running errands for and with mom and grandma

Running through the sprinkler

Saf-T-Pops

The scent of dad's Old Spice After Shave

School carnivals and productions- singing in the elementary school Spring Concert or talent show

Scouting and Camp Fire

Scully – playing the sidewalk game

The Heyday of Muncie, Indiana

Shirley Temple

Side vent car windows - small triangular windows that passengers in the front seat could push open

Skateboarding

Sleeping on the living room floor all night to awaken early Sat. morning for cartoons

Sleeping with the windows open

Stomping on the hose that makes the bell ring at the filling station

Sunburst wall clock

Surfing

Swim Lessons at the Y

Swimming at Buck Creek

Talking back to your parents, remember how that worked out for you?

Talking or singing into the fan in the living room window to make a robot voice

Tearing the slice of bread by trying to spread cold butter on it

Teeter-Totters – your teeter-totter friend, would jump off, and your seat rudely hit the ground. Remember that feeling?

Telephone Operators that were always there

Telephone Party Lines

Telephones had a loop circuit that was shared by more than one subscriber. There was no privacy on a party line. Imagine talking with a friend, a stranger picking up the phone to make a call, and hearing what you say.

Television antenna made from a coat hanger

Tents – playing in them and making them by hanging blankets across the clothesline

Tetherball

Tomato pincushions

Tooth Fairy

Toy Cookies created by Sunshine Biscuit Company

Training Bras

Trick-or-Treating- used to be two nights on Oct. 30 and 31

30 Thermos Bottles

Tube Tester

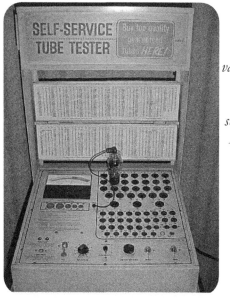

31 Bringing in your radio and TV vacuum tubes for testing. Different tube sizes had different test sockets. The user looked up the tube number and selected the test machine settings. Tube Amplifiers and Tube Rectifiers were replaced by transistors and diodes.

Tupperware Parties

Turning the TV antenna on top of the set by hand

32 Remember these?

TV repairman coming to the home

Unlimited sweets

Velvet paintings on the wall

Watching the *Wizard of Oz* for the first time

Water balloons

Water Beds

Waving at airplanes from the local airport as they flew over the backyard

33 Alarm Clock

Winding the clock before going to bed

Wishbone – pulling the wishbone from the turkey, making a wish

Wishing upon a star and genuinely believing it would come true

    Children did not require gadgets or structure for amusement. It was a rare parent who would spend long periods "entertaining" their child. When one child on the street had a swimming pool, it seemed to belong to every child. Others on the block would quickly slip into their swimsuits and prepare to jump in, even showing up at a neighbor's pool, uninvited.

    Playtime did not necessarily stand on formality. There were no "play dates." Sleepovers in the backyard with a pizza delivery from Pizza King was the best! Mom would get $3.00 from dad for their child to go to the fair for the day.

    One of the more popular rides in the 1960s was the Flying Coaster. The ride followed a circular pattern and flew off a ramp into the air. A shock-absorbing system allowed the car to land softly and spin for another trip.

Another fun ride was the Round-Up. Riders stood against caged walls - secured by a chain fence, the platform would rotate, and then the arm that holds the platform arises, so the ride is tilted. There was plenty of centrifugal force. Surprisingly, most of us did not get dizzy.

34 How about a ride on the Mad Mouse…or did you call it the Wild Mouse?

Did you ride the Caterpillar? A cover would extend over the top, and the seated riders would travel in a circular motion. As a teenager, I fearlessly rode the Double Ferris Wheel without incident. I was already dingy enough without getting lost in the House of Mirrors, though! I will just say getting lost in that maze can be scarier than any amusement ride.

35 *Bel Air Dashboard*

Cars

Imagine:

No GPS

No ABS

No Air Bags

No Injection

No Stop-Start

No Power Steering

No Central Locking

No Air Conditioning

No Electric Windows

    Did we ever have class and style! In the 1960s, the big-three auto manufacturers, Ford, GM, and Chrysler, seemed to own the car market. Foreign-made cars accounted for only a small fraction of U.S. auto sales. In 1960, Americans owned about one car for every three people.

Joy Charlene Henley

Popular cars were ones with large V-8 engines and plenty of horsepower, such as a 327, 350, 400, and 427 cubic inch big blocks by General Motors; the 427 cubic inch Chrysler Hemi; and Ford's 351 and 427 cubic inch models. Many people did not want small 6- cylinder engines even though all three American automakers had product offerings. There were exceptions for the Ford Mustang with a more modest 289 cubic inch V-8, which was purchased by over one million customers in the first 18 months on the market. Ford had expected to sell only 100,000 units in the first year of production.

General Motors outfitted many of their muscle cars from 1963 to 1975 with a hopped-up transmission called the Muncie 4-Speed, named for the manufacturing plant in Muncie. The Muncie 4-Speed transmissions became legendary in cars like Chevy Corvettes, Camaro, Pontiac Firebirds, and the Trans Am.

Station Wagons seemed to be more popular than vans. There were a few SUVs such as the 1963 Jeep Wagoneer and the International Harvester Scout 800. Ford introduced a Bronco in 1966, and the CJ Scout and Land Cruiser were the primary offerings in the small, two-door SUV market. While the Jeep CJ Cherokee and original Ford Bronco were the two best-selling two-door SUVs in the 1960s, the introduction of the full-sized Jeep Blazer paved the way for the popularity of larger models. Based on the short-wheelbase version of Chevy's pickup, the Blazer offered more power, room, and luxury (air conditioning) than the competition.

Volkswagen Beetles were popular. Ford and GM cars were for the working class, with a few exceptions. If you wanted to show off, you probably had a GM Cadillac or a Mercury (Ford) Lincoln. The only real sports car was said to be the Chevy Corvette. The "poor man's Corvette" was the Ford Mustang, released in the mid-1960s. GM's sporty offerings for the middle class in the mid-1960s included the Pontiac Firebird and the Chevy Camaro. Ford offered the Cougar. Marquis and Grand Marquis were exceptionally popular. Others making the scene were the Ford Falcon, Chrysler Valiant, Buick Riviera and Chevrolet Corvette Stingray

If you headed into a drive-in on a warm summer evening, there was plenty of excitement seeing locals take slow laps around the parking lot. A teen driver could certainly rev up that engine, the object of their pride! Gone were the Hot Rods of the 1950s. Now, hopped-up Chevys, Fords, Dodges, Plymouths, Mercuries, and Pontiacs made the scene. The "Muscle Cars" were the favorites, but anything with a sporty flair could catch the eyes & ears of the envious admirers as they sat eating their cheeseburgers, coney dogs, and fries fresh off of the tray affixed to their car door windows. So many of the cars vying for attention had their mufflers replaced with Glasspacks for an authoritative rumble or no muffler at all- with only straight pipes delivering a roar from the exhaust.

36 Chevrolet Impala

There was a grand parade of cars that ranged from the mid-to-late 1950s Chevy Bel Airs to the impressive offerings from the 1960s. Some Ford Mustangs, with their "GT" stripes and boastful "350" emblazing the lower door panels, were eye-catching. Pontiac GTOs were larger and roomier. Chevys had transformed into the Nova, Malibu, and Impala. They added the designation of SS (SuperSport) to their sportier models for extra zing in their advertising. Dodges and Plymouths boasted "Hemi" engines for even more zip, and they had models like the Barracuda, the Road Runner, Chargers, and Challengers. Mercury had its Cougar.

Many of these cars either came with or later added Hood Risers, Hood Stripes, Mag Wheels, Pin Striping, Rear End Spoilers, and other "enhancements." Custom Horns blasted a variety of non-conventional, attention-getting sounds.

The owners of these impressive beasts never tint darkened their windows as they wanted to be visible. A few had probably cajoled their parents into buying them, but most vehicles were likely the rewards of the many part-time jobs that were available to high schoolers back then. For a while, the drivers were stars, at least at the local drive-in restaurants!

In the 1960s, it was possible to get a new car – depending on the year and make/model, in the $1,500 to $3,000 range.

Chapter 6

Anthony

Back in the day, education was about "The Three Rs"- the necessary skills of reading, writing, and arithmetic. Students knew they were in class to learn, and the teacher was in charge. No gum chewing, throwing paper or spitballs, bad words, outbursts, or temper tantrums. You would be sorry.

37 Former Anthony Elementary School

It was emotional entering the building that once housed Anthony Elementary School.

Of all the schools I attended throughout life, this was my favorite. I expected the building to appear worn and torn as I had not been inside it since the mid-1960s. The building later became the Muncie Community Schools Building (as it was when I visited) and then, a part of Ball State University. It is well maintained and immaculate. When I went to the reception desk, I explained that I attended elementary school there, and asked permission to wander the halls. The receptionist's face lit up, and she smiled, "I get two or three people a week who come in wanting to do that." I got the go-ahead and was gone!

The Heyday of Muncie, Indiana

I darted down the hall to the end classroom by the playground. I remembered the small kitchen area that separated my kindergarten room and the one beside it. There was a refrigerator below the counter that housed our cartons of milk. We had milk every day and had to remember to bring our 15 cents for milk money each week. Our teacher, Miss Shroyer, preferred to sit in her blue child-sized chair, and each student scrambled to make sure she had it. I could not imagine the closets where we hung our coats, still being there. How I hoped the room looked as I remembered. Well, I was sure it had not changed since I last saw it in 1959, right?

As I entered the room, I slowly looked to the right. There were the three closets where we hung our outerwear. Well, maybe not "the" ones from back in the day, but they could have fooled me. I looked at my area- the one in the center and remembered the yellow ball picture affixed to it, so my coat always landed in the correct place. I slowly peeked into the kitchen area, and to my surprise, there was a refrigerator below the counter, where our milk cartons were chilled.

My former kindergarten room appeared to be used for light storage and occasional meetings, as did most of the rooms. The restroom at the end of the hall by the office looked small – not nearly as large as I remembered. Once upon a time, I stood in front of the mirror, fixing my hair and wanting to be pretty. My friends and I were often pushed aside by the big 6th graders who seemed so grown-up. We were just little kids to them.

How did the saying go?
1st-grade babies
    2nd-grade tots
        3rd-grade angels
            4th-grade snots
                5th-grade peaches
                    6th-grade plums
                        All the rest are dirty bums

Education was traditional, proper, and age-appropriate. Classes were structured. Some were also quite large, with some classes having 30-40 students with one teacher. All eyes would be forward on the teacher at the blackboard. I recognized Mrs. Bartlett's classroom. She was my 5th-grade teacher, who was so patient and kind. Then, there were Mrs. Hoover's classrooms, where I sat in 4th and 6th grades. My mind became a flurry of Spelling Bees and how one year, our class won the Spelling Bee Trophy. Children also participated in a classroom game called "Spelling Baseball." The class divided into teams with each speller moving to the following base when spelling a word correctly. The competition was keen to see who could spell the best and get the "home runs."

I remembered addition, subtraction, multiplication, and division Flash Cards, music class with Miss Warner, and the music cart that traveled from room to room that housed recorders or flutes and bells. I flashed on Mrs. Hoover, telling me to spit out my gum. When she first told me to get rid of it, I tossed it in the trash. Good girl! Later, I pulled out another stick of Fruit Stripe. I was usually an "eager to please" student and followed the rules. Apparently, not that day. I must have decided to test the limits and be a brat. I landed in a chair out in the hall, and it was devastating.

I smiled, recalling the annual May Festival and how each classroom transitioned into a game room with prizes. Students would sell May Festival tickets, going door-to-door for several streets. There would later be an assembly in the gym to award prizes to the students who sold the most tickets. We felt safe knocking on the doors of strangers because we were in Muncie.

It was especially neat to see the gymnasium! One year, my class performed the Disney song, "Whistle While You Work," on stage for the annual Spring Concert. There was a problem, and it was huge for this seven or eight-year-old. I could not whistle. I was told to fake it despite being self-conscious. The imagined cold stares and secret laughs of the audience told me they knew I was not whistling. Unfortunately, the audience was fixated on my lips as I increasingly became the star of the song. I had never been so glad to get off that stage.

From the 3rd/4th grade choir to Summer Recreation, the Anthony gym was a happening place. I noticed the shiny gymnasium floor and the area where we used to have refreshments. Then I remembered the dreaded P.E. Classes. Why couldn't the fact I was not the most coordinated, agile student escape my memory? I always felt awkward in relay races, slow on the wheeled, square scooter as I slid across the floor, and I could not master the cartwheels quite like my girlfriends. I would stare in awe as my friend and neighbor Janie climbed the ropes to the gymnasium ceiling.

Then, there was an embarrassing incident in the 6th grade. Someone new entered my life, and I was not sure I was going to like her. Mother Nature. She got me good in the form of monthly cramps. As I stood in the gym after decades, I flashed on the mystery note mom sent to the P. E. teacher. This incident rates high up there as one of my "I forgot about that" moments. To this day, I have no idea what the note said. We did not talk so freely about personal issues back then. I just remember, at the time, I dreaded the next P.E. class and did not want to face the teacher. One day I was a little pig-tailed girl playing tag, and suddenly I was on the supposed brink of womanhood.

I walked outside to where we used to play Dodge Ball and Elimination. Didn't a boy plant a kiss on my lips by that boiler room? Oh yes, he was an older boy in 7th grade who would frequent the Anthony playground on summer afternoons. Gone was the laughter of children telling jokes from Bennett Cerf's *Book of Laughs*. I flashed on lunchtime and walking, running, and bicycling the three streets over to home where mom often had my favorite hot Chicken Pot Pie waiting.

Staff working in the building seemed to know why I was there and flashed me approving smiles. I felt so young. I felt so old. At that moment, my world felt quite small, as if it did not extend beyond the school walls. I felt so childish and safe.

Some heyday classroom discipline that was deemed acceptable in the 1960s would not occur today. By today's standards, it would be inappropriate and abusive. The examples people shared throughout the country are occasionally shocking.

The intent of these actions, back in the day, was not to cause harm. It was all about discipline, a part of learning. The belief was that students who learned and respected rules made the best citizens.

In the 1960s at schools in "Anytown USA":

Children said the Pledge of Allegiance with pride, every morning in class.

Paper Mache was a typical art project.

Long Division supplied plenty of frustration.

It was "in" to wear your belt buckle off-center or to the side of the hip.

Multiplication was called "Times Tables."

Joy Charlene Henley

38 On Top of Spaghetti, all covered with cheese…

Kids were singing some zany songs!

Remember "On Top of Spaghetti?" How many lyrics can you still remember? Admit you were singing it!

Children obeyed at school. When issues arose between the teacher and student, the parent often "sided" with the school. A common form of discipline was corporal punishment (paddling), and students could receive a certain number of swats from a principal or teacher, depending on the severity of the infraction. The paddle hanging on the Principal's wall (often one with holes in it) spoke volumes. Some Principals even inscribed the paddle with the names of students who experienced it. The child knew after the spanking from the Principal that punishment probably awaited at home. The teacher would not always be at fault as it was the child's responsibility to behave. Staying inside during recess, staying after school, writing repetitive lines on paper or the blackboard that the bad behavior would not be repeated, and standing in the corner were collective punishments. Children not sent to the Principal's office would sometimes have their hands or knuckle area slapped by the teacher with a ruler.

A teacher may have pulled the short hairs on the back of a student's neck, for wasting time in class.

Science class students held a ball of Mercury in their hands that the teacher passed to them.

When a student dozed off in class, one teacher connected the output terminals of a Van de Graaff generator onto the metal frame of the desk and hand-cranked the generator to create a static discharge that jumped from the metal part of the desk to the student's young body. The idea was to "shock" the student into waking up. As you have probably guessed, yes, it worked.

The Heyday of Muncie, Indiana

A couple of adults still recall being elementary school students and how the teacher "slammed" a student's head against the wall. The same teacher also "slapped around" another student.

In high school, a young, female teacher would sit on the lap of a male student and stroke his hair, as she taught the class. Once, she told him where she lived and to drop by sometime.

"Bad" children with dirty or potty mouths could have their mouths washed out with a bar of soap. In case you have not guessed, it was usually a large bar.

If a student had a "weapon," in possession, it was probably a slingshot.

Schools contained Lead Paints and Asbestos.

Students would not carry a gun to school, and it would be unlikely they would have access to one. It could probably horrify the community.

Intense bullying was unusual. Students probably did not know anyone who committed suicide because of it.

Students put their seats up on their desks at the end of the day.

Most had not heard of violent gangs in the school or neighborhood. There were "cliques" or neighborhood kids that hung out, but it was unthinkable that there would be community gangs that intentionally harm or kill others. Sometimes, parents would threaten teens if they did not mind; boarding school was the next stop. No one wanted *that*.

No long hair in school. Locks could fall over the ears, "just a hair but no more." On occasion, the principal would demand the student get their hair cut or not return to school. Even when the parents said the student's hair was acceptable. There were a few situations when the principal went with the student to get the haircut. It was necessary so the principal could tell the barber when to stop cutting. There were also similar situations when teens found themselves in court. The judge ordered a haircut.

In some school districts, female students could not wear pants to school to keep their legs warm, unless the temperature fell to 15 degrees or below. If a student showed up at school in pants and it was 16 degrees outside, she went home. Brrr...my legs were cold that morning!

At some schools, children stood in line to receive immunizations and TB (Tuberculosis) tests.

For students who acted out or seemed to have disciplinary issues, it was uncommon to have "self-contained classrooms" or "special" classrooms where they went within the mainstream school. We did not hear much about "alphabet letter" conditions; ADHD, ADD, OCD, and others.

Nor did we hear much about the medications prescribed to "manage" these conditions. Disruptive students sat in front of the class by the teacher for supervision or because the teacher said so. Teachers told the students to stop daydreaming and pay attention. They were usually not recognized as having "attention deficit" anything. If a student acted out, the class looked at the teacher to take control. Clear boundaries and expectations were set in the classroom and at home.

Some students were not allowed to use fashionable electronic calculators because they were expensive, and it was "cheating." Back in the day, it was essential to know the steps for reaching the answer. The calculator defeated learning the process.

Children received a certain amount of money for grades; an "A," a "B," and so on. It tended to be a controversial issue among parents. Many parents did not believe in paying for grades and felt children should not be "paid" to achieve. Other parents paid for grades, and their kids struck it rich on report card day. Then some were grounded for a bad grade until the next report card. Report cards were handwritten.

It was relatively healthy for children to experience competition. It was not especially devastating when a child lost. In the heyday, children competed and learned sportsmanship. A child learned early on that he or she would not always be the winner. When an opponent "won," the "loser" often shook the winner's hand and offered congratulations. Every child did not receive a trophy, and their self-esteem remained intact. When a child received recognition in the heyday, they earned it. Students probably would not be able to slip by with scribbling some crayons on a piece of paper and have people shower praise for their "work." There had to be some thought go into it.

Students learned to tell time on an Analog clock, not a digital one.

Square dancing was an activity in gym class. Holding hands was awkward. Having to hold hands with a boy? Boys felt the same way as I once learned when I put out my hand to dance, and the boy said, "Yuck." It was serious stuff, after all, we risked getting cooties!

No transistor radios or other distractions were allowed in class. There was zero tolerance for the smallest things. Students eventually learned they could not fool the teacher. It was as if the teacher had eyes in the back of her or his head at times. You can bet students learned which teachers possessed this uncanny ability.

The Heyday of Muncie, Indiana

Talking back, not being prepared with school supplies, and general disruption could make a student a social outcast. It was serious business being in trouble with the teacher. The class would not find inappropriate behavior amusing, and some students would distance themselves from the troublemaker.

The school was also for socializing, and it was critical to be in style at school. Let us just say there were some definite no-nos. For instance, everyone who was anyone knew better than to wear white socks on Thursdays. Doing this made you a "greaser," whatever that meant. It was just wise not to do it. Boys who had a "ripcord"- also called a "Fruit Loop" on the back of their shirt (the small loop where the pleat meets the yoke) would have it pulled by a girl who found him cute. She would keep it and boast that she got his "ripcord!" It sometimes resulted in the shirt ripping. Some boys eventually wised up, decided enough was enough and removed the loop before wearing it.

Pencils, erasers, crayons, and paper were kept in tidy desks. Some orderly students kept a sponge with their supplies for a clean workspace. Community crayons with adjoined tables were not the norm. If a student could not do the Flashcards in the time required, the teacher would encourage practicing the math until learned. Students did not depend on a dictionary. There was an emphasis on girls taking Home Economics and boys taking Industrial Arts.

Children succeeded in large part because of structure not only in the classroom, but at home. There were routine bed and awakening times, study habits that were fueled by proper nourishment, and parents made their expectations and standards known. Families often consisted of dad working and some moms staying home. Other moms chose popular professions, such as nursing, teaching, or secretarial jobs.

Children were to have manners. Some mowed the yard, cooked, straightened their room, and invested in the household in a variety of ways. It was a rare child who did not have responsibilities within the home. Many received allowances. That quarter each week could stretch far with the penny candy bins at Woolworths. Homework came before fun. It was common in some households to arrive home from school on Friday and do the following Monday's homework. Then, the weekend began.

39 *Pencils*

The holidays were celebrated in class. Halloween was especially fun when students would change into their Halloween costumes, and the class would try to guess who was behind the mask. Remember those hot masks? There were Halloween songs. For

Valentine's Day at school, students were given in advance, the valentine list of all class names and valentines were hand addressed. Sometimes, classmates would decorate a shoebox in crepe paper or other artistic means and make a slit in the middle of the box lid. The "mailbox" in class would soon fill with valentines from classmates. There was a prize for the best-decorated mailbox.

When Easter arrived, students would make Easter bonnets and have a "Hat Parade." Each class would take turns going through the school, modeling their Easter bonnets throughout the classrooms. Then, there was May Day! Children used colored construction paper and made a "cone" with a handle, they placed a handpicked flower in the cone, hung it on the doorknob at home, rang the bell, and ran away! Was mom surprised! Also, on May 1st, children danced around the Maypole- a tall wooden pole erected as a part of various European folk festivals. It was painted and decorated with flowers, holding long ribbons that were attached to the top of the pole.

In elementary school in the 1960s, many children learned to read with *Dick and Jane* books. Students also received the *Weekly Reader*. The delivery of the publication was a much-anticipated event, and the teacher often spent much time having students take turns reading aloud. One week, there was an especially intriguing story about the tremendous event that would occur in 1970. There would be telephones that would enable people to see one another while talking! Students tried to imagine such a concept, although it was difficult for a ten-year-old to fathom. It was a prediction in the 1960s that the primary profession of the future would be Key Punch Operators.

Students were seated in reading groups. Some students also learned reading through a program called SRA Reading Laboratory. Each student had a reading kit, which contained color-coded cards that were organized by level of difficulty. Students would read and then answer questions about the material. Much of the curriculum seemed to be based on reader comprehension and advancing to the next level and color.

It was especially exciting to learn Cursive Writing! Little fingers diligently practiced the fine art. It required not only a reliable thought process, but putting thoughts into words, and ultimately on to paper. It was huge to master Cursive writing. Students learned there was to be a space – the width of a finger between words, so it was common to see a child repeatedly placing their small finger on the paper. When the student "passed the test" on the lined paper, the teacher would hand the student a piece of crisp, white paper. It was a "graduation" of sorts.

I yearn to go back to the second row of class when a significant problem was choosing between a 24 or 48 size box of crayons. Even to that one embarrassing morning in class, when I unwrapped the foil of my fruit lunch. As children around me opened their grapes and pear slices, I opened mine.! Whoops! Mom pulled the wrong food from the fridge. I still recall one boy pointing and announcing to the class in a booming voice, "She got hamburger in her fruit lunch!"

When the time came to leave Anthony, I knew this one visit would not be enough. I vowed to return. Through the miles, years, life events, happiness, sorrow, ecstasy, grief, and bliss of life, I was back where my education started. I was very thankful to visit my elementary school because not everyone can do this. Many of the schools are long gone. I slowly headed to the car and started to put the key in the ignition. Instead, I grabbed Sister Belle, got out of the car, and approached the playground. Do you know, it is socially acceptable for an older woman to play with a doll on the playground? It is one of the perks of aging; being silly is now considered "cute."

Sister Belle, at her golden age, still talks. She "played" where I did in the 1960s.

As Sister Belle sat on the teeter-totter, I headed to the swings. I wanted to feel the wind against my face and swing so high I touched the sky! If I had the limber body of my seven-year-old self, I assure you I would do it! I made my way over to the teeter-totter, picked up Sister Belle, and glanced down at the ground. Lying there was an empty, green, Pixy Stix wrapper. Who did not love the sweet and sour powdered candy, packaged in a drinking straw wrapper? I smiled and picked up the wrapper of my favorite lime flavor. It was like the ones that were dropped in the same location decades ago. Was this some kind of "sign?" I grinned, as I acknowledged the playful "child" in me. She's back!

40 Sister Belle hangin' out

I left Anthony and suddenly had a hankering for the old school pizza! Have you craved one for decades? Then make it!

Old School Pizza

Preparation:

Half sheet pan and line with parchment paper

Crust:

2 ⅔ cups flour

¾ cup powdered milk

2 tablespoons sugar

1 packet of quick rise yeast

1 teaspoon salt

1 ⅔ cup warm water (105-110 degrees)

2 tablespoons vegetable oil

Filling:

½ pound ground chuck

½ teaspoon salt

½ teaspoon pepper

1- 8 oz block mozzarella cheese – grated

Sauce:

6 oz can tomato paste

1 cup of water

⅓ olive oil

2 cloves garlic minced

1 teaspoon salt

1 teaspoon pepper

½ tablespoon oregano

½ tablespoon dried basil

½ teaspoon dried rosemary crushed

Crust:

Preheat oven to 475 degrees

Spray pan with Pam and lay Parchment Paper down

In a large bowl – flour, powdered milk, sugar, yeast, salt – whisk to blend

Add oil to hot water (110-115 degrees) – pour into your mixture

Stir with a wooden spoon until batter forms – lumps are okay

Spread dough into pan using fingertips until it is even. If the mixture does not want to cooperate, let rest 5 minutes, and try again

Bake just the crust for 8-10 minutes – remove from oven and set aside

Assembly:

Brown meats until crumbled – set aside and drain meat

Get out the pizza sauce – to the partially baked crust add:

Sauce – spread all over the crust

Sprinkle meats

Sprinkle cheese

Bake at 475 degrees for 8-10 minutes until cheese melts and begins to brown

Remove from oven – let stand 5 minutes

Enjoy:

Cut in slices and serve!

Chapter 7

We Lived to Tell About It

In the heyday…

Commitment and marriage were emphasized.

In the case of divorce, mothers were usually given custody.

Pre-marital sex and living together were probably not socially acceptable by most…which is not to say people did not do it.

Baby showers for pregnant, unwed teens were rare. They were sadly, sometimes, "sent away" to have the baby as it helped the family avoid embarrassment and shame.

When women learned they were expecting, they did not wear a regular, stretched shirt to accompany their growing tummy. They wore specially-designed Maternity clothes.

Items were purchased with cash. Few people had credit cards. In the 1960s, banks could refuse credit cards to single women since the husband's signature was required for a woman to obtain one. For a time, women could not take out loans or mortgages.

In 1960, the pill gained approval for use as a contraceptive. Even so, the pill was illegal in some states and could be prescribed only to married women for purposes of family planning. Not all pharmacies stocked it.

People did not usually complain about being a "victim" and threaten to sue others if wronged.

Women did not inject medications into their foreheads and lip area to erase wrinkles. For most, Noxzema or other cold cream and good old-fashioned soap and water (Ivory or Camay) would do the trick. A light Max Factor or Merle Norman make-up application and red lipstick could make a woman a temptress.

Women would dress up to go downtown. A fashionable neighbor used to don earrings to walk to the end of the sidewalk to her mailbox. Or so a few moms in the neighborhood said when overheard gossiping…

Women took pride in the meals they prepared and the home they cleaned.

Shopping happened at the supermarket, the corner grocery, or a drive-through convenience store like a "Miller's Milk Barn."

Vending Machines in the U.S. and other countries were also utilized for many items: beer, books, cookies, eggs, fruit, light bulbs, nightcrawlers, nylons, pocket combs, rolls of film and whiskey.

Store lists and budgets were handy. Some shoppers kept a running total with pad and pen of the grocery costs as they put each item in the shopping cart. Others would ask the cashier to inform them when they reached a specific total handing the most needed items first.

Gas stations were full-service with the attendant pumping gas and checking the oil.

It took much leg work and time to locate lost loved ones or alumni, by writing letters and making telephone calls.

When you took pictures with your camera, you had to deliver the film to a photo processing department in a store or photo booth for development. It could take up to a week for the return of the pictures; then, you decided if you liked them and mailed them to others.

The potential for the legalization of marijuana or a female president was a dream.

It would be unthinkable for women to have tattoos. Tattoos on a man sometimes bore a stigma that he was perhaps either a rebel or someone who had possibly served time in prison.

Males wore britches that fit. They would be ostracized if they wore "gangsta" jeans down over their buttocks. A Lewd Conduct or Indecent Exposure charge could be in their future.

Young People

Smoked candy cigarettes: Camel, L & M, Lucky Strike, Marlboro, Pall Mall, Salem, Viceroy, Winston, and others. In a split-second glance, they mimicked the real thing.

Were sent to the store to buy dad's cigarettes out of a machine

Had a little nip of alcohol if dad permitted

Were the "remote control" and walked across the room to change the channels for dad

Played with toy swords and pretended to be "Zorro"

41 Basketball in the hoop

Enjoyed playing basketball and many sports

Ate worms and mud pies made from dirt

Were threatened with getting a "whippin'" if they did not mind

Were punished for saying a cuss word

Could be sitting at the kitchen table a long time if they refused to eat their vegetables

Were taken to Measles parties before the MMR vaccine for Measles, Mumps, and Rubella appeared. The practice of measles parties originated from the belief that infected children would build up immunity to the disease because once someone had the Measles, they could not catch it again. Some say they were intentionally exposed to Chicken Pox as well. Childhood diseases such as Measles, Chicken Pox, and Mumps did not make news headlines with announcements of an "outbreak."

Were grounded. Teens probably would not have dreamed of calling Children's Protective Service for intervention in a family matter. Dad and mom were the bosses. The spanking the child received would not be considered an "assault" or child abuse. There was no significant debate about spanking. If a child did not mind, they knew what could happen.

Stayed home when expecting a phone call

Had enforced, regular bedtimes

Understood what "no" meant and could "take a no." When mom or dad said no, it was final. Children knew who the head of the household was, and it was not them.

Were allowed to fail, which is a freedom in itself. Today's children do not know what they are missing.

Girls knew they were girls, and boys knew they were boys. Of course!

Girls had their restroom, and boys had theirs. If a boy walked into the girl's restroom, it would cause quite the commotion!

Negative influences like violent video games and rap songs did not exist.

Imagine a childhood without the following: CD/DVD/VCR Players, Cell Phones, Computers, Game Boys, Internet, iPads, iPods, Surround Sound, Texting, TiVo, Video Games, Wi-Fi, YouTube, and other high-tech devices. There was a "Play Station" though...it was the swing set in the backyard!

Could not download songs

Did not click a mouse to obtain answers, meet others or make purchases

Interacted socially, face-to-face

Had to be home by "curfew"- which was often indicated by seeing the streetlights

Returned pop bottles for a cash refund, then spent the change on candy

Rode their bikes to elementary school- several streets away and to the shopping center for lunch

Played with toys that by today's standards, would be considered dangerous; ones that could present choking hazards, hot plates or stoves that heated up, noxious odors and sharp metal objects

Popped wheelies

Suffered burns going down scorching metal slides

Liked to visit the soda fountain in the local drug store

There was no bottled water.

Milk vending machines dispensed the drink for 10 cents.

Donned their boots, coats, and mittens in winter, they dressed weather-appropriate

Watched mom put a coin in the scale and weigh herself in public...some children may have witnessed tears.

There was a picture of a Muncie map in the telephone directory. Within the map was a bold triangle or pyramid. It was easy to daydream about how special it was to live inside that triangle. Although there was no real significance or meaning to a child, the diagram hovering over the city cast a shadow of intrigue and importance.

Speaking of magic, Cracker Jacks contained some nifty prizes! In one box was a plastic, multi-colored ring with an oval jewel. As one youngster learned, when the jewel of the ring touched the clothes dryer, the dryer turned on! Every time, without fail. He contacted other things to see if they switched on, to no avail. Being six or seven years old and having a magical ring that could do such a thing validated that Muncie was even more magical! To this day, the once upon a time proud ring owner laughs, "I probably had the secrets of the universe in it."

Did not usually participate in beauty pageants and pushy, stage mothers would have been an annoyance

Families

Acknowledged God and said His Name when they wished

Some had "Devotionals" when children returned from school

Attended church

Prayed together before meals

Ate supper, same time each evening in their brown, avocado green, orange, turquoise, or harvest gold kitchen. Imagine a plaid refrigerator

Went to the bank to withdraw money on Friday with an estimate of how much money they would need for the weekend

Had wood paneling in their homes

Some families had their surname initial on the aluminum screen door grille at home.

Hand washed dishes were the norm.

Portable, countertop dishwashers were sometimes used

Liked to gather on Sundays for mom's fried chicken – it was deliciously fried in Crisco.

Some families served dad his plate of food at supper time first because he was the "working man."

Meatloaf could be dyed turquoise. NO, never had it. Do not want to think of having it.

Food was often made from scratch.

Many families had one car, and some moms did not drive.

Approximately 9% of children under 18 lived with a single parent in 1960.

A breadwinner father, a homemaker mother, and their children comprised 70 percent of American families. Today, "traditional" families with a working husband, an unemployed wife, and one or more children make up less than 15 percent of the nation's households.

The family often consisted of one set of parents, although blended families existed.

Moms were busy homemakers. After children entered school, some moms continued homemaking.

You did not need a certification to babysit. 12-year-olds and perhaps younger were trusted to provide childcare.

A typical workday or night had specific hours with no pagers or emails to answer at odd hours.

Without computers, employed women often calculated figures and crunched numbers all day by hand.

Microwave ovens were not typically used, although some wealthier families may have had them. The ovens became available on store shelves as the mid to late 1960s approached.

The percolator made piping hot coffee to serve.

In the 1960s, central heating and air conditioning became more affordable. Up until this time, they were considered a luxury.

Living and family rooms had wooden console televisions.

Dirty clothes meant a trip to the laundromat for many families.

Recycling became popular in the late 1960s.

Tang- the orange "Space Age" instant drink was consumed for breakfast.

One bathroom served a large family.

Families used black rotary dial phones or calls were 10 cents at a phone booth where one stood in line.

It was a secret who was calling until you picked up the receiver.

Usually, no security alarms were in homes and cars.

One black and white television with as little as three channels were adequate for a household.

Common sense dictated people needed adequate rest for the following day—no staying up half the night.

Television stations "signed off" at the end of the programming day – often with the National Anthem or a poem of sorts, about God. Stations "signed on" the following morning- often with a local broadcast. Radio stations did this as well. It would be difficult to understand the need for 24/7 news formats.

Television commercials did not usually pertain to medical conditions, medications, or personal, intimate products. Topics of this nature were considered personal care and private issues with the doctor.

Sexual identity or preference was considered more of a private matter.

Attorneys did not advertise on television.

The family could comfortably sit around the television set, as programs were usually fit for the entire family's viewing pleasure.

A trip to the Post Office was required to get stamps. Some families put the flag up on their mailbox for outgoing mail. Many preferred to pay bills in person.

When banking, people went inside to speak to a live person.

People had not heard of Parental Advisory warnings on music, TV, and movies.

The Heyday of Muncie, Indiana

Records were played on the Hi-Fi, phonograph, or record player. It required a "Diamond" needle, which was expensive - $10.00. Adapters in the center of 45 RPM records came in various colors, with yellow being the most popular. Stereo would come later.

A half of an ice cream sandwich was a nickel, and it was so-o-o thick and yummy!

Imagine matching family sleepwear- especially during the holidays. It was a rare family that wore this, but it happened.

The average cost in the U.S. for a gallon of leaded gasoline in 1965 was 31 cents. Some familiar "filling stations" included Amoco, Ashland, Chevron, Clark, Esso, Gulf, Hess, Marathon, Mobil or Mobilgas, Phillips 66, Shell, Sinclair, Standard and Sunoco.

The first mall opened in Oct. 1956 in Minnesota, and they caught on across the country.

A gunshot signaled the end of a quarter or game at Muncie Central Fieldhouse.

Drive-in movies were fun where the on-screen, concession stand advertisements reminded families to "Go to church this Sunday."

Small, downtown businesses sold American made products, and people purchased them.

Patriotism reigned for the most part, and homes displayed American flags.

People in the 1960s probably would not have known the meaning of "politically correct." I am guessing it would not have been that important in their lives, anyway.

Guests had a gay time while at the party- the word "gay" meant lively or merry.

Families financially thrived since dad's full-time job paid an excellent salary and benefits.

Mom was a queen on Mother's Day! It was apparent when she beamed while opening her electric skillet, electric razor, egg poacher, or automatic toaster.

Personal information and family business were kept more private. Families felt capable of working through and resolving their issues. In other words, it was often no one else's business. Families respected the privacy of one another.

Marriage was believed to be usually between a man and a woman.

Health and Safety

Some pregnant women smoked or drank.

A maternity stay in the hospital was approximately five days.

Rabbit tests were pregnancy tests, and "the rabbit died" meant a positive result. The rabbit only died if the test was positive, although the rabbit supposedly died either way. Or so they say.

A husband's signature could be required for a Cesarean Section.

Infants went to sleep on their stomachs.

Some mothers added soda or 7-Up to their baby's milk.

Babies drank out of plastic baby bottles in assorted colors.

Abortion was illegal in each state of the union…some states allowed exceptions.

Better shoe stores had shoe-fitting Fluoroscopes or Pedoscopes. These x-ray tube machines would supposedly provide better-fitting shoes. The only "shielding" between the feet and the device was a one mm thick aluminum filter. Some units allowed the operator to select one of three different intensities: the highest magnitude for men, the middle one for women, and the lowest for children. A standard x-ray, the exposure time was 15-20 seconds. Children thought these were toys and played on them, repeatedly putting their feet in the machine.

Bright, colored, lead-based paints covered some baby cribs.

Cloth diapers attached with safety pins were used.

Soiled cloth diapers went in pails. The pail lid had a space for a deodorizing disk.

Three or four friends shared one bottle of soda.

Children drank water from the garden hose- with unsafe levels of lead.

People headed to the nearest public water fountain when thirsty.

Children were told by mom not to shower during a thunderstorm; they could get struck by lightning and die.

Children had to wait for a half-hour or hour to go swimming after eating. After a big meal, blood will be diverted away from your arms and legs towards your stomach's digestive tract. And if your limbs do not get enough blood flow to function, you are at risk of getting cramps or drowning.

The Heyday of Muncie, Indiana

There were no childproof lids on medicines.

There was no question if the vaccinations children needed, could harm them. Parents trusted the doctor, and if he said the child needed it, the child needed it.

Children received a Smallpox vaccination on their arms that would leave a faint imprint on many, for life.

Children could get Cradle Cap- crusting of white or yellow scales on the scalp. It blocked sweat ducts and trapped sweat beneath the skin.

For an earache, the parent would blow cigarette smoke in the child's ear.

For Poison Ivy, apply wet mud to the affected area.

Registered Nurses wore white uniforms with a cap that had a black stripe. In some regions, two thinner lines signified the award of a Bachelor of Science in Nursing (BSN).

Camel cigarettes were known as the doctor's favorite brand.

Television viewers watched smoking advertisements that showed Santa and doctors smoking, with the appearance of babies and children. "Before you scold me, mom...maybe you'd better light up a Marlboro," one child suggested. Camel, Chesterfield, Lucky Strike, and Winston were popular advertisers.

Second-hand smoke was inhaled by many.

People probably did not know too many patients in treatment for "rehab" or "addiction."

Patients did not always have to go to the doctor's office because the doctor made house calls.

Some doctors smoked while reading and writing in the patient's medical charts or during exams.

Smart moms had Mercurochrome (Merbromin - a compound containing Mercury and Bromine) on hand, to apply to those scraped, bleeding knees that happened while riding the bike.

For a sore throat, some moms mixed Mercurochrome, Listerine, and Aspirin for a Mercurochrome gargle. Or, in the early 1960s, the throat would be painted with Mercurochrome. In 1998, the U.S. Food and Drug Administration declared that Mercurochrome- which contained Mercury, halt its distribution in the United States over fears of potential mercury poisoning. All Mercurochrome made today is made without Mercury.

Whiskey concoction to beat a cold – whiskey, lemon juice, sugar

Mom put a few drops of kerosene on a teaspoon of sugar and made the child swallow it. Although the person who shared this story does not recall precisely why, it may have worked as a laxative.

Mom could blow gently on a burn and make the pain go away. Psychological? Maybe, but it worked.

In Canada, a pharmacy had a front window display of old medicines, including a jar of Petroleum Jelly. The Petroleum Jelly jar and label looked very old. Instructions were for both external and internal use- for coughs, sore throats, and congestion. It raises a serious question, did people eat this stuff?

Smith Brothers cough drops were a kid favorite. People joke that the drops tasted so good they ate the whole box. Maybe they are not kidding.

Cough syrups containing Codeine were an over- the- counter purchase.

Children took aspirin during illness. No one had heard of Reye's Syndrome and that aspirin should not be administered to children under age 17. Bayer or St. Joseph aspirin for children worked fine.

Anacin worked wonders for adult pain and was said to enter your bloodstream in 22 seconds, speeding relief to your nervous, tension headache.

Alka-Seltzer was deemed useful for everything from fatigue to hangovers.

Take Dristan for Sinus Congestion and Colds, "Dristan's like sending your sinuses to Arizona."

Geritol (an alcohol-based, Iron, and B-Vitamin tonic) provided women with vitamins and minerals for "iron-poor tired blood."

Apply Unguentine for sunburn

Patients took their prescriptions, written on the pad, and signed by the doctor to the pharmacy.

Sleeping disorders were rare, especially for children. Merely playing outside could be exhausting. The kiddos would probably sleep well that night.

People were generally not hospitalized for "exhaustion." They knew to go to bed when tired and would not allow the fatigue to escalate to this point.

Adults usually did not need afternoon naps or Energy Drinks to make it through the day.

Those who were not outgoing or "social butterflies" were not labeled as having "Social Anxiety"- let alone given medication to "treat" it. They were known as introverts.

Most people did not know what anxiety and Panic Attacks were, and trips to the E.R. to treat them would have been considered unusual. Instead, they took some "Miles Nervine" to calm down. Bromide was the main ingredient- used as a sedative. Bromide is still found in photographic chemicals, in some well water, and as the Bromide salt of numerous medications. Miles Nervine remained on the market as a "calmative" for nervous exhaustion, until the late 1960s.

It was common knowledge that all of us occasionally get moody and feel "down," so prescribed anti-depressants were given sparingly.

Electroshock Therapy (ECT) was occasionally used for every type of "disorder," including depression, mania, schizophrenia, and even homosexuality and truancy – until the end of the 1960s.

The Americans with Disabilities Act (ADA) and "handicapped accessible" communities did not exist.

The victim's rights were more important than the criminal's rights. If a person committed repeated crimes, he or she could be a "bad seed." A "rough childhood," for instance, would not be an excuse. Criminals would have a tough time "working" or manipulating the Criminal Justice system for a lighter sentence.

Mom and dad taught the basic rule that children do not speak to strangers. Children being taught tactics predators use to attract them would be considered odd. It was not a requirement to be street smart. Today, depending on where one lives, being street smart can be necessary to survive.

The waif-like look of "Twiggy" Lawson became popular. In the late 1960s, eating disorders emerged at an alarming rate, because women wanted to look like the supermodel.

Metrecal was a commonly used diet drink. The plan consisted of consuming four self-prepared or portion-controlled canned shakes, daily. It also came in wafers. Sego and Slender were other popular diet drinks.

Children brushed their teeth with toothpaste containing fluoride.

There was little discussion about "Cholesterol numbers," sugar making children "hyper" or meat injected with chemicals and hormones.

In the early 1960s, the FDA approved about 300 chemicals that would mix in foods. Today, the FDA approves over 5,000+ chemicals for consumption.

Lard and Crisco were "staples" of sorts, found in many kitchens.

People enjoyed consuming bacon, greasy eggs, and juicy cheeseburgers.

Saccharin was a calorie-free food sweetener. After the discovery of an elevated bladder cancer risk found in rats, it was learned the threat did not transfer to humans. It was the foundation for many low-calorie and sugar-free products around the world, tabletop sweeteners, baked goods, jams, chewing gum, canned fruit, candy, dessert toppings, and salad dressings; it returned to the market in 1981.

No hand sanitizer

With the promotion of child bike safety, came fear tactics of being harmed.

42 Baby in the back window of a car

While riding in the car, children would lay in the back window of the vehicle. They would press their noses to the glass window. They would giggle when the car stopped, and they fell out – onto the seat below.

There were no airbags in vehicles.

Some neighborhoods were so safe that children could run home from several streets away in the dark.

Most children would not have access to guns, let alone consider shooting anyone. A child merely discussing suicide- the fact it was in their thought process, could be regarded as bizarre, and this is a child who would undoubtedly receive mental health services.

If you were a danger to yourself or others, it was "criteria" for being committed.

Domestic Violence was not a common term, and although it was happening, it was not known or acknowledged to be happening at an alarming rate.

Some kids would grab the back bumper of the city bus in the winter and squat down as the bus pulled them along the snowy, icy streets.

Chapter 8

Feminine Wiles

Advertisers knew sex could sell just about anything! A TV ad for Noxzema Medicated Instant Shave about male facial hair showed seductive Swedish model, actress Gunilla Knutsson (sometimes spelled Knutson, Knudson, or Knudsen) telling men to "Take it off...take it all off." The man in the commercial shaved to the David Rose song, "The Stripper." Actress Edie Adams encouraged men to smoke Muriel Cigars. What man could resist a cigar that boasted "extra length and taste?" Pair that cigar with an icy Falstaff or Stroh's beer, and a woman who had waited all day for her hubby to return from work would have a recipe for romance.

Even sweet-natured, perky "Donna" on *The Donna Reed Show* could pitch advice about how to land a husband. One episode came to mind when there was a comparison between men and fish, and women just had to use the right bait!

Feminine wiles were a woman's power. She used her curvy figure and allure to influence her man, or any man, to attempt to get what she wants. There was none so glamorous as a 1960s heyday woman. She could be flirty, sultry, and submissive, which transformed into a mystical power, and she was not afraid to use it. She knew she could get much further with honey than vinegar. Suffice to say she was a strong female capable of outsmarting the most unwitting man.

In an ideal setting, the husband is on his way home from work. He will open the door to the aroma of a dinner fit for a king. Before his arrival, mom double checks dinner in the oven and makes sure she has a welcoming home. She clears away any remaining clutter, tends to her hair by removing the pink Spoolies, and changes her necklace because the pearls look softer. She delicately dabs perfume behind her ear lobes and on her wrists. She pauses as she looks in the mirror at her curvy figure. That midriff bulge she has tried so hard to remove is slimming down. Jack LaLanne is her friend, and she promptly turns on the TV each day to exercise with him.

Mom removes her apron and slips into something more feminine. She prepares the children for dad's arrival. She will keep noise to a minimum, she knows he does not want to arrive home to problems, and she will let him speak first. She gives a quick reminder to, "Stop fighting; your dad is on the way home." On this particular night, she has prepared meatloaf, scalloped potatoes, sweet peas, orange JELL-O with carrot shreds, and the bread slices and butter are near-by. Angel Food Cake awaits the family for dessert. Mom softly sings along with Dinah Shore when "It's So Nice to Have A Man Around the House" plays on the countertop radio. After dinner, she will gladly get her husband's slippers to help him unwind after his exhausting day. He sits down to read the newspaper and dozes off. It may sound like a fantasy, but back in the day, this scenario could keep the sizzle alive. The home was a man's castle, and a wise woman knew it.

The household was not always serene, though. Sure, there were bad days and out of control times when mom shrieked at the children, "Just wait until your father gets home!" Any heyday kid who heard those words shaped up real fast!

Many homes were tidy with everything from the oven scrubbed to the shag carpeting "raked." Yes, wives used a long-handled "rake" that kept the shag rug in perfect condition. Many homes were immaculate. After all, homemakers cleaned with Ajax liquid, and it cleaned like a white tornado!

The 1960s ads, slogans, and advice could be hilarious, inappropriate, insulting, and blunt. Well, and a bit naughty!

Remember these sayings, slogans, and products?

Cigarettes are like women. The best are thin and rich.

Women do not want to compete in the workplace with men; they want to marry them.

Does your husband look younger than you?

A woman's hair, eyes, and teeth will not look as beautiful if she does not wear deodorant.

Husbands admire wives who keep their stockings perfect.

Romance will die if you have dishpan hands.

A blemish can wreck a romance.

Have a good girdle

Looking for health and happiness? Eat more lard.

No gray hair- you could lose your job.

"I love my husband far too much to risk getting dry, lifeless middle-age skin."

The Heyday of Muncie, Indiana

The essential quality of coffee is how much it will please your man.

Wives are desperate for home appliances and will cry to get them.

Wives are for cooking.

Butter is slippery. That is why we eat as much as possible to lubricate our arteries and veins.

Imagine Vitamin Donuts with B1...on second thought, don't do it! That sulfuric Thiamine odor is mighty unpleasant.

Some instructions detailed how a man could measure his wife for an ironing board.

In one ad, a desperate woman was upset that her hair was out of place. She held a gun to her head, poison in the other hand and had a noose around her neck. "If my hair looks such a mess one more night, I'll kill myself," she agonized.

Push-up bras told the story of how women "trapped" their men.

Ads implied if he was not interested in her, it was because she failed to use a feminine hygiene product. In a day when personal health was often kept private, some ads were bold, daring, and certainly pushed the envelope. One ad showed a woman locked out of her house by the husband. Another revealed a broken marriage being the result of the wife who failed to use a feminine hygiene product. Bottom line: if there is something wrong in the marriage, the woman is probably to blame.

Nature's Chlorophyll was supposedly in every bar of a popular green soap...suggesting this is what gave the soap its color.

"My men wear English Leather, or they wear nothing at all."

One vintage car ad showed a woman with her legs inappropriately spread, enjoying maximum legroom in her new car.

A woman in an ad was spanked over her husband's knee because he discovered she did not "store test" for fresher coffee.

Prepare yourself, ladies! A trip to the beauty parlor may be in order. Is the perm still holding up?

A faded newspaper ad encouraged husbands to "Train Your Wife."

Fetch his pipe

Answer "Yes, dear" to all requests

Massage his feet wearing only cellophane wrap

Fragrances

Ambush

Avon

Cachet

Chanel No. 5

Chantilly

Charles of the Ritz

Coty Imprevu and Jungle Gardenia

Estee Lauder

Evening in Paris

Faberge Aphrodisia, Tigress & Woodhue

Fidji

Golden Autumn

Heaven Sent

Interlude

Le De Givenchy

Love's Baby Soft

Muguet de Bois

My Sin by Lanvin

Oh! de London

Revlon Jean Nate'

Rive Gauche

Shalimar

Tabu

Tweed

White Shoulders

Wind Song

Yardley English Lavender

Bar Soaps

Camay

Cashmere Bouquet

Dial

Dove (pink Dove introduced in the 1960s)

Ivory

Lava

Lifebuoy

Lux

Old English

Woodbury

Zest

Cold or Face Creams

Bleach and Glow

Bonnie Bell Ten-O-Six

Happy Face (Washing Cream)

Jergens

Nivea

Noxzema

Ponds Cold Cream

Tussy Skin Care

Remember how the cream felt cold to the touch, fresh out of the jar?

43 Woodbury Cold Cream

Cosmetics

Almay

Avon

Aziza

Charles of the Ritz

Clairol

Cover Girl

Dorothy Gray

Elizabeth Arden

Elvis Presley Lipstick

Flame-Glo

Germaine Monteil

Max Factor

Maybelline – especially Cake Mascara

Merle Norman

Pan-Stik

Revlon

Tangee

Tussy

Yardley

Deodorants

Arrid

Ban

Degree (initially named Rexona antiperspirant and known as Sure in various parts of the world)

5 Day Antiperspirant and Deodorant Pads

Fresh Stick

Lady Speed Stick

Mennen Speed Stick

Mum

Right Guard

Secret

Soft & Dri

Tussy

Women's Hair Products

Adorn Hair Spray

Aqua Net Hair Spray

Dippity-Do

Hidden Magic Hair Spray

Lilt Home Permanent

Miss Breck Hairspray

New Dawn Hair Spray

Ogilvie Home Permanent

44 Hairstyles

45 Curlers made a woman beautiful!

Rave Home Permanent

Roux Fanci-Full Rinse

Tame Clean Rinse

Toni Home Permanent

VO 5 Conditioning Hair Dressing

Shampoo

Breck

Bright Side

Clairol

Dial

Halo

Head & Shoulders

Helene Curtis

Lustre Crème

Mini-Mist Dry Shampoo

Minipoo Dry Shampoo

Prell

Redken

Suave

Tame

Tandem

Twice as Nice

Vaseline

White Rain

Toothpastes

Colgate

Crest

Gleem

Ipana

Macleans

Pepsodent

Stripe

Ultra Brite

Lotions

Dermassage

Helene Curtis Magic Secret Skin Lotion

Jergens – remember pouring it out of the glass bottle?

Pond's Angel Skin

46 *He's ready for a date…*

Men's Grooming Products

Afro Sheen

Afta by Mennen

Aqua Velva Classic Ice Blue

Aramis

Avon for men

Barbasol Shaving Cream

Brilliantine

British Sterling

Brut

Brylcreem

Burma Shave

Butch Wax

Canoe

Eau Sauvage

English Leather

Groom & Clean

Hai Karate

Jade East

Jovan Musk

Lectric Shave

Old Spice

Pomade, gels, waxes

Pub

Rapid Shave

Spruce After Shave

Vitalis

Chapter 9

Near-Death

We nearly "died" many times as teenagers...in fact, we are lucky to be alive. It did not take much to put us at the brink of death. The teen years were turbulent regardless of where we resided. Life was an emotional roller coaster, and some of those rides were bumpy. When life was good, it was like being on a high. When it was bad, well, it could be the end of the world. Like being stranded at home and not having a ride to the local teen dance club on a Friday or Saturday night. Remember when she wanted to break up because she found someone new? It was like a stab through the heart, and self-esteem ripped to shreds. Remember when a pimple the size of Jupiter appeared on picture day or the day of the prom? When an acquaintance called and told you that your boyfriend was "with" someone at a party, your heart shattered into a million pieces. These were real problems.

The teen years were a time of discovery and, of course, raging hormones. As several men courageously admitted, they felt continuously "horny" as teenagers. One amusingly referred to his teen years as "bra unfastening training for guys!" Love commenced in the back seat by cornfields near the airport, or at the Muncie or Ski-Hi Drive-Ins. She had such innocence and playfulness, and she smelled so good! Lovestruck teenagers awkwardly swayed together at the junior high school dance, ditzy girls enveloped themselves in endless phone chatter- either with their guy or with their girlfriends talking about the guy, and each crush could be "the real thing." Scribbling his name on a notebook during class, sure beat listening to that drab teacher.

Parents usually wanted to meet the date, know where the couple was going, and gave a time to be home. Several mothers said they always made sure their daughters had at least a dime when going on a date, in case they needed to call home. Some teens kept the dime in their shoes. Parents were trusting until there was a violation of that trust. Wise teens knew they had better return home on time. Or else...

Who could forget?

After school jobs

Attending the Battle of the Bands

Babysitting for 50 cents an hour and 75 cents an hour after midnight

"Bases" and making out: "First Base" – kissing, "Second Base" – caressing, "Third Base" - fondling other areas, and "Home Run" - going all the way. Some guys say what the heck, they just started at "First Base" and went straight to the Home Run!

Becoming "Blood Sisters" or "Blood Brothers" - two friends make a tiny cut (usually on the finger) and when it bleeds, press fingers together

Boys having paper routes

Breaking up - repeatedly playing the same 45 RPM record on the record player/Hi-Fi, while the tears flowed…

Busy Signal Dating – Teens called their telephone number to reach a busy signal. In between the loud sounds, they would yell (often, at the top of their lungs) each digit of their phone number. It sometimes took a while, and it was difficult for the person on the other end of the phone because the numbers, of course, had to be yelled louder than the busy signal and be in sequence. Many teens spent hours doing this, just another way of being silly! Interestingly, it did not seem so strange at the time. I gained personal experience with the Busy Signal, where I met my long-term friend Kenny. Kenny and I met when I was 14. The magnitude of this encounter and friendship would last for decades. Shortly before he passed, Kenny showed me his original Social Security card that had my faded, penciled, Muncie phone number from the 1960s in the upper corner. Hey, I did write that!!! I assume this remained in his wallet until the day he took his last breath.

Cassette tapes – opening the insert to read the song lyrics

Curfew – Police informing you that you are in violation

Dating – one-on-one when you turn 16

Deciphering the lyrics of "Louie Louie" and rumor has it, there was a "dirty" version…A few girls got caught by a parent singing it, and you do not want to know what happened next.

Dick Clark Caravan of Stars

Drinking Royal Crown (RC) Cola

Drive-in movies

Driver's Ed at school and sitting in the simulator, pretending to drive to get a burger and fries

Drooling over Carl Storie and The Chosen Few

Hairdryers and sitting under a hooded bonnet – the plastic, hatbox held a flexible hose which laid circular in the box

Hickeys - either wearing a low-cut shirt to show them off to friends or covering them up so mom and dad could not see them.

Large empty juice cans used as hair rollers

Learner's Permit and first Driver's License

47 *Portable Record Player with LP (Long Play) 33 RPM vinyl record*

Listening to all 17 minutes of "In-A-Gadda-Da-Vida"

Listening to Bill Craig, Jr. at Muncie's WLBC radio play the favorites

Listening to Larry Lujack at WLS radio in Chicago

Listening to Motown

Listening to "White Room"

Listening to Wolfman Jack

Listening to WOWO radio's broadcasts from "the little red barn" in Fort Wayne

The Loft – located in "The Village" near Ball State University

Pajama parties

Paul Petersen – watching him sing "My Dad" on *The Donna Reed Show* and playing the song on the record player

Pen Pals

The Heyday of Muncie, Indiana

Pinball Machines

Playing "Spin the Bottle" and "Post Office"

Record Hops

Restrooms - using them for their intention and not for taking selfies

Rings - going steady, receiving a pre-engagement ring, and wrapping angora around his ring

Sadie Hawkins dance

Self-piercing ears with an ice cube and needle

Shelley Fabares - watching her sing "Johnny Angel" on *The Donna Reed Show* and playing the song on the record player

Singing, "I got a brand-new pair of roller skates; you got a brand-new key..."

Sleeping in curlers overnight (O-U-C-H)

Sneaking and having a boy over – despite the consequences from parents

Sometimes when a guy defied the house rule and dad came home, he chased the guy up the street! What a sight!

Stridex Medicated Pads for acne

Teachers, you could talk to about anything! No subject was off-limits. Annette Fuson- a teacher at Storer Junior High in Muncie, taught Home Economics and Dating. She was way ahead of her time. She made students feel so comfortable asking about sex, that they knew they could even call her at home. Now, all teenagers can benefit from Fuson's expertise, with her book, *Straight Talk for Teenage Girls*, available through Amazon.

48 Typing in Hot Pants and Go-Go Boots

Telephone calls and laying on the floor playing with the phone cord

Magazines were a considerable part of a teen's world:

Calling All Girls (CAG)
Cheetah
Crawdaddy
Creem
Guitar Player
Hullabaloo/Circus
Ingenue
Life
Mad
Playboy
Reader's Digest
Rolling Stone
16 Magazine
Soul Magazine
Teen Life
Teen Time
Tiger Beat
Young Miss

Icons and others, we loved during the heyday

Paul Anka
Desi Arnaz, Jr.
Jane Asher
Frankie Avalon
Lucille Ball and Desi Arnaz
Tony Bennett
Pattie Boyd
Angela Cartwright
Veronica Cartwright
Richard Chamberlain
Tim Considine
Johnny Crawford
James Darren
Doris Day
James Dean
Sandra Dee
Troy Donahue
Tony Dow
Patty Duke
Clint Eastwood
Vince Edwards
Shelley Fabares
Fabian
Mia Farrow
Sally Field
Jane Fonda
Annette Funicello
Kathy Garver
Don Grady
Andy Griffith
Billy Hinsche
Eddie Hodges

Ron Howard
Anissa Jones
Don Knotts
Art Linkletter
Peggy Lipton
Lisa Loring
Allen Ludden
Ann Margret
Dean Martin
Dean Paul Martin
Jerry Mathers
David McCallum
Hayley Mills
Elizabeth Montgomery
Mary Tyler Moore
Billy Mumy
Ken Osmond
Butch Patrick
Paul Petersen
Elvis Presley
Vincent Price
Debbie Reynolds
Kurt Russell
Jean Shrimpton
Nancy Sinatra
Connie Stevens
Sharon Tate
Twiggy
Robert Wagner
Raquel Welch
Johnny Whitaker
Betty White

Back in the day, every kind of music was acceptable. From Johnny Mathis to Petula Clark to Chet Atkins to Freddie and the Dreamer, the music collection offered a wide variety.

Popular Recording Artists

A

Aaron Neville
Al Kooper
Amboy Dukes
American Breed
Andy Williams
The Angels
Anita Bryant
Archie Bell and The Drells

49 The Archies - #1 Billboard Top 100 for the year 1969

Aretha Franklin
Arlo Guthrie
Arthur Conley
The Association

B

B. B. King
B. J. Thomas
Barbara Lewis
Barbara Mason
Barry McGuire
The Beach Boys

50 The Beatles: John, Paul, George and Ringo

The Heyday of Muncie, Indiana

The Beau Brummels
The Bee Gees
Beverly Bremers
Bill Anderson
Bill Hailey and The Comets
Bill Monroe
Billie Holiday
Billy J. Kramer & The Dakotas

Billy Joe Royal
Black Sabbath
Blind Faith
Blood, Sweat, and Tears
Blues Image
Blues Magoos

51 Bob Dylan and Joan Baez

Bob Dylan
Bob Lind
Bobbie Gentry
Bobby Darin
Bobby Freeman
The Bobby Fuller Four
Bobby Goldsboro
Bobby Hebb
Bobby Rydell

Bobby Sherman
Bobby Vee
Bobby Vinton
Booker T. and the MGs
The Box Tops
Brenda Lee
Brian Hyland
Brook Benton
Brooklyn Bridge

Buck Owens
The Buckinghams
Buddy Miles Big Band
Buffalo Springfield
Burt Bacharach
The Byrds

C

Canned Heat
Captain Beefheart
The Casinos
The Castaways
Cat Stevens
Chad and Jeremy
Chambers Brothers
Charley Pride
Charlie Rich
Cher
Chet Atkins
Chicago Transit Authority
The Chiffons
Chris Montez
Chubby Checker
Chuck Berry
Cilla Black
Clarence Carter
Classics IV
Cliff Nobles and Company
Cliff Richard
Connie Francis
Connie Smith
The Contours
Conway Twitty
Count Five
Country Joe and the Fish
The Cowsills
The Crazy World of Arthur Brown
Cream
Creedence Clearwater Revival
Crispian St. Peters
Crosby, Stills, and Nash
The Cryan' Shames
The Crystals
The Cuff Links
Cyrkle

D

Darlene Love
The Dave Brubeck Quartet
Dave Clark Five
David Cassidy
Dean Martin
Dee Sharp
Deep Purple
Del Shannon
The Delfonics
Derek and The Dominos
Dinah Washington
Dion and the Belmonts
Dionne Warwick

52 Have you ever seen a jukebox with all Elvis songs?

The Dixie Cups
Dolly Parton
Don Gibson
Donny Osmond
Donovan
The Doors
Doris Day
Dottie West
The Drifters
Duane Eddy
Dusty Springfield

E

Eartha Kitt
The Easybeats
Eddy Arnold
Edison Lighthouse
Electric Flag

Electric Prunes
Ella Fitzgerald
Elvis Presley
Emmylou Harris
Engelbert Humperdinck
Eric Burdon and The Animals
Ernest Tubb
Essex
Everly Brothers
Every Mother's Son
Eydie Gorme

F

Fabian
Faron Young
Fats Domino
Ferlin Husky
The Fifth Dimension

Flatt and Scruggs

The Fleetwoods

Floyd Cramer

The Flying Machine

Fontella Bass

The Fortunes

The Foundations

The Four Seasons

The Four Tops

Frank Sinatra

Frank Zappa & The Mothers of Invention

Frankie Avalon

Frankie Valli and the Four Seasons

Freddie and The Dreamers

Freddy "Boom" Cannon

Freddy Fender

Friend & Lover

Friends of Distinction

G

Gene Pitney

Gene Vincent

The Gentrys

George Benson

George Jones

Gerry and the Pacemakers

Gladys Knight and The Pips

Glen Campbell

Glenn Yarbrough

The Grass Roots

Grateful Dead

Guess Who

H

Hank Locklin

Hank Williams

The Happenings

Horst Jankowski

Hugh Masekela

The Human Beinz

Helen Reddy

Henry Mancini

Herb Alpert and The Tijuana Brass

Herman's Hermits

The Hollies

Humble Pie

I

Ian Whitcomb

Ides of March

Ike and Tina Turner Review

Iron Butterfly

The Isley Brothers

J

J. Frank Wilson and The Cavaliers

Jackie DeShannon

Jackie Wilson

The Jackson Five

James Brown & The Famous Flames

Janis Ian

Janis Joplin

Jay and The Americans

Jay and The Techniques

Jeannie C. Riley

Jeff Beck

The Jimi Hendrix Experience

Jimmie Rodgers

Jimmy Clanton

Jimmy Dean

Jimmy Gilmer and The Fireballs

Joan Baez

Joe Tex

Joey Dee and The Starliters

John Fred and His Playboy Band

Johnny Cash

54 Somebody to Love- Jefferson Airplane peaked at #5 on Billboard Top 100. #33 for the year 1967.

53 Johnny Mathis recorded 73 studio albums, 18 of which went Gold and 6 were awarded Platinum for selling over 1 million copies.

Jerry Lee Lewis

Jewel Akens

Jim Reeves

Johnny Rivers

Johnny Taylor

Johnny Tillotson

Johnny Winter

Jonathan King

Joni Mitchell

Judy Collins

Judy Garland

Julie London

June Carter Cash

Junior Walker and The All-Stars

K

Keith

Kenny Rogers & The First Edition

The Kingsmen

Kingston Trio

The Kinks

The Knickerbockers

Kris Kristofferson

Kyu Sakamoto

L

Lawrence Welk and His Orchestra ("The Champagne Music Makers")

Led Zeppelin

Left Banke

Lefty Frizzell

The Lemon Pipers

Len Barry

The Lennon Sisters

Lenny Welch

Lesley Gore

The Lettermen

Linda Jones

Linda Ronstadt

Little Anthony and The Imperials

Little Eva

Little Peggy March

Little Richard

Little Stevie Wonder

Lonnie Mack

Loretta Lynn

Lorraine Ellison

Los Bravos

Lou Christie

Lou Rawls

Louis Armstrong

The Lovin' Spoonful

Lulu

M

The Mamas and The Papas

Manfred Mann

Marianne Faithful

The Marketts

Marmalade

Martha and The Vandellas

Marty Robbins

The Marvelettes

Marvin Gaye and Tammi Terrell
Mary Wells
Mason Williams
The McCoys
Mel Carter
Melanie Safka
Mercy
Merle Haggard
Merle Travis
The Mermaids
Merrilee Rush and The Turnabouts
Mitch Miller
Mitch Ryder & the Detroit Wheels
Moby Grape
The Monkees
The Moody Blues
Muddy Waters
Mungo Jerry
Music Explosion

N

Nancy Sinatra
Nat King Cole
Nazz
Neil Diamond
Neil Sedaka
The Newbeats
1910 Fruitgum Company

O

The Ohio Express

The O'Jays
The O'Kaysions
Oliver
Olivia Newton-John
Otis Redding
The Outsiders

P

The Partridge Family
Pat Boone
Patsy Cline
Patti Page
Patty Duke
Paul and Paula
Paul Anka
Paul Petersen
Paul Revere and The Raiders
Peaches and Herb
Peppermint Rainbow
Percy Faith
Percy Sledge
Perry Como
Pete Fountain
Peter and Gordon
Peter, Paul, and Mary
Petula Clark
Pink Floyd
Procol Harum

Q

Question Mark & the Mysterians

R

Ramsey Lewis Trio
Randy and The Rainbows
Rare Earth
The Rascals
Ray Charles
Ray Conniff Singers
Ray Price
Ray Stevens
Richard Harris
Ricky Nelson
The Righteous Brothers
Roger Miller
The Rolling Stones
The Ronettes
Rooftop Singers
Roy Clark
Roy Head
Roy Orbison
Royal Guardsmen
Ruby & The Romantics

S

S/Sgt. Barry Sadler
The Safaris
Sam and Dave
Sam Cooke
Sam the Sham and The Pharaohs
Sandy Nelson
Sandy Posey
Santana
Scott McKenzie
The Searchers
The Seeds
The Seekers
Sergio Mendes & Brasil '66
Shades of Blue
The Shadows of Knight
The Shangri-Las
Shelley Fabares
The Shirelles
Shirley Bassey
Shirley Ellis
Shocking Blue
Simon and Garfunkel
Sir Douglas Quintet
Skeeter Davis
Sly and the Family Stone
Small Faces
Smith
Smokey Robinson & The Miracles

55 Single (45 Revolutions Per Minute) record adapter needed to play singles on a phonograph

Sonny and Cher
The Soul Survivors
Spanky and Our Gang
The Spencer Davis Group
Spiral Staircase
Spirit
The Standells
Starbuck
The Statler Brothers
Status Quo
Steppenwolf
Strawberry Alarm Clock
The Supremes
The Swingin' Medallions

Terry Stafford
Three Dog Night
Todd Rundgren and Nazz
Tom Jones
Tommy James and the Shondells
Tommy Roe
Tony Bennett
Tony Orlando and Dawn
The Tornados
The Toys
Traffic
The Tremeloes
Trini Lopez
The Troggs
The Turtles
The Tymes

56 Peace Sign

T

The T-Bones
Tammi Terrell
Tammy Wynette
The Temptations
Ten Years After

V

Van Morrison
Vanilla Fudge
Vanity Fair
Velvet Underground
The Ventures
The Vogues

W

The Walker Brothers
Waylon Jennings
Wayne Cochran and The C.C. Riders
Wayne Fontana & the Mindbenders

We Five

The Who

Willie Nelson

Wilson Pickett

Y

The Yardbirds The

Youngbloods

Z

The Zombies

There were silly songs like:

"Green Giant"

"Hello Muddah Hello Faddah"

"Itsy Bitsy Teenie Weenie Yellow Polka Dot Bikini"

"Monster Mash"

"Tiptoe Through the Tulips"

"Who Put the Bomp (in the Bomp, Bomp, Bomp, Bomp Bomp)"

"Wooly Bully"

Oh yes, and we were doing a little something that goes like this: Shirley! Shirley, Shirley bo Birley, Banana fanna fo Firley, Fee fy mo Mirley, Shirley! "The Name Game," released by Shirley Ellis in late 1964, had all of us singing some strange words!

Speaking of "The Name Game," in the 1960s, top baby names were: Donna, Karen, Linda, Mary Susan, David, James, John, Michael, and Robert.

Beautiful Instrumental Hits of the 1960s

Henry Mancini songs:

"Baby Elephant Walk"

"Charade"

"Days of Wine and Roses"

Joy Charlene Henley

"Love Theme from Romeo and Juliet"

"Mr. Lucky "

"Moon River"

"Peter Gunn Theme"

"The Pink Panther Theme"

"A Taste of Honey" – Herb Alpert and the Tijuana Brass

"Alley Cat" – Bent Fabric

"Apache" – The Shadows

"Because They're Young" – Duane Eddy and The Rebels

"Calcutta" – Lawrence Welk

"Cast Your Fate to The Wind" – Sounds Orchestral/Vince Guaraldi Trio

"Classical Gas" – Mason Williams

"Exodus" and "Theme from The Apartment" – Ferrante and Teicher

"The Good, The Bad and The Ugly" – Hugo Montenegro

"Grazing in The Grass" – Hugh Masekela

"Green Onions" and "Hang 'Em High" – Booker T. and the MGs

"Hawaii Five-O Theme" and "Walk Don't Run" – The Ventures

"The Horse" – Cliff Nobles & Co.

"The In Crowd" - The Ramsey Lewis Trio

"Java" – Al Hirt

"Lara's Theme" from Dr. Zhivago

"Love Is Blue" – Paul Mauriat

"More" – Kai Winding

"No Matter What Shape (Your Stomach's In)" – The T-Bones

"Our Winter Love" – Bill Pursell

"Out of Limits" – The Marketts

"Pipeline" – The Chantays

"Route 66 Theme" – Nelson Riddle and his Orchestra

"Sleep Walk" – Santo and Johnny

"Soul Coaxing" – Raymond LeFevre

"Soulful Strut" – Young Holt-Unlimited

"Stranger on the Shore" – Acker Bilk

"The Stripper" – David Rose

"Take Five" – Dave Brubeck

"Telstar" – The Tornadoes

"Theme from A Summer Place" – Percy Faith

"Time is Tight" – Booker T. & The M.G.s

"Walk Don't Run" – The Ventures

"Washington Square" – The Village Stompers

"Wipe Out" - The Surfaris

57 Jukebox

Do you remember:

Pondering what Billy Joe McAllister and his girlfriend threw off the Tallahatchie Bridge?

Why it was "Judy's Turn to Cry"?

Your first 45 record?

Your first album?

The phone number of the time and temperature?

Your favorite flavor of popsicle and Kool-Aid?

Your favorite dance?

Your favorite teen year, and why?

Your wages at your first after school job?

Your childhood phone number beginning with two letters? Do you remember the numbers?

Teen girls fell in love with Ricky Nelson and Davy Jones. When they left us, it was like losing a part of our youth. Many fans still know the words to every one of their songs. Whether Ricky Nelson was closing his eyes, tenderly playing the guitar, and singing, "Teenage Idol," or Davy Jones was serenading the world with "Daydream Believer," their music is a part of us.

I remember the day I received an autographed postcard from teenage heartthrobs Dino, Desi, and Billy and knew at age 12, this was true love. I ran across the street from the mailbox, screaming at the top of my lungs! After all, we were talking, Dino Martin, Jr., Desi Arnaz, Jr., and Billy Hinsche! I became an instant celebrity with my friends. I was even on the radio, discussing this legendary postcard! In a roundabout way, they made *me* famous!

Dance Crazes

The Batusi

The Boogaloo

The Bristol Stomp

The Bug

The Bump

The Chicken

The Drag

The Freddie

The Frug

The Funky Chicken

The Hitch Hike

The Hully Gully- Did you know the Sam the Sham and the Pharaohs 1964 hit "Wooly Bully" was initially titled "Hully Gully," but the band could not record it under that name due to the prior existence of a recorded song by that title? Also, the speed of the beat did not coordinate with the steps of the "Hully Gully."

The Jerk

The Limbo

The Locomotion

The Madison - a line dance featured in the movie Hairspray that continues in the Broadway musical

The Mashed Potato

The Monkey

The Pony

The Roach

The Shake

The Shimmy

Shingaling

Shotgun

The Skate

The Stroll – created in the 1950s and still prevalent in the 1960s

The Strut

The Swim

The Tighten Up

The Twist

The Watusi

"I'd rather wear flowers in my hair than diamonds around my neck."

Anonymous

Chapter 10

Groovy Things

It was all part of being a teenager…

Autograph Books

Avon fragrances – Bird of Paradise, Blue Lotus, Brocade, Candid, Charisma, Cotillion, Field Flowers, Occur! Persian Wood, Rapture, Skin So Soft, Somewhere, Sweet Honesty, To A Wild Rose, Topaze, Unforgettable, Wishing

Baby Doll pajamas

Bangs- the longer, the better

Beads (Love Beads)

Beatles record player

Bell Bottoms

Belts- wide ones around a mini skirt

Bikinis

Black Lights

Blouses- Chiffon

Body painting

Bows in hair

Boys with mop-top hair

Bras- padding them

Bright, colorful menswear

"Bubble Gum" music

Candles- all scents, homemade

Cardigan sweaters

Cashmere sweaters

Chains and chain belts

Choker necklaces

Class Rings

Collars and lapels

Cruising

Culottes

Double-breasted suits (in the style of Brian Jones of The Rolling Stones)

Dresses in vivid colors – red, orange, yellow, blue

False eyelashes

Fish Net stockings

Floral patterns

Fringe hanging off of jackets

Fringed shimmy tops

Girls making their dresses from Simplicity Patterns to show off at dances

Go-Go Boots

Granny Dresses

Gypsy-like clothes with flowery patterns

Hairstyles: Beehive, Bouffant, Flip, French Twist, long, Pageboy, parted down the middle, ratting/teasing hair to give it that "poof," short

Hats – large and floppy

Headbands

High collars

High waisted pants

Hip-Hugger pants

58 VW (Volkswagen) "Hippie" Van

Hippies

Incense

Ironing hair (with an iron on the ironing board)

Jackets (collarless)

Jeans

Jumpers

Knee-High socks

Leather boots

Lip gloss

Long hair on guys

Love's Baby Soft

Madras plaids

Madras Shoulder Bags

"Make Love, Not War"

Maxi dresses, skirts, and coats

Medallion necklaces

Midi Dresses

59 Mini Dress in Go-Go Boots

Mini Skirts – in all colors/designs

Moccasins

Mood Rings

Nehru jackets

Oversized earrings

Oversized soft sweaters

Paisley shirts (men)

Pantyhose in colors, many still wore seamless stockings with garter belts

Pea Coats

Peace Signs

Peasant blouses and ones that bared the midriff

Penny Loafers

Pierre Cardin suits for men - single breasted collarless jacket and slim pants

The Heyday of Muncie, Indiana

Plaid, button-down shirts for men

Plaid, Mohair sweaters

Platform shoes

Polka Dot printed fabrics

Polo Neck shirts – guys

Ponchos

Puka Shells

Rickie Tickie Stickies – vinyl, flower hippie stickers

Saddle Shoes

Sewing Machines

Shifts – simple, geometric dresses available in a variety of colors and patterns

Shimmy skirt (the more fringe, the better)

Shirts- button-down Oxford cotton

Slacks – comfortable styles for men

Sleeves - "bubble" style, puffed and long

Sports Team jackets with logos

Stirrup pants

Sunglasses – over-sized, tinted sunglasses, that had gold frames, and a pinkish rainbow tint

Suntan lotions/oils – Bain de Soleil, Bonnie Bell, Coppertone, Hawaiian Tropic, QT, Sea & Ski, Sudden Tan, Tahitian Tan, Tanfastic, Tanya

Sweaters – polo-necked, ribbed, striped

Tent Dresses

Tie-Dye shirts were fashionable.

Ties with prints- some five inches wide, with vivid stripes and patterns

Tight trousers

Tights

Trouser straps

Tube Tops

60 Tie-Dye - produce patterns by tying parts of a garment or piece of cloth to shield it from the dye

V-neck sweaters

Velvet

Velvet trousers

Vests

Waterbeds

Wet look, vinyl fashions

Winged Sleeve dresses

Wool Kilt Skirts with pleats

Wool Shorts in winter (often plaid) with knee-high socks- college students often wore these.

Wrap - Around skirts

Zits (pimples) – Clearasil, Ice-O-Derm, and Phisohex used

Teens in the heyday spoke a language/slang all their own:

Ape - crazy or mad

Bad – awesome

Ball- go all the way

Blitzed - drunk

Boss- cool or fantastic

Bread- money

Cat - guy

Catch some rays - get out in the sun

Chicken – Playing chicken is when two cars race toward each other; the first driver to pull to the side is the chicken

Cool - good

Crash- go to bed

Cut Out – leave the area quickly

Don't Flip Your Wig – don't be upset

Dungarees – blue jeans

The Heyday of Muncie, Indiana

Five Finger Discount - stolen

Flake off – leave

Fox – good looking woman

A Gas – having a lot of fun

Going steady – dating only one person

Groovy – nice or neat

Hairy – awkward or out of control

Hang loose – take it easy

Heat – police or law enforcement

Hunk – good looking guy

It's Snowing Down South – girl or woman's slip is showing

Keep the Faith – a phrase often said. Ask several people the meaning, and you will probably receive different answers. A good-bye greeting, keep believing, keep religious faith, be true to yourself, or a sort of verbal peace sign

Ken Doll – guys who cared too much about their looks

Love Bite- hickey. Red mark made by the suction of the lips often on the neck

Lump It- learn to live with it

Moo Juice – milk

Moon – drop your pants and show your bare bottom

No sweat – no problem

Outta Sight – wondrous, unbelievable

Pad – where you sleep or live

Petting - most often involved kissing, embracing, and caressing

Pig – police officer, cop

Popped – arrested/caught

Punch It - hit gas pedal and go fast

Queer – dorky or dumb

Rad- short for "radical," good or great

Rap – to talk

Rat Fink – someone who informs on you

Rave On – please keep it going

Roach- the butt of a marijuana cigarette

Rubbers - boots

Rule – to have control of the situation

Scarf- eat super-fast, a large quantity or any type of indulgence

Score – going all the way

Scuzz – low down, disgusting person

Shotgun – To "shotgun weed" was when one person forced marijuana smoke into the mouth of another person. Most common way; when smoking a joint, one person turned it backward, so the lit part was in their mouth (usually between their teeth)

Silent Majority – term used by President Nixon. An unspecified large group of people in a country or group who do not express their opinions publicly.

Skag or Skank – an ugly girl

Skin – a handshake, "give me some skin"

Skirt – a girl

Slug Bug – Volkswagen Beetle

Sock It to Me – let me have it or lay it on me

Submarine Races – parking next to the water to wait for the submarine races. Excuse to park and make-out

Swapping Spit – French Kissing

Tapped Out – has no money

Threads - clothes

Tight – very friendly

Tough or Tuff – some young girls were known to answer their phones with "Miss Tuff's residence." It meant they were "hot stuff."

Tube – television

Way out – beyond explanation

"What's Your Bag?" - what's your problem?

The Wild Thing - sex

61 Go-Go Dancer

Go-Go Dancers or Cage Dancers, like one pictured here, were popular in the 1960s! They were famous, and some appeared at Hullabaloo, the teen night club between Muncie and Yorktown. Often clad in mod outfits with white Go-Go Boots, their endless energy demanded attention. With hair swirling from ear to ear and gyrating movements, they were an essential part of the music scene.

62 Larry Carmichael

One Muncie musician was smitten. He admits, "The only reason I begged for the Hullabaloo gig was that Barbara Costerison was a cage dancer at the stage. When I got the gig opening for The Lemon Pipers, Barbara was off that night. I was devastated, never got over it." -Larry Carmichael

> *"I will continue when you recover."*
>
> -Andres Segovia during his performance at Emens Auditorium at Ball State University, February 7, 1969

Chapter 11

Superstars!

It was the concert of a lifetime for teen guitarists Rod McClure and Randy Henzlik. On February 7, 1969, they headed to Emens Auditorium on the Ball State University campus to see the 75-year-old master, a classical guitarist from Spain. They could not fathom the significance this concert would have in their lives. Especially in the music they played.

Andres Segovia

According to McClure, Emens Auditorium was the perfect venue because it was extremely efficient with acoustics. McClure recalls the evening with the great Andres Segovia, "That night at Emens, you thought you were in the presence of God. He was plucking the strings of your heart with his guitar. He was so impressive at his advanced age then. He sat there and played a whole evening of concert level material, note for note, by memory. All of the complex, phrasing, passages, classical guitar. In the last three or four rows in the balcony, there was a heckler who was coughing." McClure remembers how Segovia stopped playing, casually looked up at the guy in the back of the balcony, and announced, "I will continue when you recover." It was the class of a polished, genius guitarist.

After the concert, McClure and Henzlik were outside when they spotted some Segovia posters and decided to remove them. They went back inside, figuring maybe they could get lucky and get the posters signed. To their surprise, an entourage of about six men approached. Segovia was in the group! The group saw McClure and Henzlik and subtly motioned with their arms for Segovia to "runoff," as McClure interpreted it. Segovia put his arms out to the entourage, which seemed to give the message that perhaps *they* needed to back off. Segovia approached McClure and Henzlik, and both shook hands with the legend. Speaking in broken English, Segovia asked if they enjoyed the program. He also signed their posters.

Today, McClure still holds the enthralling encounter in his heart and remembers Segovia's discipline and control. As he emotionally explains, "I never knew a player like him. It was a merging of knowledge and soul...it flowed out of him effortlessly. He played with absolute perfection. This is as good as it can be done...this was as perfect as it gets. Segovia would play everything the same thing, note for note- memorized. It was stunning...it was just absolutely stunning. If God can play guitar and I'm sure He can, He would play like Andres Segovia.

63 Rod McClure back in the day

McClure was one of many aspiring, talented Muncie teen musicians in the heyday, and music was his life. His first electric guitar, a Domino Californian model, cost $69.00 at Miracle Mart. He sold his stingray bicycle to raise the money for the guitar. It seems like yesterday that he purchased his first Hendrix record at Kresge's in downtown Muncie. Albums were $2.99 in mono and $3.99 in stereo. 45 rpm records were 79 to 99 cents. Those were the days when musicians could walk through Kresge's, a Five and Dime store while eating a chopped BBQ sandwich from the snack bar. McClure was really into local music back in the day and believed, "The local acts were the biggest things around. I used to watch when they would play. I would watch to see what they were playing – how they were playing. Dave Bennett, guitarist with the Chosen Few... the tone and the nuance he put into his playing- the way he emphasized notes... all of that was kind of a revelation to me. He was outstanding, really good with tone."

There were other celebrity encounters in McClure and Henzlik's lives as well.

Jimi Hendrix

The date was March 27, 1968, and guitarist Jimi Hendrix was going to be at the Teen America Building at the Delaware County Fairgrounds. Tickets were $2.50 in advance or $3.00 at the door. It was a concert forever etched in the minds of Muncie teens. Hendrix had recently come off tour with The Monkees.

McClure knew many things about Hendrix, one of these being that Hendrix was left-handed. He could never imagine the significance of knowing this until one precise moment when he was about to have the thrill of a lifetime! Before Hendrix entered the Teen America Building that evening, McClure extended his left hand to shake hands. The two shook hands and talked a moment as Hendrix asked, "Do you play?"

Enter Jimi Hendrix. Live, on-stage to a crowd of approximately 400-500 people. Appearing in an open neckline and "psychedelic" shirt, he wore a carved jade pendant with a gold medallion. As he tuned his guitar, a guy yelled, "Take off your hat!" Hendrix was quick to retort, "Well, first of all, if I take off my hat, will you take off your pants?" The guy and a few others started yelling, "Yeah..." Hendrix flipped him off with his middle finger and an "f-you." It appeared for a few seconds, like a Deputy Sheriff who began to get on stage, might arrest Hendrix for a lewd gesture. Hendrix spun around and started playing an extended intro into "Hey Joe." It was rather amusing when Hendrix told the audience how glad he was to be in "Muncie, Indianapolis!"

McClure recounts, "He started playing this amazing stuff. It sent chills up your backbone; the sounds were so unreal." On this particular night, Hendrix wowed the young audience with "Foxy Lady," "Purple Haze," and "Red House"- material from his first album. In keeping with Hendrix tradition, he destroyed a guitar at the end of the show. The neck, however, remained intact. After the show, McClure was given a drumstick by Mitch Mitchell. years later, McClure sold a Jimi Hendrix ticket on eBay to this very concert he and Henzlik attended, for over $800.00! Considering the low cost of the Hendrix concert tickets and the fact the ticket sold on eBay for over ten times the amount WERK radio's Larry McCabe netted promoting the concert, it was quite the takeaway for McClure!

The Who

On Nov. 23, 1967, McClure and Henzlik were in the audience of The Who concert. After the Muncie concert, they went to the band's blue bus – an old school bus converted into a tour bus. It sat behind the Teen America Building at the Delaware County Fairgrounds.

Back in the day, it was no big deal to approach bands. McClure believes, "They were one of the bands working at the time but not yet real famous. They had success with 'I Can See for Miles.'" Venturing back behind the building certainly paid off because Keith Moon was there. Moon was toweling off his sweat and smoking a cigarette at the time. "He was really personal – he gave me a drumstick and asked what we thought of the

show," McClure says, although admitting, "I was kind of let down that Pete Townsend was not back there yet."

64 Randy Henzlik

For two impressionable, hopeful guitarists, seeing Andres Segovia, Jimi Hendrix, and The Who provided the ultimate inspiration. McClure says the experiences of meeting both Segovia and Hendrix and shaking their hands were so compelling that his mind was totally blown. When he discusses meeting the two, he exclaims, "I got to see two absolute masters of the guitar who were icons, from two completely different realms. If Andres Segovia is the god of guitar, then Hendrix was the devil…he just let it fly!"

For McClure, these concerts were some of the best of times with Henzlik, who left us way too soon. Henzlik's sister still has and covets the poster signed by Segovia for her beloved brother.

Muncie resident Virginia Southard also, well remembers the Hendrix concert. Her brother Ronnie purchased a guitar from Hendrix after his show, behind the stage. Ronnie eventually fought in the Vietnam War and, sadly, did not survive. The guitar passed on to Virginia's middle son, Jason. Jason went on to enter and win – of all things, a Jimi Hendrix talent competition with the guitar. Virginia also had a celebrity encounter of her own! One of her most memorable events happened at the Muncie Fieldhouse at the Dick Clark Caravan of Stars. The year was 1963, and The Supremes were on the program. Southard happened to be in the restroom when Diana Ross rushed through the door. Ross inquired, "Oh honey, please can you help me? I need a safety pin." Southard took a pin out of her bra. A seam had split in Ross's outfit, and Southard will never forget putting her hand under Ross's clothing, "below her butt." Southard does not remember uttering a word, and to this day, the experience seems surreal.

Back in the day, Muncie's Pat Vandegriff remembers hitching a ride with Rick Derringer and Randy Zehringer of The McCoys, who had two of the nicest Harleys he had ever seen. Vandegriff was also at the Muncie Airport on April 4, 1968, when Senator Robert F. Kennedy was there. Most of Vandegriff's family went to the airport to see the Senator off. Vandegriff stood by the fence, next to the runway, holding his brother Brian, who was almost 3. They waved at Senator Kennedy, and he waved back as he prepared to leave for Indianapolis to give a campaign speech. Sadly, Senator Kennedy and the world soon learned that Martin Luther King, Jr. had not only been shot but died that evening. Senator Kennedy told the Indianapolis crowd the tragic news.

Wayne Cochran and The C.C. Riders

Years ago, on his show, Jackie Gleason lit a cigarette and gave a whooping introduction for the next act. If you were watching at home, you probably remember that single night. He grinned, "Occasionally, I go to a nightclub. I like to bounce around town and see what's going on. One night I dropped into a place called 'The Barn,' and what I saw there I have never seen before and don't expect to ever see again. I am going to introduce to you the wildest combination and the wildest guy I've ever seen in my life." Wayne Cochran was in the house!

After a blasting, grand musical intro by the C.C. Riders, Cochran eventually made his way to the stage. A chair dancing crowd went wild as Cochran made a spectacular entrance fitting of royalty. If this was your first time seeing the legend, your jaw had to drop to the floor. There was no mistaking the glitzy outfit, and famous, big hair belonged to a superstar. Now, this guy knew how to strut a pompadour! He also did not miss a beat with his gravelly voice and slick, on-stage dance moves.

It seems like yesterday that the incomparable Wayne Cochran appeared at 1730 Broadway in Muncie, Indiana. Woodbury's Sixty-Seven Supper Club was a hot spot for Cochran fanatics. The talk of the town often centered on outrageous stories about Cochran and his supposed, latest escapades, which fans say included losing control and poking holes in the ceiling. Word traveled fast that he threw a chair through a glass window at the venue. Everyone wanted to experience the hysteria!

Years ago, if you were to ask Cochran to describe himself, he would have told you, "I'm a hillbilly with a sixth-grade education." Casting his modesty aside, he was an enormously talented musician, songwriter, and record producer.

In 1963, Cochran formed his group, the C.C. Riders ("Cochran's Circuit Riders") in Shreveport, Louisiana. Muncie jump-started Cochran's career by being the band's first road club and job. Cochran was known to boast about Muncie back in the day. The group also lured a considerable following in the South and Midwest by extensively touring and performing at various clubs, lounges, and seedy dives throughout the region.

If you were lucky enough to catch one of Cochran's floor shows, you knew you would probably never in your lifetime see another artist like him. Elvis Presley used to watch Cochran's performances and was especially impressed with his wardrobe and act. Ike and Tina Turner were also big fans. Whether playing Miami or Las Vegas, Cochran hobnobbed with the entertainment industry's elite. He was a huge draw, gaining a reputation as one of the hottest performers in Las Vegas.

The Heyday of Muncie, Indiana

Taking time out of his busy day at Wayne Cochran Ministries in Hialeah, Florida, a soft-spoken Pastor Wayne Cochran told, via telephone, of ministering to people through his church, records, tapes, books, and television. He also found time to talk a little Muncie even though that period in his life was a long time ago.

He admitted his memories were a bit sketchy, but he recalled staying at a Muncie hotel where "I was broke and rehearsed all day." He quickly gained the nickname, "The White Knight of Soul," - which he said was a reference to James Brown. Cochran laughed, "That was ok at the time. You did not have to be politically correct."

65 The great Wayne Cochran and WERK Radio DJ Larry McCabe

Cochran and Gleason were close, and Cochran enjoyed being on *The Jackie Gleason Show*. It was apparent by the enthusiasm in his voice. "That was really great! He was like a father to me during that time. He came to my club every Friday night and brought the whole cast, and the June Taylor Dancers came by usually every week," Cochran shared. Cochran's club, The Barn, in Miami, was a hot spot, and it was known as the number one club in South Florida. Taylor acquired many of her ideas for the dance steps used by the dancers from Cochran's show. Cochran loved those days and explained, "Everybody came to The Barn, from well-known actors, actresses, recording artists, and singers ranging from Connie Francis to Tom Jones, and Lloyd Bridges to Bob Conrad. We played soul music, rhythm, and blues music with horns. They called it the 'Home of Soul.'"

Cochran recorded his debut single "My Little Girl" for the Scottie label in 1959. He was just getting started! There were other recordings throughout the 1960s for such labels as Gala ("Funny Feeling," "Liza Jane"), Confederate ("Linda Lu"), Aire ("Cindy Marie"), King ("Harlem Shuffle," " Little Orphan Annie") and Mercury ("Get Down With It" and "Goin' Back to Miami"), the latter, a song that would be covered by The Blues Brothers. Cochran's popularity soared like a rocket!

He soon appeared on such entertainment shows- both in the U.S. and internationally as *The Johnny Carson Show*, *The Merv Griffin Show*, *The Mike Douglas Show*, *The Dinah Shore Show*, and many others. He worked 3-6 months a year at The Flamingo and The Las Vegas Hilton.

The C.C. Riders and Ike and Tina Turner with their band played with Elvis. Cochran would play from Miami to Las Vegas and eventually celebrated an incredible 20 years with the C.C. Riders. He also had a couple of bands before the C.C. Riders, so his musical career spanned 25 years.

All crazy antics aside, there was a deep, compassionate side to Cochran. It is this side that he chose to focus on later in life. When asked about yesteryear, he did not mention the wild days. Far from it. He decided to focus on the tender story of his song, "Last Kiss," his best work, and claim to fame. No amount of wild, out-of-control stage presence can compare to this masterpiece.

The song details the real-life tragedy of 16-year-olds Jeanette Clark and J.L. Hancock, who were on a date a few days before Christmas in 1962. It was Jeanette's 16th birthday. The 1954 Chevy they were riding in (borrowed from J. L's father), hit a tractor-trailer truck on the road in rural Barnesville, Georgia. Jeanette, J.L. Hancock, and Jeanette's friend, Wayne Cooper, who was riding with them, were killed instantly. Two other friends, Jewel Emerson and Ed Shockley, survived with serious injuries. Cochran named the song "Last Kiss" because it was the dramatic high point of the song. The tragedy also hit too close to home since Cochran's drummer had been dating Jeanette Clark's sister at the time of the crash.

Cochran said he resided on Route 1941 in Georgia, which was about 15 miles away from the crash. It was a busy road. He had been writing a song about the many accidents on the strip of highway that was unfinished until he heard about the tragedy on the strip of the Georgia highway known as 1921 South 2L (Highway 341) in Barnesville. There was an intense emotional response from the community after the tragedy, and Cochran used those feelings to complete the song.

He dedicated the song to Jeanette Clark. Copies of Cochran's original version sold out of the trunks of cars, and the song was a local hit in Georgia. Major Bill Smith (Producer of "Hey Paula" by Paul and Paula) bought a copy and persuaded J. Frank Wilson and The Cavaliers to record it.

Released June 1964, the song reached the Top Ten in October of that year, eventually placing at #2 on the Billboard Hot 100. It sold over one million copies, earning a Gold Record. Cochran promised never to forget Jeanette Clark. "She was a sweet little girl, and it was one of the biggest songs in that period of music," Cochran said with unmistakable emotion and sorrow in his voice.

Once upon a time, Cochran lived the life of a superstar. It was a road fraught with partying, women, and drugs. Whether belting out rock 'n' roll or a hymn, music was phenomenal in Cochran's life. Who would ever imagine Cochran would one day celebrate 40+ years in the Ministry?

Cochran spent his final years in the limelight of serving The Lord. He shared that he humbly looked back at his life and gave thanks. "I'm glad for the popularity. I traveled all over the world. I've had a good career, and The Lord really blessed us," Cochran added, as our conversation was about to end. Muncie and its importance in Cochran's career were worth one more mention. Cochran recollected, "It played a huge part. We enjoyed it. Tell everybody, hello."

Wayne Cochran

May 10, 1939 – November 21, 2017

Jim Davis

Do not be surprised if you are out and about in Muncie and happen to see Jim Davis- creator of the comic strip character "Garfield!" People in the know say he enjoys dining at Vera Mae's in downtown Muncie and at the Delaware Country Club, where he is known to squeeze in a round or two of golf.

David Letterman

David Letterman can be easy to spot. You may find him at the David Letterman Communications and Media Building and Emens Auditorium at Ball State University. The school- where he is a generous financial donor, is his Alma Mater (1965-1969). Do not be surprised also if you happen to see him strolling downtown.

Bob Ross

The late artist, Bob Ross, filmed shows in and lived in Muncie. His presentation was taped and produced by WIPB in Muncie from 1984 until the show ended in 1994. It is said, during his lifetime, Ross only allowed one public institution to display his work- the Minnetrista Cultural Center in Muncie.

Kade Puckett- National Fingerstyle Guitar Champion

The media loves Fingerstyle guitarist, Kade Puckett. Indiana folks frequently see and hear him featured on TV, radio, and in magazines. He plays with every piece of his heart and soul.

Joy Charlene Henley

When this super talent is going to be in the house, the seats fill fast! Puckett is a third-generation Fingerpicker who, in July 2013, won the National Fingerstyle Guitar Competition. Before this, he won the Indiana State Fingerstyle Guitar Competition. In 2012, he was the Second Place Winner in the same contest.

Puckett is a versatile musician. He enjoys playing all genres of music, has dynamic vocals, and interacts with the audience on a personal level. I dare you...no I "double" dare you to try to stump him with a request! If you say it, he can play it! He knows his music, that is for sure. Heads turned when Puckett took front and center at the annual Chet Atkins Appreciation Society convention in Nashville, Tennessee.

The day I headed to Bloomfield, Indiana, to see Puckett will always be near and dear to my heart. I became a huge fan the first time I watched his online videos. I immediately spread the word about Puckett to other guitarists throughout the country. He similarly plays Fingerstyle in Tommy Emmanuel and Chet Atkins style, yet, his talent is in a realm all its own. His sound can be rockin' and upbeat or tender and smooth. Puckett plays a variety of songs from "The Christmas Song" (one of his best) to Queen's "Crazy Little Thing Called Love" to "The Rainbow Connection."

Whether he plays a soft ballad, a song he wrote, a new rendition on some old favorites like "Summertime" or "Walk Don't Run" or picks on some Van Halen or Merle Travis; he astounds audiences. He is a spectacular one-person show.

I remember the emotion I felt as I walked toward the stage. I pinched myself, as a reminder I was really about to see "the" Kade Puckett in person! After many months of social networking, I slowly approached the side of the stage and stood there, listening to every note. It had been a long road from Seattle, Washington, to the spot where I stood at that moment. As Puckett strummed the guitar, he happened to glance over to the side of the stage, and our eyes met. We smiled. Once off-stage, Puckett and his wife Timberly Ferree pulled up a chair. Timberly manages his successful career.

66 *The phenomenal Kade Puckett*

They make quite the team. Puckett can play the swankiest venues to the informal. On this day, sitting on a bench in the sunshine amid carnival rides and folks carrying signs that offered "Free Hugs," it was the perfect setting. The audience raved about Puckett's performance, asking where he would play next. He has familiar faces at his shows because he has such loyal fans. Catching an occasional show does not do it for them. They want more, so they travel to where he performs.

Sometimes I have to hear some of those Kade Puckett songs myself, so I attend another one of his shows, listen to a CD or turn those headphones way up on YouTube. The guy can play some serious guitar. You are going to be impressed.

Armed and Famous

Then, there was the CBS Show, *Armed and Famous*. The series followed five celebrities: Latoya Jackson, Trish Stratus, Erik Estrada, Jack Osbourne, and Jason Acuna (aka "Wee Man" on MTV's *Jackass*) as they trained to become Reserve Police Officers for the Muncie Police Department.

Upon graduating and being sworn in on December 5, 2006, the celebrities went on patrol with the same training officers who traditionally ride with new officers. The American reality television series premiered on January 10, 2007, with an estimated 8.2 million viewers.

The celebrities have returned to Muncie on occasion, especially at Christmas, to shop with local families. So, if you happen to encounter Jack Osbourne or his dad Ozzy in Muncie, do not be surprised. Estrada has spent several occasions as a Reserve Officer in Muncie and helping local charities. In the past, he assisted the Muncie Crime Stoppers holiday food basket program at Meijer and the Muncie Fraternal Order of Police Shop-with-a-Cop program at Target. He has also worked the 11:00 p.m. to 7:00 a.m. shift for the Muncie Police Department, patrolling the streets.

Roger Overbey

Every city needs a citizen like Roger Overbey! If you have watched online videos of Muncie and the surrounding areas, seen pictures of community events, and tuned-in to Cable Channel 60-the Public Access Channel in Muncie to the *Community Focus* program, you have seen the master at work! From conducting impromptu to official interviews, heading to the scene of the action, Drone Photography, captivating Videography, and more, Overbey's skills and expertise are in high demand. As they should be for the former City of Muncie Media Director, whose achievements are renowned. Initially contracted by former Muncie Mayor Dan Canan, for 10 years, Overbey's experience in Public Access Media and Photography spans decades. He has an unsurpassed ability to capture the essence of people just being themselves. Be sure to catch his "Happy Muncie" video on YouTube!

67 *Cynda Williams, actress and singer (former wife of Billy Bob Thornton), festive and ready for the holidays with Overbey. She knows Muncie. She attended Northside High School and Ball State University.*

68 Roger Overbey left a legacy as the Media Director for the City of Muncie, and for Channel 60 - the Public Access Channel. His company, Millennium Productions, continues to do great things in Muncie! Seen here with buddies, Jack and Ozzy Osbourne, Overbey has an extensive circle of celebrity friends.

69 Renowned Author, Dr. Gregory H. Williams, who wrote the masterpiece, Life On The Color Line, visiting Overbey

70 Overbey with CHIPS actor, Erik Estrada who always receives a warm welcome in Muncie!

Even a local laundromat has had brushes with celebrities. *Armed and Famous* filmed at The Laundry Basket, as evidenced by a giant neon sign in the business. Nancy, who referred to herself as "the German lady" over at The Laundry Basket in Muncie, has done the laundry of Willie Nelson and a particular Race Car Legend with the surname of Andretti. She also visited with Red Skelton years ago at Ball State.

Kim Ousley

71 Kim Ousley

Oh, and there is one more celebrity! Well, she is more of a hero! Meet Kim Ousley of Anderson, Indiana!

Joy Charlene Henley

Ousley and I had emailed for at least ten years, and soon after I arrived in Muncie, we finally met in person at a local bookstore. Ousley is a Cancer survivor, amputee, and writer. She is a strong advocate for people with disabilities, often volunteering 10-15 hours a week at Social Service and faith-based organizations. Having been diagnosed with Sarcoma in August of 2010, after noticing a large bulge or swelling on her ankle/lower leg area, she underwent several surgeries and the eventual amputation of her lower leg. She has survived a Cancer diagnosis not once, not twice, not thrice, not four but five times. Ousley spends much of her life helping others and being supportive by answering questions from those facing the fears she once encountered. She knows the feelings associated with learning a tumor is present, and she is quite familiar with the word "metastasized." She understands the fears of Chemotherapy and radiation, the struggles of living with long- term side effects, and being forced to let go and grieve the life one had planned.

72 Kim making a difference in the lives of others

The Heyday of Muncie, Indiana

Ousley turned a dream into reality with Kim's Art Kart. It was an idea she expanded with her personal touch, after seeing a similar one in action at the Indiana University Simon Cancer Center in Indianapolis. She hosts Kim's Art Kart at St. Vincent's Hospital at the outpatient Erskin Infusion Lab in Anderson, Indiana. The St. Vincent Anderson Foundation, the community, and friends sponsored the Art Kart. When it was unveiled, staff had surprised Ousley by decorating it!

Mounds State Park, located near Anderson, Indiana in Madison County, is a sort of second home to Ousley, where she has obtained advanced Certification as a Master Naturalist. Her certification authorizes her to volunteer at any State Park nationwide. She also has a heart for supporting and helping single mothers identify and develop skills to help them rise from poverty. Her faith is "stronger than ever." If anyone in this world has a positive attitude about life, it is this gal. As if her life is not already full, Ousley is working on a book that tackles the personal issues and hard stuff about moving forward. She is a lifeline to many.

Chapter 12

The Boob Tube with Rabbit Ears and Rooftop Antennas

Can you name the products or missing words in these commercials?

It takes two hands to handle...

In the valley of the jolly, ho-ho-ho...

Plop, plop, fizz, fizz...

10, 2, and ...

I'd like to teach the world to sing...

When it says Libby's, Libby's Libby's...

Does she or ...

Breakfast of...

He likes it, hey Mikey…

Promise her anything but give her...

The best part of waking up is...

Melts in your mouth...

Double your pleasure...

When it rains it...

Two all-beef patties, special sauce, lettuce, cheese, pickles…

Baseball, hot dogs, apple pie, and...

Put a tiger in your...

What would Tareyton smokers rather do than switch?

"You've come a long way, baby, to get where you've got to today...!"

Nothin' says lovin' like somethin' from...

It's not nice to fool...

See the U.S.A. in your...

The Heyday of Muncie, Indiana If you've got the time, we've got the...

Western Air Lines, the only way to...

Good to the last...

I'd walk a mile for a...

Breakfast of ...

A little dab...

You'll wonder where the yellow went...

Does she or...

Rice-A-Roni, the San Francisco...

Winston tastes good...

Everyone knows it's ... (hint: a toy)

"I cannot believe I ate the whole thing."

What was 99 and 44/100% pure?

Leave the driving to us...

Were you glued to the TV watching these shows?

Adam-12

The Addams Family

Adventures in Paradise

The Adventures of Ozzie and Harriet

The Adventures of Rin Tin Tin

Alfred Hitchcock Presents/The Alfred Hitchcock Hour

The Alvin Show

American Bandstand

The Andy Griffith Show

The Andy Williams Show

Another World

Archie Comedy Hour

As the World Turns

Atom Ant

The Avengers

Baby Huey

Bachelor Father

The Banana Splits

The Barbara Stanwyck Show

Batman

Bat Masterson

Beany and Cecil

Ben Casey

Joy Charlene Henley

- *The Beverly Hillbillies*
- *Bewitched*
- *The Big Valley*
- *The Bing Cosby Show*
- *The Bobby Darin Show*
- *Bonanza*
- *The Brady Bunch*
- *Branded*
- *The Brighter Day*
- *The Bugs Bunny Show*
- *Bullwinkle and Friends/The Bullwinkle Show*
- *Burke's Law*
- *Candid Camera*
- *Captain Kangaroo*
- *Car 54, Where Are You?*
- *The Carol Burnett Show*
- *Casper the Friendly Ghost*
- *Cheyenne*
- *Cimarron Strip*
- *Columbo*
- *Combat*
- *The Courtship of Eddie's Father*
- *Daktari*
- *Daniel Boone*
- *The Danny Kaye Show*
- *The Danny Thomas Show*
- *Dark Shadows*
- *Davey and Goliath*
- *Davy Crockett*
- *Days of Our Lives*
- *The Dean Martin Show*
- *Death Valley Days*
- *The Defenders*
- *Dennis the Menace*
- *Deputy Dawg*
- *The Dick Cavett Show*
- *The Dick Van Dyke Show*
- *The Dinah Shore Show*
- *Discovery* (*Discovery '65* was especially popular)
- *Disney's Wonderful World of Color*
- *Divorce Court*
- *Dobie Gillis*
- *Doctor Kildare*
- *The Doctors*
- *The Donna Reed Show*
- *The Doris Day Show*
- *Dragnet*
- *The Ed Sullivan Show*
- *The Edge of Night*
- *FBI*
- *Fair Exchange*
- *Family Affair*
- *The Farmer's Daughter*
- *Father Knows Best*
- *Felony Squad*
- *The Flintstones*

The Heyday of Muncie, Indiana

The Flip Wilson Show
Flipper
Flying Nun
For Better For Worse
Fractured Flickers
The Fugitive
The Garry Moore Show
General Hospital
Gentle Ben
George of the Jungle
Get Smart
The Ghost and Mrs. Muir
Gidget
Gilligan's Island
The Girl from U.N.C.L.E.
The Glen Campbell Goodtime Hour
Gomer Pyle, U.S.M.C.
Green Acres
Green Hornet
The Guiding Light
The Guns of Will Sonnett
Gunsmoke
The Gypsy Rose Lee Show
The Hathaways
Have Gun Will Travel
Hawaii Five-O
Hawaiian Eye
Hazel
Heckle and Jeckle

Hee-Haw
Here Come the Brides
Here's Lucy
High Chaparral
Highway Patrol
Hogan's Heroes
The Hollywood Palace
Honey West
The Honeymooners
Hootenanny
House Party (Art Linkletter)
The Huckleberry Hound Show
Hullabaloo
The Huntley-Brinkley Report
I Dream of Jeannie
I Love Lucy
I'm Dickens…He's Fenster
Iron Horse
The Invaders
I Spy
It Takes A Thief
It's the Great Pumpkin, Charlie Brown
I've Got A Secret
The Jack Benny Show
The Jack Lalanne Show
The Jack Paar Tonight Show (and The Jack Parr Program)
The Jackie Gleason Show
The Jerry Lewis Show

The Jetsons
The Joey Bishop Show
The Johnny Cash Show
Jonny Quest
Judd for the Defense
The Judy Garland Show
Julia
Kindergarten College
The King Family Show
Kraft Music Hall
Land of the Giants
Laramie
Laredo
Lassie
Laurel and Hardy
The Lawrence Welk Show
Leave It to Beaver
The Lone Ranger
Looney Toons
The Loretta Young Show
Lost in Space
Love American Style
Love is a Many Splendored Thing
Love of Life
Love on a Roof Top
The Lucy Show
The Magilla Gorilla Show
Make Room for Daddy
The Man from U.N.C.L.E.

Mannix
The Many Loves of Dobie Gillis
Marcus Welby, M.D.
The Mary Tyler Moore Show Maverick
Mayberry R.F.D.
McHale's Navy
The Merv Griffin Show
The Mickey Mouse Club (Spin and Marty and The Hardy Boys)
Mighty Mouse
The Mike Douglas Show
The Millionaire
The Milton Berle Show
Mission Impossible
Mister Ed
The Mister Magoo Show
Mister Rogers' Neighborhood Mod Squad
The Monkees
The Monroes
The Mothers-In-Law
The Munsters
Mutual of Omaha's Wild Kingdom My Favorite Martian
My Friend Flicka
My Mother the Car
My Three Sons
Naked City

The Heyday of Muncie, Indiana

The Name of the Game
National Velvet
Nightmare Theater
The Nurses
One Life to Live
One Step Beyond
Our Five Daughters
The Outer Limits
Outlaws
Ozzie and Harriet
The Patty Duke Show
Pepe Le Pew
Perry Mason
Pete and Gladys
Peter Gunn
Petticoat Junction
Peyton Place
The Phil Donahue Show
Pink Panther
Please Don't Eat the Daisies
Popeye
Porky Pig
Quick Draw McGraw
Rat Patrol
Rawhide
The Real McCoys
The Rebel
The Red Skelton Show
The Rifleman

Rin Tin Tin
The Road Runner Show
The Rockford Files
The Rocky and Bullwinkle Show
Romper Room
Room 222
Route 66
Rowan and Martin's Laugh-In
The Roy Rogers Show
Saturday Night at the Movies
Scooby-Doo, Where Are You!
Sea Hunt
Search for Tomorrow
The Secret Storm
Sergio Mendes & Brasil '66
Sesame Street
77 Sunset Strip
The Shari Lewis Show
Shindig
Sing Along with Mitch
60 Minutes
Sky King
Smothers Brothers Comedy Hour
Sonny and Cher
Space Ghost
Speedy Gonzales
Spider-Man
Star Trek
The Steve Allen Playhouse

Superman

Surfside Six

Tarzan

Tennessee Tuxedo

That Girl

The Three Stooges

The Time Travelers

The Time Tunnel

The Today Show

Tom and Jerry

The Tonight Show- Johnny Carson

Top Cat

Twelve O'clock High

The Twilight Zone

Underdog

The Untouchables

The Verdict Is Yours

The Virginian

Voyage to the Bottom of the Sea

Wacky Races

Wagon Train

Walt Disney's Wonderful World of Color

What's My Line?

Where the Action Is

Where the Heart Is

Wild Kingdom

Wild West

Woody Woodpecker

The Yogi Bear Show

Young Doctor Malone

Zorro

The *I Love Lucy* episode of Lucy giving birth to "Little Ricky" (Keith Thibodeaux) celebrated huge ratings. Viewed by over 70% of all U.S. households, it had higher ratings than the inauguration of President Dwight D. Eisenhower. The storyline coincided with Lucy's real-life pregnancy with Desi Arnaz, Jr.

Popular TV Shows that started as Radio Shows

The Adventures of Ellery Queen

The Adventures of Superman

The Aldrich Family

Amos 'n Andy

Arthur Godfrey's Talent Show

Dragnet

Fibber McGee and Molly

The Gene Autry Show

The George Burns and Gracie Allen Show

Grand Ole Opry

The Green Hornet

Guiding Light

Gunsmoke

I Love Lucy

The Jack Benny Program

The Life of Riley

The Lone Ranger

The New Truth or Consequences

Ozzie and Harriet

People are Funny

Perry Mason

The Red Skelton Hour

This Is Your Life

Joy Charlene Henley

Game Shows

Alumni Fun

Beat the Clock

Beat the Odds

Bowling for Dollars

Call My Bluff

Camouflage

Candid Camera

College Bowl

Concentration

The Dating Game

Dream House

Eye Guess

The Face Is Familiar

The Golden Shot

Hollywood Squares

I've Got A Secret

Jackpot Bowling

Jeopardy!

Let's Make A Deal

Make That Spare (a 15-minute show that spanned four years)

Match Game

Missing Links

Name That Tune

The Newlywed Game

PDQ

Password

People Are Funny

Play Your Hunch

The Price Is Right

Queen for A Day

Say When

Seven Keys

Snap Judgment

Stump the Stars

Supermarket Sweep

Tic-Tac-Dough

To Tell the Truth

Truth or Consequences

University Challenge

Video Village

What's My Line?

Who Do You Trust?

You Bet Your Life

You Don't Say?

The Heyday of Muncie, Indiana

Movie Actresses of the Era

Julie Adams
Ursula Andress
Julie Andrews
Eve Arden
Anne Bancroft
Brigitte Bardot
Candice Bergen
Polly Bergen
Ingrid Bergman
Karen Black
Ellen Burstyn
Dyan Cannon
Diahann Carroll
Julie Christie
Joan Crawford
Bette Davis
Doris Day
Sandra Dee
Catherine Deneuve
Angie Dickinson
Patty Duke
Faye Dunaway
Barbara Eden
Samantha Eggar
Anita Ekberg

Britt Ekland
Mia Farrow
Barbara Feldon
Annette Funicello
Judy Garland
Judy Geeson
Olivia de Havilland
Rita Hayworth
Audrey Hepburn
Katharine Hepburn
Olivia Hussey
Glynis Johns
Shirley Jones
Deborah Kerr
Dorothy Lamour
Hope Lange
June Lockhart
Tina Louise
Lulu
Shirley MacLaine
Dorothy Malone
Dorothy McGuire
Dina Merrill
Sarah Miles
Vera Miles

Hayley Mills
Mary Ann Mobley
Elizabeth Montgomery

73 Agnes Moorehead as "Endora"

Patricia Neal
Suzanne Pleshette
Vanessa Redgrave
Debbie Reynolds
Diana Rigg
Katharine Ross
Eva Marie Saint
Connie Stevens
Inger Stevens
Stella Stevens
Susan Strasberg
Barbra Streisand
Sharon Tate
Diana Rigg
Katharine Ross
Eva Marie Saint
Connie Stevens
Inger Stevens
Stella Stevens
Susan Strasberg
Barbra Streisand
Sharon Tate
Elizabeth Taylor
Deborah Walley
Jessica Walter
Tuesday Weld
Lana Wood
Natalie Wood
Joanne Woodward
Susannah York

Movie Actors

Eddie Albert
Morey Amsterdam
Alan Arkin
Ed Asner
Fred Astaire
Frankie Avalon
Gene Barry
Warren Beatty
Jack Benny
Milton Berle
Humphrey Bogart
Marlon Brando
Lloyd Bridges
Charles Bronson
Raymond Burr
Richard Burton
Red Buttons
James Caan
David Carradine

John Carradine
Richard Chamberlain
Lon Chaney, Jr.
James Coburn
Sean Connery
Jackie Coogan
Bob Crane
Richard Crenna
Robert Cummings
Tony Curtis
Sammy Davis, Jr.
Robert De Niro
Robert Duvall
Clint Eastwood
Henry Fonda
Glenn Ford
Harrison Ford
Clark Gable

Joy Charlene Henley

Gale Gordon	Peter O'Toole
Cary Grant	Gregory Peck
George Hamilton	Sidney Poitier
Dwayne Hickman	Elvis Presley
Dustin Hoffman	Vincent Price
Bob Hope	Anthony Quinn
Rock Hudson	Ronald Reagan
Tab Hunter	Cliff Robertson
Boris Karloff	Cesar Romero
Tony Kirk	Mickey Rooney
Don Knotts	Robert Stack
Burt Lancaster	Robert Taylor
Jack Lemmon	Spencer Tracy
Peter Lorre	Peter Ustinov
Karl Malden	Dick Van Dyke
Steve McQueen	John Wayne
Sal Mineo	Orson Welles
Paul Newman	Cornel Wilde

74 Marilyn Monroe

Sex Symbols

Julie Adams	Yvonne Craig
Ursula Andress	Catherine Deneuve
Lauren Bacall	Angie Dickinson
Carroll Baker	Diana Dors
Brigitte Bardot	Clint Eastwood
Warren Beaty	Anita Ekberg
Jacqueline Bisset	Lola Falana
Dyan Cannon	Barbara Feldon
Claudia Cardinale	Jane Fonda
Sean Connery	Peter Fonda

Anne Francis	Marilyn Monroe
Eva Gabor	Paul Newman
Zsa Zsa Gabor	Kim Novak
Tom Jones	Elke Sommer
Eartha Kitt	Stella Stevens
Janet Lee	Elizabeth Taylor
Michele Lee	Lana Turner
Gina Lollobrigida	Mamie Van Doren
Sophia Loren	Deborah Walley
Carol Lynley	Raquel Welch
Jayne Mansfield	Natalie Wood
Ann-Margret	
Yvette Mimieux	

Some Popular Movies of the 1960s

Alice's Restaurant
The Apartment
Babes in Toyland
Barefoot in the Park
Batman

Beach Movies:
    Beach Blanket Bingo
    Beach Party
    Bikini Beach
    Muscle Beach Party

Ben-Hur

The Birds
Bob and Carol and Ted and Alice
Bonnie and Clyde
Born Free
Breakfast at Tiffany's
Bullitt
Butch Cassidy and the Sundance Kid
Cactus Flower
Cape Fear
Casino Royale
Charade
Chitty Chitty Bang Bang

The Heyday of Muncie, Indiana

The Cincinnati Kid	*In Cold Blood*
Cool Hand Luke	*In Search of the Castaways*
Days of Wine and Roses	*In the Heat of the Night*
The Dirty Dozen	*It Happened at The World's Fair*
Doctor Dolittle	*It's a Mad, Mad, Mad, Mad World*
Dr. Strangelove	
Dr. Zhivago	James Bond movies:
Easy Rider	*Dr. No*
Exodus	*From Russia with Love*
Flipper	*Goldfinger*
Funny Girl	*On Her Majesty's Secret Service*
Georgy Girl	*Thunderball*
Girls! Girls! Girls!	*You Only Live Twice*
Gone With The Wind	
The Good, The Bad and the Ugly	*Jungle Book*
The Graduate	*Lawrence of Arabia*
The Great Escape	*The Leopard*
The Greatest Story Ever Told	*Lilies of the Field*
Guess Who's Coming to Dinner	*The Love Bug "Herbie"*
Hang 'Em High	*Love Me Tender*
A Hard Day's Night	*The Magnificent Seven*
The Haunting	*A Man for All Seasons*
Hello Dolly	*The Man Who Shot Liberty Valance*
Help!	*Mary Poppins*
How the West Was Won	*Midnight Cowboy*
Hud	*The Miracle Worker*
Hush...Hush, Sweet Charlotte	*The Moon-Spinners*
The Hustler	*The Music Man*
I Saw What You Did	*My Fair Lady*

National Velvet
The Nutty Professor
Ocean's Eleven
The Odd Couple
Old Yeller
Oliver!
101 Dalmatians
Peter Pan
The Pink Panther
Planet of The Apes
Pollyanna
The Prime of Miss Jean Brodie
A Raisin in the Sun
Romeo and Juliet
Rosemary's Baby
Rudolph the Red-Nosed Reindeer
The Shaggy Dog
Some Like It Hot
The Sound of Music
Spartacus

The Spy Who Came in From the Cold
Summer Magic
Swiss Family Robinson
The Ten Commandments
That Darn Cat!
13 Ghosts
The Three Lives of Thomasina
The Time Tunnel
To Kill a Mockingbird
Toby Tyler
Tom Jones
Tonka
True Grit
2001: A Space Odyssey
Viva Las Vegas
West Side Story
Who's Afraid of Virginia Woolf?
Wild Bunch
Zorba the Greek

News Highlights

The 1960s spanned everything from Viet Nam war protests, love, race riots, drugs, earning the reputation of being the "Swinging Sixties" with sexual liberation, man walking on the moon, to peace and freedom.

Soon-to-be President John F. Kennedy made five appearances in Muncie.

The first Presidential Election debate was televised between Kennedy and Nixon.

Lunch counter sit-ins happened until store owners integrated people.

The invention of The Pill

The founding of Motown

Alfred Hitchcock's *Psycho* terrified movie-goers and became one of the year's (1960) most successful films, as well as one of the most memorable, logical thrillers of all time.

75 President John F. Kennedy and First Lady Jacqueline on a leisurely afternoon

Newly elected President John F. Kennedy and Vice President Lyndon B. Johnson took office.

The creation of the Peace Corps

76 The Kennedy Children, Caroline and "John-John," play in the White House

77 Mercury Space Capsule

The Heyday of Muncie, Indiana

Alan Shepard was the first American in space during a 15-minute suborbital flight on Freedom 7 in the Mercury Space Capsule.

John Glenn became the first man to orbit the earth on February 20, 1962, in the Friendship 7 Mercury Space Capsule.

The Beatles released their first single, "Love Me Do" in the United Kingdom.

The Cold War

Marilyn Monroe left us.

The Assassination of President John F. Kennedy

Vice President Lyndon B. Johnson became President.

U.S. Civil Rights Leader Martin Luther King Jr. gave his famous "I Have a Dream" speech.

Introduction of Zip Codes in the U.S.

Beatlemania! The Beatles appeared on *The Ed Sullivan Show* twice, and teenage girls fell in love. At concerts, they cried, screamed, pulled their hair, spiraled into a frenzy, some fainted, and ended up on stretchers. Over 70 million people watched each show. "Meet the Beatles" graced many record collections.

United States President Lyndon B. Johnson signed the Civil Rights Act of 1964 into law and the Voting Rights Act of 1965.

Sidney Poitier won the Academy Award for Best Actor, becoming the first black actor to earn that honor. *Lilies of the Field* (1963)

Medicare was signed into law, and benefits became available on July 1, 1966.

A Charlie Brown Christmas was featured for the first time.

3,500 U.S. combat troops were initially sent to Vietnam. Eventually, 190,000 American soldiers were in Vietnam.

The Vietnam War escalated, and opposition to it began to mount as anti-Vietnam protests became more frequent. 250,000 people marched into Washington to protest the Viet Nam War.

Muncie celebrated the 100th anniversary of becoming a city with a community celebration. People gathered for a parade and festivities at the Delaware County Fairgrounds.

All U.S. cigarette packs had to carry the warning label, Caution: Cigarette Smoking May Be Hazardous to Your Health.

Batman debuted on TV.

The first *Star Trek* episode, "The Man Trap," was broadcast. The plot involved a creature that sucked salt from human bodies.

Elvis married Priscilla and broke a million hearts.

Dr. Christiaan Barnard in Cape Town, South Africa, performed the first heart transplant.

Thurgood Marshall became the first African American appointed to the Supreme Court.

Civil Rights Leader Dr. Martin Luther King Jr. was assassinated.

The assassination of Senator Robert F. Kennedy

At a Harlem rally, Malcolm X was assassinated.

The Civil Rights Act of 1968 was signed into law by President Johnson.

Richard Nixon was inaugurated after winning the United States presidential election.

60 Minutes first aired as a Sunday night Prime Time News Program with a fall season debut on September 24, 1968.

78 Man on the Moon

Astronauts Neil Armstrong and Edwin "Buzz" Aldrin were the first men to land on the moon on July 20, 1969.

Oliver won the Academy Award for Best Picture.

The First Philadelphia Bank installed the first cash dispensing machine.

Woodstock

Famous Hoosiers

Alexandria

Gaither, Bill - Singer/Songwriter

Bedford

Bowersox, Ken – Astronaut

Walker, Charles D. - Astronaut

Beech Grove

McQueen, Steve - Actor

Bippus

Schenkel, Chris - Sports Broadcaster

Bloomington

Carmichael, Hoagy - Composer, Pianist, Singer, Actor

Brazil

Redenbacher, Orville - Popcorn Entrepreneur

Columbus

Pence, Mike -48th Vice President of the United States, 50th Governor of Indiana from 2013 to 2017 and member of the United States House of Representatives from 2001 to 2013

Stewart, Tony- Hoosier Race Car Driver

Crown Point

Ross, Jerry - Astronaut

Dale

Henderson, Florence - Actress, Singer

Dana

Pyle, Ernie - American Journalist/Legendary War Correspondent during WWII

Elkhart
Smith, Connie - Vocalist

Elwood
Canary, David - Actor

Evansville
Glass, Ron - Actor

Fairmount
Davis, Jim Creator/Cartoonist of *"Garfield"*

Frankfort
Geer, Will – Actor

Fort Wayne
Lombard, Carole - Actress

Long, Shelley – Actress

York, Dick - Actor

Gary
The Jackson Five - Pop Music Quintet originally consisted of Jackie, Tito, Jermaine, Marlon, and Michael

Malden, Karl - Actor

Helmsburg/Martinsville
Helms, Bobby -Singer

Henryville
Sanders, Colonel Harland -Founder of KFC

Indianapolis
Dillinger, John - Criminal

Fox, Vivica A. - Actress

Fraser, Brendan - Actor

Hiatt, John - Singer/Songwriter

Letterman, David - Television Host

Lilly, Eli - Founder of Pharmaceuticals company

Montgomery, Wes - Jazz Guitarist

Pauley, Jane - Television Journalist

Pugh, Madelyn - Writer, *I Love Lucy*

Quayle, J. Danforth - Senator and 44th Vice President of the U.S.

Tarkington, Booth - American Novelist

Wolf, David - Astronaut

Jeffersonville

Schnatter, John - Founder and CEO of Papa John's Pizza

Kokomo

Kroft, Steve - Journalist, and Correspondent

Logansport

Kinnear, Greg - Actor

Lafayette

Rose, Axl - Guns N' Roses Singer

Stradlin, Izzy (born Jeffrey Dean Isbell) - Guitarist, singer, songwriter, Co-founder and former rhythm guitarist of Guns N' Roses

Lowell

Worley, Jo Anne - Actress

Marion

Dean, James - Actor

Millville

Wright, Wilbur - Aviation Pioneer

Mitchell

Grissom, Virgil Ivan "Gus" - Astronaut

Muncie

Bonham, Ron- Professional Basketball Player

High School

Attended Muncie Central High School

As a senior, he averaged 28 points per game and earned Indiana's "Mr. Basketball" award as he led his team to the State runner-up spot.

He graduated in 1960 as the school's all-time scorer for the State of Indiana.

79 Ron Bonham in action!

College

In 1986, inducted into the University of Cincinnati Athletics Hall of Fame

In 1991, inducted into the Indiana Basketball Hall of Fame

NCAA Champion 1962

Consensus first-team All-American 1963

Consensus second-team All-American 1964

3-time First-team All-MVC 1962-1964

Professional

2-time NBA Champion 1965, 1966

Career NBA and ABA statistics: Points: 723 (6.1 PPG), Rebounds: 170 (1.4 RPG), Assists: 44 (0.4 APG)

Muncie (Continued)

Braverman, Michael - TV Producer, Director, Screenwriter

Buzzington, Ezra – Actor

Croft, Mary Jane - Actress

Mussler, Mark - Original member of the musical group Village People (his persona was the construction worker) and make-up artist

Ross, Ellen (born Mary Ellen Nelson) -1940s actress

New Castle

Indiana, Robert (born Robert Clark) - American artist in the Pop Art movement. His "LOVE" print, first created for the Museum of Modern Art's Christmas card in 1965, was the basis for the widely distributed 1973 United States Postal Service "LOVE" stamp.

Peru

Porter, Cole - Songwriter

Seymour

Mellencamp, John - Singer/Songwriter

Stam, Katie - Seymour Indiana Junior Miss 2005, Miss Duneland 2008, Miss Indiana 2008, and Miss America 2009

South Bend

Everett, Chad - Actor

Speedway

DeWitt, Joyce - Actress

Terre Haute

Crothers, Scatman - Actor

Valparaiso

Brown, Mark N. - Astronaut

Vincennes

Skelton, Richard Bernard "Red" - Comedian

Wabash

Gayle, Crystal - Singer

West Lafayette

Earhart, Amelia - Pioneer Aviator

Jones, Anissa - Actress

Children's TV Personalities in Indiana

Bill Jackson – Children's TV host, Cartoonist, and Educator

Bob Glaze – *Cowboy Bob's Corral* (previously called *Chuckwagon Theatre*)

Captain Star - Larry Vincent, Horror Host. "Captain Starr" on WFBM in Indianapolis in the 1960s, was one of a trio of hosts, along with Harlow Hickenlooper and Curley Myers in children's programming. They featured the old *Three Stooges* shorts, as well as skits for an in-studio audience of children. As the program progressed, watchers could expect pie-in-the-face comedy and songs from the hosts.

"Janie" - Janie Hodge hosted the WTTV-4 cartoon show *Popeye and Janie* weekdays from 1963 to 1986.

Curley Myers – Starred in *Curley's Cowboy Theater* for eight years and then a Saturday morning kids show with co-hosts and friends Jerry Vance and Hal Fryar.

Dave Garrison and Dudley – Hosted the program, *This Side Up* in Indianapolis

Harlow Hickenlooper –Local programming for Muncie and Indianapolis, featured Harlow Hickenlooper/*The Three Stooges,* at WFBM/WRTV out of Indianapolis. Hal Fryar rose to fame as Harlow Hickenlooper with Curley Myers as his co-star. This program and other Hickenlooper shows, such as *Fun Time* and *All Hands-on Deck*, spanned 12 years, from 1960 to 1972.

Hoosier Hank – hosted cartoons

"Miss Annette" and "Miss Julie" - hosted *Romper Room*

Pat Garrett Rooney – hosted *Kindergarten College*

Sammy Terry – Horror host

Chapter 13

Actress Kathy Garver Dishes on the Hit CBS Show Family Affair

From 1966-1971, Americans were glued to the TV watching a sweet-natured sitcom about a carefree bachelor raising his nephew and two nieces- with the reluctant help of his English butler, after their parents died in a car accident. Actress Kathy Garver played Catherine "Cissy" Patterson-Davis on the top CBS show, *Family Affair*, from September 12, 1966, to September 9, 1971. The show ran for 138 episodes. The popular series focused on bachelor Bill Davis- played by actor Brian Keith. He attempted to raise his brother's orphaned children in his luxury, New York City apartment at 600 East 62nd Street. Anissa Jones and Johnny Whitaker played 6-year-old twins, Elizabeth "Buffy" and Jonathan "Jody" Patterson-Davis. The children provided quite a contrast in the life of wealthy, engineer Bill Davis, who was known to date socialites. As the storyline goes, Bill's brother Bob and sister-in-law Mary had died in an automobile accident.

Their children, teen Cissy, and her younger twin siblings Buffy and Jody had been passed among relatives in Terre Haute, Indiana, to temporary homes. Relatives attempted to give the responsibility to Bill. "Uncle Bill" is not keen on the idea at first, but the children endear themselves to him. First, Buffy comes along, followed by Jody, and finally, Cissy. Initially unsure of the situation is Mr. French – played by Sebastian Cabot, who effectively becomes the children's nanny, in addition to his valet duties.

Interestingly, the siblings in the storyline are from Terre Haute, and actress Anissa Jones was from Indiana in real life. Right away, Garver enthusiastically mentioned that we have something in common, "The Indiana connection!" Speaking from her California home, Garver admits to being noticed from her *Family Affair* fame. People say she has the same smile and has not aged. She is recognized, on occasion, as pig-tailed "Buffy" with her current blonde hair.

During filming, life was busy for 18-year-old Garver, who played 15-year-old Cissy on the show. She would report for make-up at 6:30 a.m. Jones and Whitaker ("the kids" as Garver refers to them) would come at 8:00 a.m. Garver was not only on the set bright and early but was often the last to leave. Brian Keith only worked for about half of the production schedule so that the remaining cast would film scenes for many different episodes in one day.

Like Don Fedderson's other program, *My Three Sons*, *Family Affair* used a 60-day production schedule for Keith. All of his scenes for the season would be shot in two thirty-day blocks, while his co-stars would fill in after the actor's work completed. In the 1960s, a season of shows was 38 episodes, as opposed to today's 28 episodes.

Garver enthusiastically recalls her days on *Family Affair*. She says, "There was a naturalness I had. The whole show was incredible, memorable, and lovingly done." She courageously approached the producer of the show with a push to include miniskirts. As she told him, "We need to get hip!" The producer saw it differently, responding, "If you do that, then you really date the show." Garver believes he knew his stuff, as evidenced 50+ years later. A look back at *Family Affair* finds a set that is, for the most part, in sync with today's world. It does not have a definite 60s flair. Garver believes, "If you look at the show, the décor and clothing are the same. They aimed for something classic and would endure."

Garver remembers her co-star, actor Brian Keith with fondness and admiration. His role on *Family Affair* earned three Emmy Award nominations for Best Actor in a Comedy Series. She was impressed with Keith's talent. "Brian was a fabulous actor not probably getting the recognition he deserved. He was an ex-Marine and had a wonderful combination of 'manly man' and unbeatable, sensitive heart and soul," Garver recounts. On June 24, 1997, two months after the suicide of his daughter and having lived with Cancer for some time, Keith was found dead of a self-inflicted gunshot wound at the age of 75. With sorrow, Garver also speaks of Jones, "Anissa was an absolutely loving, sweet, talented person that drugs destroyed." Anissa was found dead on August 28, 1976, at the age of 18. Sebastian Cabot, who played Giles French ("Mr. French"), died of a stroke at age 59 on August 22, 1977. Johnny Whitaker has worked as a Drug Counselor in California.

Garver started acting at age seven when she appeared as a young slave in the epic movie, *The Ten Commandments*, with Yul Brenner. She has appeared on *Nash Bridges, Matlock, and Simon and Simon*, among other shows. She has also garnered critical acclaim in movies, stage, and voice-over animation.

She hosts live presentations, has been a spokesperson, appeared on talk and game shows (she is super at winning top money for charities), and makes personal appearances at charity events, celebrity autograph signings, celebrity tennis tournaments, and more. She has used her experience to help guide new actors in the business. She is also involved in such charities as "Child Help" (which aids abused children), the Rose Resnick Lighthouse for the Blind, and the Make-A-Wish Foundation.

Garver's parents were instrumental in her success as they emphasized education and normalcy. She is quick to give credit to them and shares, "I had great parents who saved all of my money, and I never took drugs. Without getting the Coogan Law passed, there would still be parents taking advantage." The California Child Actor's Bill (also known as the Coogan Act or Coogan Bill) is a law applicable to child performers, designed to safeguard a portion of their earnings for when they enter adulthood. It was put into effect in 1939 in response to the plight of Jackie Coogan. He played Uncle Fester on the TV show, *The Addams Family*. He earned millions of dollars as a beloved child actor only to discover, upon reaching adulthood, that his parents had spent almost all of his money. Since then, the California Child Actor's Bill had revisions. The law requires the child's employer to set aside a portion of the child's earnings in a trust fund. It makes the separate earnings property of the child, rather than community property of the parents according to California Community Property laws.

80 Kathy Garver yesterday and today

A conversation about the Coogan Law prompts mention of Paul Petersen. Garver and Petersen are close friends. Petersen, of course, played "Jeff Stone" on *The Donna Reed Show*. He starred on the show with Donna Reed, Carl Betz, and Shelley Fabares. Today, Petersen is the President of the non-profit, tax-deductible group, "A Minor Consideration" – formed in January of 1991. The organization's website states it provides guidance and support to young performers, past, present, and future.

The group's members are always on call to assist parents and their professional children on a no-cost basis. By providing a strong emphasis on education and character development, plus helping to preserve the money these children generate, the members of A Minor Consideration are always available to help with the tricky transition issues that for many child stars, prove to be so troubling. The group presents an educational program, both public and private, to share its knowledge of what can happen in the world of juvenile Hollywood. Petersen's organization has been instrumental in educating the public and sharing vital information and updates about The Coogan Law.

When Garver is encouraged to share one of her favorite memories of the heyday, one quickly comes to mind. She comments, "The first time I heard The Beatles! It was fun! The loving, sharing, and a harkening to peace..."

Life is good! Garver spent her early acting years like many in the profession. Her comment is profound that "80 percent of your life is spent getting your next gig." She met her husband on the tennis court (a true "love match") and has been married for over 30 years. She has a son. When we chatted, Garver had just returned from Kentucky- where she participated in the International Mystery Writer's event and in Tennessee, where she starred in the musical, *Summer Magic*. Hayley Mills starred in the 1960s production.

Garver was recently honored with The Young Artist Former Child Star Lifetime Achievement Award at the 31st Young Artist awards ceremony for her role as "Cissy" on *Family Affair*. It is bestowed by the Young Artist Foundation to recognize former child actors and child singers for lifetime achievement within the motion picture, television, and radio industries. She has also been awarded the Golden Halo award for excellence in the entertainment field.

Kathy Garver is the author of four books:

The Family Affair Cookbook – "… because I like to cook. I like to eat. I thought it would be interesting to make that my first foray into publishing."

Surviving Cissy: My Family Affair of Life in Hollywood

X Child Stars: Where They Are Now - chronicles the shows and lives of child stars from favorite TV series of the 1950s, 1960s, 1970s, and 1980s

Holiday Recipes for a Family Affair- a follow-up to her first book

The obvious question for Garver is if she watches Retro TV. That is a definite yes! You guessed the show...*Family Affair!*

Garver has a website at www.kathygarver.com that is chocked full of more information about her exceptional career.

Chapter 14

Magic in the Air

Wherever your heyday was lived, you probably remember that small, off the beaten path Sundries store or the shoe store where your Keds were purchased. Remember how you felt when you were there? Who was there with you?

Muncie had its share of happening places!

A & P Grocery

81 A &W Root Beer Stand

Allison's Apparel Shop

Apple Tree in the Village

The Armory

Aultshire Addition

B & B Loan

BK Drive-In

Ball Brothers Corporation

Ball Family Historical Homes

Ball Memorial Hospital

82 Welcome!

Ball State Duck Pond

Ball Stores

Banner Whitehill

The Barn

Battle of the Bands

BCJ Productions

Betty's Hum-Dinger Drive-in

Big Dipper

Big Wheel

Blackford Drive-In Theater

Blue Dipper

The Blue Note

Bonanza Steak House

Bowl-a-Mat

Boys and Girls Club

Brazier Burger

Bryant's Food Shoppe

Burger Chef (people still rave about "The Works" salad bar)

Burger Time

Burkie's Drive-In

Burns Sweeper Shop

Burris School

Butterfield's

Camp Crosley

Camp Munsee

Camp Red Wing

Candle-Lite Bowling Lanes

Cantrell's Barber Shop

The Cardinal Shop

Carmen's Drive-In

Carriage House

Carter's Drive-In

Catalina Swim Club

The Cave

Charleen's Dress Shop (in The Meadows)

Charlie Gill's Grocery Store

Chevrolet Plant

Christy Woods

Chug-A- Mug

Cinderella Shop

Clara's

Clark's Dairy Isle

College Sweet Shop in The Village

The Collegienne Shop

Collins Ice Cream

Colonial Baking Company

Community Sing at the Fieldhouse

Concannon's Pastry Shop

Country Clubs

Covalt Meadow Gold Dairy

Cozy Lodge

Dairy Dream

Dairy Queen

Dalby's Drug Store

Davis Restaurant

Deb-n-Heir Shop

Delaware County Airport

Delaware County Fair

Delaware Hotel

Delaware Machine

Delco Remy

Dog n Suds

Dorothy's Variety Store

Downyflake Donut Shop

Drug Stores- Haag, Haney, Hook's, Owl

Duff's Smorgasboard

The Dug Out

Eavey's Grocery

Eleanor Cole Dance Studio

Emerald Lake

Flamingo Cocktail Lounge

Frank's Foundry

Freddie's Record Shop

Friendly Foster's

Frisch's Big Boy

Full - Service Gas Stations

Fuller Brush Man

Gamble's Department Store

Gill's Grocery

Goff's Dairy Isle

Goff's Restaurant

Gommel's Market

Harvest House Cafeteria

Heekin Park

Henry's Hamburgers

High Street Methodist Church

Hills Brothers Shoes and Clothing Mart

Home Shows

Hotel Roberts

Howard Johnson's on Broadway

Huddleston's Fruit Market

Hullabaloo

Ice Cream Shops

83 The genuine Mr. Freezer Fresh ice cream truck of yesteryear

Ice Cream Trucks – Mr. Freezer Fresh and Mr. Softee

Italian Villa

Jack's Camera Shop

Jimmy Carter's Skyline

Johnson's Donut Shop

Kaleidoscope

Kmart slide/toboggan

Kentucky Fried Chicken and the rotating bucket sign

King's Corner

Kresge's

L.S. Ayres

The Lighthouse Restaurant

Madison Street Market

Mandarin Inn

Manor's Lounge – Northwest Plaza

Marhoefer and the annual picnic

Mark III Tap Room

Marsh Supermarket

Marshall Carter's

84 The Masonic Temple

McCulloch Park

McDonald's Dairy Bar

McQuithy's Fruit Market

Meadow Gold Dairy

Meadows Shopping Center

Miller Milkhouse

Miracle Mart

Mister B's Lounge

Mister Fifteen

Mom and Pop businesses

The Moose Lodge

Morningside area of Muncie

Muncie Bowling Center

Muncie Central High School

Muncie Children's Home

Muncie Civic Theatre

Muncie Community Schools

Muncie Dragway

Muncie Drive-In

85 Muncie Fire Station #1

Muncie Music Center

86 Muncie Public Library

Muncie Roll-A-Way/Gibson's Skating Rink

Murphy's Grocery

Murray's Jewelers

Nixola's Beauty Salon

North Star Drive-In

Northwest Plaza

Oasis Tavern

Oliver's Food Market

The Omar Man/Omar Bakeries

One Accord

Orv's

Osco Drugs

The Palms

The Patio

The Penguin

People's Studio

Phillip's Pool

Pig and Whistle

Pixie Diner

Ponderosa Steak House

Pop's Place

Putt-Putt Golf

Q.L.'s

Record House

The Reservoir

Riggin's Dairy

The Rivoli Restaurant

Rivoli Theatre

Robert Hall Clothing Store

Robert Q's

The Roberts Hotel and the bowling alley underneath it

Rocky's Music Center

Roselyn Bakery

Rosie's

Rosinski's Grocery

Ross' Corner & Ross Flagpole Cafeteria

Ruble's Record Rack

Rustic Cabin

S. H. Green Stamp Store

St. Lawrence

St. Mary's Church and Festival

Scott's in The Meadows Shopping Center

Shedtown Garage "Confectionery" with a jukebox, sodas, and sweets

Silvers Dairy Bar

Skate-a-Way

Ski-High Drive-In

The Heyday of Muncie, Indiana

Skyline Restaurant

Souder's Music

Southside High School

The Spot lunch and cigar store

Spring Water Park

The Squire Shop

Steck's Clothing

Stillman's Department Store (and the shoe fitting Fluoroscope /Pedoscope)

Stonehenge Records

The Strand

Sudlow's Potato Chips

The Tally or "Tally Ho"

The Teen Club

Thomas Park

Tiger Raceway (Model Cars)

Tom Thumb Raceway (Slot Cars)

Tony the Tiger

Tower Lanes

Tuhey Pool

Uni-Mart Restaurant

Uptown Theater

Vickie Lynn Pastries

The Villa

Walgreen's downtown

Walnut Street at Christmas

Warner Gear

The Water Bowl

Welles Department Store

Westinghouse

Westside Park

White River

White's Market

Whitely Neighborhood

Wise Food Markets

WERK Radio

WLBC Radio

Wolfe Ice Cream

Woodbury's Sixty-Seven Supper Club

Woolworth's

Wysor Grand Theatre

Ye Olde Donut Shop

YMCA

87 Muncie YWCA

Zayre

    Many smaller, family-owned businesses did not merely thrive but were successful. Families worked from sun-up to sun-down, serving the Muncie community and surrounding areas. Soda fountains and Mom and Pop diners reigned!

    Lee Anne Richardson Parsons, who resides in Florida, remembers the good old days. "We are like brothers and sisters; our memories are shared and touch without even knowing the person by name. I remember the egg salad at Woolworths, the warm cashews, and the Coke man actually delivered Cokes to our house. My mom also worked downtown at Greens Dime Store, and years later worked at Woolworths. We would catch the bus or walk to town on Saturdays with our allowance to buy a record, fingernail polish, or that sandwich.

My favorite winter coat was bought at Sears, with the squeaky wooden floors, and I marched right upstairs to get my picture with Santa. We played outside until my friend Cindy's dad would whistle them home at dark. A broken baby buggy became a horse for pushing each other around in, and a big cardboard box was transformed into an airplane. We actually found some glue in one box, said it could be used on open wounds, so I

88 Le Anne Richardson Parsons

volunteered my newly gouged leg up for an experiment. I still have the hole that was left when it healed. We hunted the new kids and would leave them in the alleys while we all had a snack at the closest house and would fight over the skate key. Those were the days and even without all the new electronics. The beginning of the end was the elimination of the alleys, no alleys in the new additions, and our alley was like the superhighway to each other's house. How many received their first kiss in one? Alleys were where we learned and talked and shared everything with our best friend. Alleys, such a simple thing!"

Shedtown

The Thomas Park/Avondale neighborhood is known as Shedtown, and it was a place of love for those who grew up in the area. It has a reputation of being one of Muncie's most impoverished neighborhoods, and there were some tough, brutal times through the decades. You will find some of the homes quaint- a sort of throwback to the days of simple housing. Homes may be old, but the revival and positive vibes today, speak volumes. The flip side of a rugged Shedtown childhood is that many fondly remember it as a time of frolic and getting lost in play and adventure. You will hear this straight from the source... people who grew up and blossomed there.

Jack Dudley, a many moons ago youngster, was happy to describe some of the ways Shedtown kids passed the time. "Did you ever play the game 'Animals?' It had to be pitch dark with no moon. A child would choose the animal he or she wished to be the children would determine who would be 'It' and turned off all the lights in the house. The animal that was 'It' had to growl all the time and try to find the others. If 'It' touched anyone else, they were out of the game. Another game was called 'Handy Over,' which involved throwing a ball over the roof of a house and seeing if someone could catch it on the other side. Whoever threw the ball yelled 'Handy Over,' and if someone on the other side caught it, they shouted, 'Pigtail.'

Then, there was ' Tin Can Alley.' A tin can was situated in the middle of the alley. Whoever was 'It' tried to guard the tin can to keep the others from kicking it. If anyone managed to get by 'It' and kick the can, that person was the winner. There was also a nighttime game called 'Slips,' which was a form of Hide and Seek. Of course, most boys were always up for a good game of cowboys with their cap guns! If they did not have a 'weapon,' they made rubber band guns.

The Colonial Bread truck would pass by the homes each day. The driver would often tell some of the children if they yelled in a loud voice, 'Colonial is good bread,' he would give them a free, small loaf. It was fresh baked and delicious. Every time the bread truck would approach, it was common to see a small group of children run into the street, screaming, 'Colonial is good bread,' and the driver obliged! A popular place in Shedtown was Gill's Grocery at 12th Street and Perkins Avenue. Early each morning, the bakery truck would arrive and fill the bread box in front of the store with bread and pastries before the store opened. It was never locked.

Then, there were the gypsies passing through the area, who would have a stage show at Thomas Park. After the show, they would try to sell different kinds of medicines. Children tended to fear the gypsies because they had heard they sometimes kidnapped young children.

It was routine to get hard water from a well and soft water for washing clothes and shampooing hair from the downspout at the corner of the house in a 55-gallon drum."

Many who grew up in Shedtown say they benefited from independence and responsibility and described a Shedtown childhood as "the best." Perhaps sometimes, the story is about more than unemployment, failing economics, and statistics. The other story is one of the determinations of families to survive. Many Shedtown families were unstilled in unimaginable circumstances and found a solid foundation, of sorts, that others may not even consider.

Families shared an anchor of love, courage, and strength that was so secure they rose above the most challenging of times. Perhaps it is worth remembering that our circumstances do not necessarily define us.

89 *Thank you for the memories, Norval Jack Dudley. September 16, 1932 – October 14, 2014*

People are re-discovering Shedtown every day. With new faces and energy in the area, it is an exciting time! The families who proudly hail Shedtown as their home keep its legacy and future alive. They promote the area on the Facebook page, "Growing Up Shedtown." You will see the following: "This page is for people who grew up in Shedtown, arguably Muncie's best and most colorful neighborhood." If you speak with folks or read between the lines, there are comments woven with emotion. There are so many heartfelt memories.

While one woman recalls nearly setting her home on fire while trying to keep her new baby doll warm, another person remembers being given beer for mowing a yard. Whether people remember eating 10 cent hamburgers at the Blue Dipper, small burgers at Friendly Foster's, the live monkey at the Ross Grocery Store- and the live elephant ride there in the parking lot, or the apple pie at the Flagpole Cafeteria, they smile. There is also a Facebook page, "Our Lovely Home in Shed-Town, Muncie, Indiana."

Many say they loved their Shedtown upbringing and will always be proud of it. One native said she is thinking of making flags that say, "We're Shedtown Proud...Alive and Loud!" Perhaps there is a moral to the creativity that launched the legacy of Shedtown. Give a child a loving family, and the imagination can take that child anywhere.

.

Chapter 15

What Was Happening Out at WERK-AM 990?

You heard it here first! We are going behind the scenes of 990 AM on the old radio dial to WERK in Muncie, Indiana. Some of the things you are about to read have a shock factor! And you thought all they did was play music! It was the mid-to-late 1960s, and the WERK Radio on-air personalities quickly achieved "celebrity status" among teens. Some of these voices belonged to Bill Shirk, Larry McCabe, Tom Cochrun, Dave Barr, Gary Demaree, Gil Hole, Bruce Munson, Joe London, and a relatively unknown Ball State University student at the time- David Letterman.

Once upon a time, I had an encounter with two of the DJs! Our eyes met, like when one experiences love at first sight from across a crowded room. It was powerful. My heart fluttered. Ok, so it was from a distance, and Larry McCabe and Bill Shirk just happened to look at me from their remote location while broadcasting at the fair. I had a crush on one of them at the time. It is what giddy 14-year-olds sometimes do!

No matter where McCabe and Shirk have traveled in this world, it is obvious when speaking with them, that WERK is near and dear to their hearts. They remember the sign-on day at WERK as if it happened yesterday. McCabe references it by saying, "Nat King Cole died on February 15, 1965, the day after WERK started. The station did a tribute to the singer. The day WERK became a reality, Valentine's Day and National Heart Month were the two themes. Dave Barr was the first to 'Break the Ribbon' by speaking on the air." McCabe was second for the honor. On this first day, WERK solicited on-air donations and interviewed heart specialists and patients treated at the time for heart ailments. The first month, the station adopted the slogan, "The Station That Is All Heart." Generous donors gave WERK significant dollars for the Heart Association, and the event created goodwill in the community. From the time WERK launched, the community embraced it. There was no doubt success was on the way!

It was an especially exciting time for a young, Bill Shirk, who, with his father, R.J. "Bob" Poorman, Sr., dreamed of owning a radio station. Back in 1961, Poorman applied for the FCC Broadcasting License for that very initial day of operations. Father and son had collaborated about the project, discussing many avenues, and listening to various radio stations. Their brainstorming resulted in endless, unique conversation. They knew what it would take to build a successful radio station, and these two dreamed big! Shirk had only one thing to say when the two unleashed their ideas about owning a station, "Dad, if you did this on a radio station full-time, you would have a hit!"

A popular jock needed to be hired, and McCabe was the man. Gil Hole- a Muncie native, known for his creative, dry wit, was also in demand. Hole would eventually broadcast the early morning shift and oversee the WERK SHEET – the station's weekly survey review of the top hits of the day. Young talent came into the station- some being as young as 14 and 15 years of age.

Shirk quickly impressed everyone at WERK with his versatility. From 1968-1972, he rolled up his sleeves and wore a variety of hats- those of General Manager, Station Manager, Sales Manager, Program Director, Production Manager, afternoon DJ, and Janitor.

90 Broadcast Microphone

If there was work to be done, he was the man. When Shirk reminisces about those early days, it is easy to forget he is describing a time over half a century ago. He declares, "I was always the nuts and bolts, and dad was the creative juices. Within a matter of a year, our rating was 68 shares. Not bad for a small, 250-watt daytime AM station!" Shirk would be instrumental in bringing Blood Sweat and Tears, The Who, Dick Clark, and many others, to Muncie. At the time, WERK was the second radio station in the U.S. to connect with Dick Clark.

Shirk attended Burris High School in Muncie and graduated from Ball State University in 1967 with a B.S. Degree in Education. He taught school in Selma, Indiana- east of Muncie. He also owned Granny's Nightclub out on Highway 32 in Muncie- which was a favorite place during the heyday.

Then, there was Larry McCabe. Whether you knew him as McCabe, Lar-On-The Air, or Larry McKay, (as he was later identified in the broadcast industry), 49 years in radio broadcasting molded a legend. McCabe knew back in 1965 that Muncie and the surrounding area radio listeners were "thirsty" for a new voice. It bordered on miraculous that so much action was happening at WERK with such a severely dysfunctional power station.

The station's signal would drastically fade- especially on Muncie's eastside. Listeners would lose the station on their car radios at Muncie's city limits, usually in the same general spot. The studio had bare minimum broadcasting equipment; two or three automatic cart machines (not yet even mounted) sitting precariously on top of the empty boxes they arrived in and the least expensive, new Gates Radio Mixer. The station was limited in what it could do. In the early days and times with no sponsors, WERK was almost commercial-free, except for two or three live messages. It did not phase the community

WERK was situated at a farmhouse with a near-by garage, approximately three and a half miles south of Muncie on State Road #3 - on the way to New Castle. The station sat on the east side of the highway. There were a few acres to the south and east where the six directional towers and extensive ground wires were situated.

McCabe grew up in Muncie on North Broadway- just outside the Muncie city limits, at the junction of state highways 67, 3 and 35. His parents owned the Candle-Lite Bowling Lanes at 3325 North Broadway in Muncie. The establishment was originally a lounge. McCabe's mother, Marjorie- who was only 17 years old when he was born, diligently worked behind the counter as a chief cook at the bowling alley and was, in some ways, more like a sister figure to him. McCabe believes the time he spent at the Candle-Lite is crucial because it was here where he became "hooked on" music. Tunes often played from the jukebox as well as the live music for the night-clubbers, many of whom were servicemen and women.

His mother and stepfather Bob McCabe believed bowling would be the next passion and big money maker in the U.S. So, the Candle-Lite Lounge transitioned to the Candle-Lite Bowling Lanes. There were 12 lanes. McCabe's parents divorced in 1948, and he and his mother moved in with his aunt and her husband on West 8th Street in Muncie. In the summer of 1949, McCabe contracted Polio during a nationwide epidemic, which would eventually paralyze him from the waist down. He believes having to wear heavy metal braces and walk on crutches slowed him down somewhat but did not deter his desire to be a dynamic sportscaster and DJ.

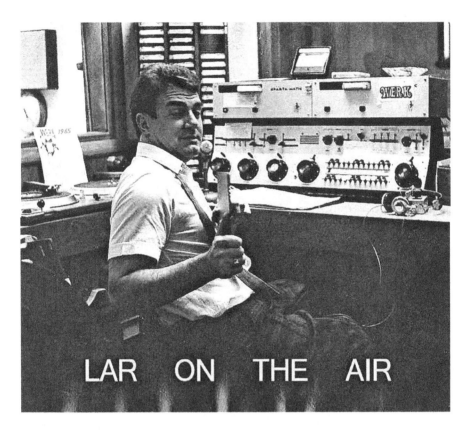

91 Larry McCabe spinning the hits, 1965

Ask McCabe about Muncie, and he will tell you, "It was a great place to grow up; it was bustling and just thrilling!" He still applauds the companies that brought jobs to the community, such as Acme-Lees, the General Motors/Chevrolet plant, and Ball Brothers. He recalls the railroad track that ran through the center of town, when the Beatles, the British Invasion and Motown hit Muncie and when Wayne Cochran and the C.C. Riders played at Woodbury's Sixty-Seven Supper Club on Broadway. One of his most cherished moments was meeting the great Joan Crawford at the Pepsi Cola Bottling Company on North Walnut Street in Muncie and the Bob Hope Troop's appearance at the Muncie Fieldhouse.

McCabe attended Muncie Central and Wes-Del High School. In 1958, he graduated from Indiana University on a State Rehab Grant, with a B.S. Degree in Radio and Television. He then broke into part-time radio in Clearwater, Florida, in 1959 and later got his first, full-time break at Muncie's WLBC in 1960 over the morning airwaves. In approximately 1962 and after drifting back to Florida, where McCabe could not locate decent work, he was lucky to find a job at WMRI in Marion, Indiana, where he became the Program and Sports Director. McCabe and his wife Judy made Marion their home, and their son Michael was born in 1963. After nearly three successful years there, a door opened for McCabe to return to Muncie and become the Program and Sports Director at WERK in early 1965.

McCabe also sang with some of the bands who performed at the Muncie YWCA, "Cats Cave" and at local clubs like Woodbury's Sixty-Seven Supper Club and The Oasis when the groups "jammed" on Saturdays.

Shirk's father created the WERK KREW. McCabe explained that their "Great Savior," R. J. Poorman (described as "a brilliant Marketing and Promotions genius" by McCabe), decided soon after he bought complete control of the station to call the team the WERK KREW. Poorman often came up with ideas to implant positive images in listeners' minds and developed long-term loyalty and bonds with them. In this vein, he came up with the plan to add Valentine's Day (the date WERK first signed on-the-air) as a sort of local holiday, celebrating Feb. 14th each year with a virtually free WERK birthday party with live bands, free birthday cake, soft drinks, door prizes, etc.

Many festivities were broadcast live on 990 AM. WERK's first birthday party was held at Gibson's Roller-Skating Arena. The National Guard Armory, across from the North Walnut Street Fieldhouse, was the venue the second year. The third year, the birthday bash happened at the Lions Delaware County Fairgrounds, in what was then, the Industrial Building. It was a large, corrugated steel structure that was ideal for the station's purposes. WERK charged a nominal "cover charge" of something like 35 cents admission to defray some of the overall expense. The WERK annual "Birthday Blasts" were always a huge success, at least for the six+ years McCabe was at WERK.

McCabe recalls, "One of Bob's first ideas was to initiate a contest over the air in which listeners received calls at random from the telephone book. Anyone who answered their phone when WERK called with 'It's fun to WERK all day' would win a prize. Some of these prizes included portable radios, cameras, movie theater passes, etc. Merchants were eager to trade these gifts for airtime. A 'Be Kind To (whoever) Day' was introduced. The station solicited cards and letters from listeners who nominated bosses and other worthy persons, of whose hard work and dedication (and charitable goodwill) benefited the community." McCabe's high school classmate, Gordon Miller of Gordon's Flowers, agreed to deliver a bouquet of flowers to each daily "Be Kind To" recipient, which fostered even more community spirit.

Shirk and Poorman added innovative ideas about progressive radio programming to WERK-AM 990 and had the determination to take on new challenges. McCabe, on the other hand, admits he was a little "old fashioned" in his radio programming ideas. He believes though that most of Shirk and Poorman's plans for the direction WERK would take, were right on target. Father and son monitored other highly successful stations like WABC in New York City to help create ideas for WERK. McCabe holds Shirk in the highest regard and believes that much of the success of WERK originated from him. McCabe knows why. It's a simple explanation, "He pushed the boundaries. In short, he would try anything!" It was Shirk's idea to broadcast the talk show, "The Hot Line," which featured the Mayor, Police Chief, and other notables.

Tom Cochrun was brought on board, while a Freshman at Ball State University. He walked and hitchhiked to his WERK job interview in October of 1964. Cochrun learned a new radio station was going on air. Staff was impressed that "a kid" walked into the radio station. Well, just as long as "the kid" would have a car by the time he started work! Cochrun noted the day of sign-on, "I sat on the floor in the control room, holding alligator clips together so Larry could use the turntable to play records. I was not sure what I had gotten into, but it was exciting! At the time, I was just a college kid, and I do not think Larry, Gil Hole, or Paul St. John really paid me much attention and probably wondered why I was hanging around." Then there were what some would see as the "perks." As Cochrun tells it, "I remember our first-anniversary remote- there were screaming girls, people wanting autographs, lots of adulation. Heavy stuff for a college kid." Cochrun reported news on weekends and helped as needed during the week. He would stop at the police station to read the police reports and talk to officers before going to WERK. In those days, the station presented hourly newscasts, in addition to occasional half-hour segments.

One Christmas especially stands out for Cochrun. He recalls, "I had the Christmas sign-on, and it was the Christmas of '66 or '67, I believe. I had an old clunker of a car that I drove to Indianapolis after I signed off the station in Muncie around 5:30 p.m. I drove the old car through a snowstorm so I could spend some time with my family. I got up in the middle of the night and drove back to Muncie, again in a snowstorm and on very treacherous roads, to get to the station Christmas morning with whoever might be listening. Larry and the other guys were going to come out to relieve me. Well, I kept getting calls from all of the staff saying as to how they were snowed in and could not get out of their drives, or that the roads were too snow-covered. So that Christmas, I spent the day alone at the station. Thank heavens, mom had packed a turkey sandwich. Ah yes, the good old days!"

92 WERK Sheet- A weekly list of the top 40 songs

In April of 1969, Cochrun planned to get married and to spend the spring and summer in Europe. He could take a leave of absence at WERK if he could get someone to fill in for him. Cochrun had a plan, and it involved one of his friends. He shares, "David Letterman was a friend from Ball State. He also did a radio program on the campus station, which had a kind of cult following. It was pure if young, Letterman humor. Letterman welcomed the chance to try his hand at a professional station." McCabe gave input for hiring Letterman after listening to the audition tape. "So, from April until August, he took over my shift at WERK, playing music and reading the news," Cochrun remembers. Letterman and McCabe became friends. In fact, Letterman would later contact McCabe when he moved to Los Angeles with hopes of being a Comic Writer.

After returning from Europe, Cochrun realized he wanted to concentrate on the news and in a broader market, so, in September 1969, he bid farewell to the WERK KREW. He moved on to reporting at WIBC/WNAP in Indianapolis, later working at WTHR TV, became the President/CEO of Nineteenth Star - a television production company, and was then News Director at WISH-TV. Cochrun retired in January 2007. Cochrun looks back at the WERK days and has ideas about the super station's popularity. He concludes, "The memories are many and remain indelible. The station was a smashing success because Muncie needed something new, fresh, alive, and energetic. Times were right for a rocker to have a big impact. The late 1960s were a time of turbulence and change, and a hip, fast-moving radio station helped to choreograph the life and times of East Central Indiana. It was a rare moment. Seldom could you find the confluence of events - social change and upheaval, the emergence of the boomer impact on music, fashion, culture, and a new station that played the music of the time."

Then, there was Gary Demaree, who sensed the magic of radio at the ripe age of 13. A neighborhood friend, Randy Hatcher, had cobbled together a "pirate radio" right in his bedroom using a Crude Signal Generator, a tiny reel-to-reel tape recorder, and a record player. The two named the station WRKH, using Hatcher's initials. Together, Demaree and Hatcher mimicked their favorite DJs from WOWO, WLS, and CKLW and broadcast rock 'n' roll to an area that probably spanned the equivalent of several city blocks. It was a massive hit with the neighborhood kids. There were at least two other similar pirate stations at the same time in other Muncie neighborhoods. The teens negotiated deals with local record shops to provide records in return for advertising credit on their handwritten or typed "hit lists." So far, it was easy. However, it was about to get a little more complicated. The guys drew the attention and irritation of a higher-up over at WLBC, who threatened to turn them into the FCC for unlicensed broadcasting. Demaree remembers it causing much fear and alarm among their little "pirate" community- especially for their parents. He can share a happy ending, though, because the person at WLBC eventually offered Demaree and a few friends the opportunity to host an early Saturday morning radio program on WLBC.

Over time, the pirate station faded away. It was not long before Demaree, and a couple of other teenagers used their previous broadcasting experience to spin records during the live band breaks at the teen nightclub, Hullabaloo. The Yorktown club was a short distance from Muncie. Demaree had a new project, "I became a member of the Teen Council at Hullabaloo and through personal contacts developed there, became a 'groupie' at WERK, which enabled me to hang out at the studios on State Road 3 South on weekends. Eventually, Station Manager Bill Shirk Poorman gave permission for me to voice the weather reports on Saturdays and Sundays. It developed into a kind of informal internship that continued until I graduated from Muncie Central in 1969." Demaree was eventually offered a part-time position at WERK.

Some things happened back in the heyday at WERK, that well...let us just say were hush-hush! You heard it here first, and it is probably the only time you will hear about it! One of the most memorable episodes in those early days of WERK occurred in the first year or two when McCabe received a telephone call at WERK from a promoter of recording artist, Brook Benton. Benton was popular in record sales and personal appearances in the mid-1960s with "It's Just a Matter of Time," "Endlessly," "The Boll Weevil Song," and his mega 1970 comeback hit, "Rainy Night in Georgia."

The promoter phoned McCabe and informed him Benton was heading by automobile to Indianapolis for a concert and would be passing through Muncie. He asked if WERK would like to do a brief, on-air interview with Benton. Plans were for Benton to arrive in approximately two and a half hours, so McCabe promoted it on the air. He told listeners the great Brook Benton was on his way to WERK, and they would be chatting live. McCabe estimates he mentioned it ten times in the following hour and a half. He tried to not panic as the end of his shift neared, within a half-hour, and Benton did not appear. There was also no call explaining his absence. McCabe had more or less guaranteed listeners they were going to hear an interview with Brook Benton. Desperate times call for desperate measures so, here we go! McCabe asked the janitor at the time, named James, to come into the main broadcast booth, he explained the situation to him, and informed him he was going to be "Brook Benton" for about five or six minutes. James had two words, "No way." But McCabe quickly assured him he would introduce questions that would require him to answer in a super concise manner, mostly yes or no. James happened to be an African American about Benton's age with a beautiful, deep, baritone voice. Somehow,

James pulled it off! They were so convincing that about seven or eight carloads of listeners showed up in the WERK parking lot within the next hour or so, after the approximate six-minute "Interview with A Star." Many of the listeners wanted Benton's autograph. The explanation was that Benton had such limited time, and "He was behind schedule and had several interviews lined up, waiting for him to do in Indianapolis, so he just had to be on his way." McCabe never learned why Brook Benton did not appear. He laughs about it now as he reasons that perhaps Benton and the promoter simply lost their way. Yeah, cornfields can do that to you!

Muncie had an active nightlife! The Castle Nightclub on Kilgore, The Palms, and The Pixie Diner on South Madison were hang-outs for the WERK KREW. After jock meetings on Monday nights, the gang would head to Pizza King on Madison for pizza, beer, and some laughs. They also enjoyed watching the hottest network show at the time, *Laugh-In*.

*93 Larry McCabe working hard on a typical day.
It was a tough job, but someone had to do it.*

Some would later head out north Broadway to Woodbury's Sixty-Seven Supper Club. McCabe developed such a great relationship with all of the Woodburys - Harry, Harriet, and their son John, that he would give them free, on-the-air "plugs," which resulted in not having to pay for his drinks. His guests received free drinks, as well. Later, McCabe nearly landed in serious trouble with Poorman over this indiscretion. McCabe remembers preparing to leave Muncie with high, mixed emotions in April 1971. He experienced a recurring nightmare that the Woodburys handed him a bar bill for over $6,500. He insists that he would wake up in a cold sweat and is thankful he never received the invoice in reality.

McCabe believes, "WERK's success had a lot to do with the fact that all of us respected and even loved the people we worked with, and we loved being 'hams' (aka creative artists) on the air. This was not only true for the full-timers but even weekend and part-time jocks like young Chuck Crane, Steve Michaels, and David Letterman."

Then, there was "Sybil!" Everyone loved her! Sybil "Bubbles" Bennett was a celebrity in her own right. She was often a topic of conversation for the gang and the target of their many sneaky, outlandish jokes. McCabe is quick to offer some wacky examples of the gang's humor! He laughs, "We would constantly be pulling pranks on her, much of the time involving her big, old midnight blue, four-door Cadillac - which could have been Gen. Rommel's staff car in better times. We would go to Kirk's Sporting Goods and buy an auto bomb, which would explode with a deafening whistle and explosion sound, pouring out black smoke when she turned on the ignition switch, not damaging her car, but scaring the 'bejeebers' out of her. Another time we had our newsman, who was a reserve Deputy Sheriff, go run into Sybil's office and breathlessly tell her that he was extremely sorry that he had accidentally shot holes in her Caddy's front windshield while doing target practice with his service revolver outback. We had stuck some very realistic-looking bullet hole decals on her windshield. She was mortified, to say the least. Later, the newsman got his dose of our perverted humor when we put a live chicken into the small booth where he was reading the farm market reports one morning. The hen laid an egg right on the desk in front of him while he was attempting to regain his composure."

Now, this is zany stuff about Maudie Frickert! McCabe is the one who brought "her" to life! As only he can tell it, "Maudie was the star of my 'Noon Day Rush-Hour Traffic Report,' heard weekdays around noon on WERK," McCabe begins. "It was a serial-like audio soap opera of Maudie, in her personalized helicopter, 'high above the Eaton expressway' (Cammack, Skyway, Modoc freeway, etc.) reporting on the congestion (or total lack of it) below. The reports were very topical and even seasonal. At Christmas, devilish Maude scares Santa on Christmas Eve (innocently flying in his reindeer-powered sleigh, filled with toys) by firing 'dummy' machine gun rounds at him from her 'copter. Maudie herself is 'skyjacked' to Cuba for one week's harrowing episode, to eventually encounter Fidel at his gigantic refinery complex called Castro Oil.

By the way, all these pulse-quickening episodes were hand-written by me- usually on the back of teletype paper. I recorded each one, with Maudie's part separately, including helicopter sound effects with Maudie's voice on a filter, as if on a two-way radio, leaving my part to be done 'live' so I could actually talk over her at times and make it sound more realistic. This really fooled a lot of listeners into believing that Maudie and I were two separate people, especially when I interrupted her report in mid-sentence. Maudie could genuinely 'get away' with saying outrageous things that I would never dream of uttering. It was a classic case of 'altered ego.' The total time of each 'episode' only lasted three to five minutes maximum. Still, I later discovered to my complete surprise that the 'Noon Rush-Hour' report actually developed quite a cult following, especially with the 'hip' Ball State University student listeners back then."

Bruce Munson has a take on the WERK adventure, "The personalities made it what it was… ones like Larry McCabe, Bill Shirk, Sybil Bennett, Horace Smith, and Gil Hole- who had 'Mr. Showbiz' painted on the door of his vehicle. The big difference between WERK and WLBC is that WERK was more youth oriented. WERK was about more of an adventure, and there was an element of mischief. Nobody at WLBC put a live chick in the broadcast booth! A WERK broadcast was more fun. It was the people behind the scenes who had more fun too! WERK was a remarkable experience!"

94 James Brown, the "Godfather of Soul," and Larry McCabe

In the summer of 1965, WERK sponsored the Dick Clark Caravan of Stars. McCabe was the Emcee for the show, which headlined Herman's Hermits. Through decades, celebrities have swarmed to McCabe. Perhaps due to his radio promotions or his charm. Maybe a bit of both. If McCabe were ever to compile a list of celebrities he has never met, the list would have to be short. Sure enough, he claims he never met Frank Sinatra, Elvis, Marilyn Monroe, and John Wayne.

They were golden days, especially when McCabe joined the Shirks for dinner in their home. He remembers Poorman would offer a drink, and Betty (his wife) would prepare a great meal. Then, Shirk, McCabe, and Poorman would sit in the den, watch Dean Martin and chat about radio. It was a good life!

McCabe eventually left WERK in 1971 but not because he was unhappy there. Quite the opposite. He had a yearning to see how far his abilities would take him. He had a strong feeling that if he did not do it, he would regret it for the rest of his life. He left amid numerous mixed emotions because he was saying good-bye to the best and funniest job he had in radio, to date.

McCabe's work eventually took him to various stations in the Los Angeles area, such as KHJ, KIIS, KFI, KFWB, KRLA, KMPC – where he worked alongside such icons as Robert W. Morgan, Wink Martindale, and Jim Lange. Ultimately, he landed at K-EARTH 101 in the Los Angeles area and acquired the name, Larry McKay.

National commercials have featured McCabe, ones for notable clients such as Princess Cruises, Honda, Walt Disney Productions, Jack-in-the-Box, and the Professional Golf Association, among many others.

95 Dick Clark and Larry McCabe in the hallway of the Muncie Fieldhouse in 1965

He was also associated with national sitcoms such as *Cheers, Married with Children, Fresh Prince of Bel-Air, Frazier, The Simpsons,* and *Family Ties*. McCabe was the Public Address Announcer for the Los Angeles Lakers for three seasons- two of them NBA Championship seasons.

He also honed his voice-over talents, gaining work and exposure in commercial and promo work.

Muncie was undoubtedly a highlight along the way in McCabe's 49-year broadcast career.

Today, McCabe is retired and resides in California. He has one more title to add to his lengthy list of accomplishments: Author! He went on to write his memoirs in the fascinating book, *Lar'-on-the-Air*, available through Amazon.

Bill Shirk, lovingly known as "Super Skirk," spent more than four decades in the radio business. With his father, he had a knack for making the creation of the WERK empire at 990 AM seem easy. The station was family-owned from 1965-1981. Shirk explains, "It was a simple plan, a little sanity, and we just played the hits. We were promotion. We did remotes. If it was going on in the city, we were there. WERK Radio was ten years ahead of its time." In addition to playing a significant role in Indianapolis radio in the 1970s through the early 2000s, Shirk made his mark as an Escape Artist. Many believe he has a "connection" to Houdini. He holds eight World Records in Escapology. His motion picture, *The Escapist*, is about a radio station owner who must perform dangerous publicity stunts to prevent his business from being taken over by a big corporation. In 2008, Shirk was the recipient of the Silver Cup Award at the World Escape Artist Convention.

You could call him a daredevil or a superhuman who cheats death. The big question, is there anything this man cannot do?

Some of Shirk's life-threatening stunts for charity include:

Being buried alive with a ten-foot python, two tarantulas, and two rattlesnakes. The feat received worldwide coverage. Shirk refused to come out until President Carter donated to his charity. Shirk received the contribution after 79 hours of being underground.

Being buried underground and while there, one of the wooden crossbeams that supported Shirk's coffin lid split from the weight of the dirt and pointed toward his heart-like a dagger

Being handcuffed and chained, hanging 20 feet in the air from triple burning ropes

When discussing hanging from cables on a helicopter, he will matter-of-factly surmise, "I always thought I had a very good, calculated risk of surviving it."

Running with bulls in Pamplona while in a straitjacket

Jumping off bridges and cliffs

Hanging 1600 feet in the air from a helicopter by an ice skate (while in a straitjacket)

Standing on railroad tracks as a train approached, at the last moment falling utterly flat between the tracks as the train rolled over him. Shirk was so precise in his timing that he reduced the time from 1.4 to 1 second.

Hanging from a burning rope, 100 feet upside down, with his head in a bag with a snake

Being plunged into a pool of sharks from a burning rope

Shirk is also the author of the book *Modern Day Houdini*, where he shares the secrets of his 25 great escapes- complete with pictures.

96 (L to R) Tom Cochrun, Bill "Super" Shirk, Larry McCabe, "Big" Joe London, and the Union 76 Girls, gather around Shirk's Jaguar

Since 1978, Shirk has raised thousands of dollars for underprivileged and disabled children and adults, along with tornado relief victims throughout Central Indiana.

When reminded he is a walking miracle, Shirk acknowledges, "I am very lucky to be alive." Although the daredevil stunts are a thing of the past, Shirk still has his zest and passion for radio. People who knew him years ago, marvel at the slew of radio stations he has acquired in his lifetime and his millions of dollars of property in Indiana. His accomplishments are extraordinary Radio Personality, Escape Artist, Broadcast Entrepreneur, and Actor. Not bad for a guy who once upon a time had a dream with his father to own a radio station in Muncie, Indiana.

Home to Shirk is in Zionsville, Indiana, with wife Liz, and he has a daughter Maxine. Sadly, Shirk's father, Bob (R.J.) Poorman died in 1980. He was a legend who touched many lives, especially over the airways in Indiana. He is remembered with exceptional honor and respect and for caring about Muncie. Shirk can undoubtedly vouch for this when he says, "He loved life. He loved Muncie- the city, and the city loved him.

When I think of Muncie, I always think of the wonderful people there. Whoever coined it America's Hometown, got it right."

Chapter 16

Our Betty Harris

You are about to read the probable, final interview of Muncie icon, Betty Harris. During the heyday, it was common knowledge more musicians came out of Muncie than any other city, far and wide. The teen musicians had one significant person in common: Betty. She was a fireball of sorts, who believed in the talents of every musician who walked through her office door.

She inspired and promoted young hopefuls. If a band needed publicity photos, she would do a quality photoshoot. Need a new bass player for that band? Tell Betty! When a band caught the eye of the famous, local newspaper columnist, it was like hitting the big time!

Her weekly column, "Where the Bands Are" was a Friday must-see in the *Muncie Evening Press* in the late 1960s and early 1970s. It was common to see long-haired musicians hanging out in her office, waiting for the latest hot-off-the-press edition. She was known as "The Dick Clark of Muncie," which was an apt description.

Betty did not just promote the music of teen musicians; she developed their self-confidence. Many musicians are still playing music today because of this woman right here.

In later years, lavishing praise on Betty for her multitude of accomplishments, and her celebrity status could be challenging because she was such a humble person. I know, when I tried, she told me not to do it.

Betty especially enjoyed hearing the stories of musicians, whom she helped along the way. Her invaluable knowledge and experience of the music scene were unique. If music events were happening in Indiana or even adjacent states, Betty was in the loop. Also, there was The Cave – the teen club located below the PAL Club on Walnut Street in Muncie. The Cave gave teens a decent, safe place to hang out on weekends. Local bands often graced the stage there. Betty saw the project as her baby! She smiled, "It was a good thing…if I hadn't done it, nobody else would. I wrote the column and built The Cave. Out of these are my favorite memories."

Joy Charlene Henley

The Beatles! Now here is a subject Betty knows! Looking back, it is hilarious that people pondered if those long "mop tops" were wigs! Mentioning this and the mere thought of it really made Betty chuckle! She once remarked, "When I saw the reaction of the teens and 'tweens' to The Beatles, I knew something big was coming in, and I wanted to be a part of it." The mention of the teen musicians who used to sit in her office with long hair, made her laugh! The reminder that most of those musicians cut off those ponytails, now have short hair and are in their 60s, *really* made her laugh!

97 Betty "at home" doing what she did best, in her small corner of the world at her Muncie Evening Press office -Courtesy of Margaret Scott

Betty was originally from Troy, Missouri. She obtained her bachelor's degree in Journalism from the University of Missouri. She began her career as an editor for the *Muncie Morning Star* and then became a photographer and reporter for the *Muncie Evening Press*, where she worked from 1949-1973. After writing the "Where the Bands Are" column, Betty went on to write "Senior Scene" from 1992-99, first for Muncie's *The Star* and then for *The Star Press*.

When covering wedding stories, Betty would travel to meet the bride to see her gown if the bride could not come to her office. She had to give the perfect description. She was extraordinary. Her long-time Muncie friend was Ruth Chin, also an accomplished photographer since 1946, who owned Chin Photography. Ruth also owned the downtown Mandarin Inn in the 1950s and 1960s. Betty was especially fond of her friend and colleague Ruth Mauzy McFadden, who, during her newspaper tenure for over a half-century, was a Reporter, Society Columnist, Editor, and Women's Editor.

After retiring from the newspaper, Betty worked on campus at Ball State University as Assistant to the Dean in the College of Business. She described herself during that time as "The MBA Coordinator for ten years." With her husband's encouragement, she eventually transitioned from employee to student at Ball State, receiving her Master's Degree.

Sharing a picture of her daughter Mary Margaret and her husband, Betty beamed, "She is my pride and joy. I gave Margaret to God"- a reference to her being a Missionary. She added, "She is also a Minister," as is Mary Margaret's husband. Both reside in the Seattle, Washington area. Betty's son Bill, who attended Muncie Central, is an Airline Pilot and musician who, with his wife Rhonda, resides in North Carolina.

Betty's blessings included several grandchildren and great-grandchildren. Her great-granddaughter Gabriella Popa is an accomplished actress who appeared in the movie *The Edge of Darkness* with Mel Gibson, among other projects.

In the heyday, Betty was encouraged to enter the political arena, which did not interest her. It was a time when she was devoted to family and everything that was happening in Muncie. She was one busy lady! Some of the interests and highlights of her life included:

Writing Books

Writing Book Reviews

Writing for *Prime Years* and other magazines

4-H activities

Gardening- especially growing her green beans, I think she used Ball Jars!

Helping at Minnetrista Cultural Center in Muncie

Job's Daughters

Holding Offices in both local and state divisions of the Muncie branch of the National League of American Pen Women

City Events

She danced with a women's troupe in Las Vegas and insisted, "There was nothing to it!"

Betty grinned, when remembering her husband's words of advice, "You should slow down more." She was a romantic who believed in love at first sight. Once upon a time, she went to a USO type of dance. The discussion of it brought out an amusing impishness. She echoed children reciting rhymes while jumping rope, "Went to the USO and picked up a beau..." She laughed with a few tears when recalling that time in her life. Having known the love of two wonderful husbands and the loss of them, Betty was rich with love and devotion.

At Ball State University, during Betty's September 22, 2003 presentation titled, "Confessions of a Rock 'n' Roll Reporter," she was known as the "hippest" reporter on the beat. Many of her once upon a time, teen musicians appeared in the audience. Betty was always one to refer to the 1960s band members as "my kids." She interviewed the likes of The Beatles, The Rolling Stones, The Who, Jimi Hendrix, Iron Butterfly, Alice Cooper, and other 1960s notables. She once admitted, "I liked 'In-A-Gadda-Da-Vida,' which is strange when you look at me." She could vividly recall the 14 amps piled high on the stage for the Jimi Hendrix concert in Muncie. She could tell you that July 18, 1969, was when Tommy James and the Shondells appeared at Emens Auditorium on the Ball State University campus. October 1970 was etched in her mind because that is the date Blood, Sweat, and Tears was in town.

Her favorite interview? She once said it was Alice Cooper! She had not arranged an interview, so she donned some jeans and a t-shirt and waited by his dressing room. The date was April 1, 1973, and the place was the Indianapolis Convention Center. Betty was a stickler for details, remembering there were 12,400 people in attendance. She had a firm belief, "You do what you do to get a story." Cooper's manager told Betty she would have to leave. But Cooper, wearing platform, leopard–print, thigh-high boots, stopped his management, instructing, "Let her be... she swings." It was a common phrase at the time for a cool cat!

People still talk about the time Betty supposedly took the band, Strawberry Alarm Clock, to her home for supper. Did her husband *really* take the group for a ride on his tractor, on their property?

Decades later, people still wonder if one of The Beatles stayed all night at Betty's home. Someone even went so far as to suggest Ringo was the lucky house guest! Betty was with The Beatles on September 3, 1964, at the Indianapolis State Fair. During a Press Conference, she asked the group if they ever dreamed about walking down the street without getting mobbed. John Lennon replied, "We used to do that with no money in our pockets, so there's no point in it. It's a dead loss." It is hearing of these encounters and experiences with famous people (that would leave the rest of us breathless), that tempt us to dream and speculate. Besides, guessing and pondering feed the grapevine an extra helping of pizzazz! Did one of The Beatles really stay all night at Betty's home? Some insist they heard Betty say no. Others just keep on talking. If anything, it probably made interesting fodder for the community at a time when Beatlemania was at its peak.

Gone are the hectic newspaper deadlines and heavily scribbled calendars of commitments. Back in the day, Betty could have quickly filled multiple calendars and day planners. On the day of our luncheon, she was busy enjoying the small things in life, which, as we know, are the big things. She enjoyed reading poetry, the daily newspaper, and writing for personal fulfillment. Betty frequently chatted with her sister-in-law about everything from visiting the ducks at a nearby park, to scenery to the clouds.

After our luncheon, I came away knowing the Muncie ride was a great one for such a talented, caring person. Did Betty remember the names of every musician? Perhaps not, but she felt oh, so loved. This remarkable lady saw the good in every person who crossed her path. She invested in the hopes and dreams of teen musicians. How many people in the world do this? Betty had a gigantic heart, and there was room in it for all of her "kids." I mentioned several names of musicians, and with each one, her face lit up. Then, her eyes welled with tears as she declared, "They were my friends."

98 Betty Harris- January 23, 1925, to March 18, 2013

> *Annoying the cook will result in smaller portions.*
>
> -Author Unknown

Chapter 17

The Secret Ingredient in the Ball Stores Chocolate Cake

Some of these foods may make your mouth water! On the flip side, you may wish you could unsee others. They have one thing in common; they were popular during the heyday! Bon appetit!

Apple Dumplings (served warm)

Banana and Potato Chip sandwiches

Banana Meat Loaf

Beanee Weenees

Beans and Cornbread - honey cornbread is a favorite!

Beans over toast

Beefaroni

Bologna Cake – made with bologna, and the "frosting" on the "cake" was cream cheese flavored with ranch powder or dressing

Bread (slice) soaked in pea juice

Chicken a la King – in the skillet, baked, soup style

Chicken (whole) in a can

Chili added to spaghetti

Chilled Prune Whip

Joy Charlene Henley

Chips on a variety of sandwiches

Cinnamon and Sugar Toast

Cinnamon Rolls dipped in Chili

Corn Casserole

Cornbread in milk

Corn Pancakes

Cream Cheese and Bologna Sandwich

Cream of Wheat

Creamed Peas on toast

Creamed Tuna- with Cream of Mushroom soup and olives poured over waffles

Dill Pickle Sandwiches – mayonnaise on bread, salt, pepper, thinly sliced lengthwise pickles

Fluffernutter Sandwiches - white bread, peanut butter, jelly, and marshmallow crème (many variations)

Foot Long Coney or "Slaw" (coleslaw) hot dogs

French Toast

Fresh Broccoli on toast with Cheese Sauce

Fried Bologna Sandwiches – with crisp-edged bologna and the hump in the middle

Fried Egg and Grilled Cheese Sandwich

Fried Green Tomato Sandwiches

Frozen Pork and Beans and Ketchup pop

Fudge Potato – pasteurized, processed chocolate poured over a slit baked potato

Gravy Bread – dipping your bread in gravy

Grits

Ham and Beans

"Ham Salad" Sandwich or Sandwich Spread -made with ham or bologna, hard-boiled eggs, relish, mayo, and a touch of mustard. Mix and spread on bread. Heydayers, still make it today!

Ham with Hollandaise sauce

Hominy with Butter

The Heyday of Muncie, Indiana

Indiana Spaghetti – add bacon and onion to spaghetti

JELL-O... get out the fruits, olives, cheese, prunes, marshmallows, celery, and get creative with decorative molds!

La Choy Noodles and Chow Main topping

Lettuce Leaf (Iceberg), topped with a scoop of cottage cheese, half of a canned peach, and a dollop of your favorite dressing – a popular dieter's lunch back in the day

Liver Loaf

Liverwurst Sandwiches

Macaroni and Cheese with ketchup

Mashed Potato Pancakes

Maters and Mayo Sandwich- tomatoes and mayo on bread

Mayo on canned pear halves

Meatballs dipped in barbecue sauce and grape jelly

Milk Chicken – chicken with a milk/cream sauce poured over it that resembled gravy

99 Olive Loaf...Yum!

Olive Loaf Sandwiches

Olive-topped hot dogs

Onion Pie - perhaps better known as a Southern delicacy, onion pie was brought to Indiana by Eastern European immigrants. Serve as a side dish. The pie crust is filled with sliced sweet onions, butter, cream, bacon, eggs, and cheese.

Joy Charlene Henley

Potato Salad Loaf

Raw Potato Sandwiches - spread butter on a piece of bread, put slices of raw potato on it, add plenty of salt and pepper and another slice of bread on top

Roast Lamb swimming in jelly

Salmon Patties – form salmon, crushed crackers, a little onion, and an egg into patties. Fry in skillet. Season to taste. Add ketchup if desired.

Saucewich Sandwiches – Scald one tall can of evaporated milk in a double broiler. Blend in ketchup and mustard. Serve hot on toasted or grilled sandwiches, closed or open-faced. Also good on toasted English Muffins. Variations: Add tuna to the sauce and serve on sliced toast. Or, add deviled or ground ham and pour over poached egg on a toasted English Muffin. Add grated cheese to cover burger on the bun

Shake 'n Bake

Smothered Tater Tots- covered with sautéed ground bison, Jalapeno Cheese, green onions and hot sauce

Spaghetti Sandwich – spaghetti on toast

Spaghetti-stuffed green peppers

Spam and Eggs for breakfast

Spam Burgers

Spam Pancakes

Spam slices baked with peaches between them, known as Fiesta Peach Spam Bake

Sugar Sandwiches – sugar and margarine, sugar and peanut butter or sugar and cinnamon slathered between two slices of bread

Tuna Noodle Casserole – can of tuna, a box of Macaroni and Cheese, Cream of Mushroom soup, and potato chips

Tuna Stuffed Eggs

Van Camp's Pork and Beans

Veg-All Soup – add tomato juice to Veg-All

Vegetable and Tuna JELL-O Wreath at Christmas

Waffle Burgers – Spread ground beef (add cheese if you like) on a squared waffle, top with butter, and garnish with Green Pepper and Chili Sauce

Wieners in a can with a pack of BBQ sauce included

Deep-Fried Foods

Deep-Fried foods are popular items at the County Fair! It is hard to believe some of these were and still are, prepared this way.

Belgian Waffle on a stick

Biscuits

Bologna in Butter sandwiches

Brownies

Butter

Candy Bars

Caramel and Chocolate Deep-Fried Ice Cream treat

Cookie Dough

Dill Pickles

Fruit (coat the fruit, deep fry it, and cover it with chocolate and powdered sugar)

Funnel Cake

Green Tomatoes

Ice Cream Burger

Klondike Bars

Oreos

Peanut Butter and Jelly Sandwich

Peanut Butter Pineapple Pork Burger

Pizza Balls

Pop Corn

Potatoes with Butter

Sauerkraut Balls

Spam-filled donuts

Spam with melted Velveeta Cheese

Twinkies

Tempting Desserts

Angel Food Cake

Baked Alaska

Banana Cream - filled Chiffon Cake

Grasshopper Pie

Mayonnaise Cake

Mock Apple Pie made with Ritz Crackers

Old Fashioned Cream Pie or Hoosier Sugar Cream Pie is the Indiana state pie. The pie is sometimes called "Chess Pie" in Southern Indiana.

Pineapple Upside-Down Cake

Pink Champagne Cake – dubbed "the elite of party cakes" that contained ¾ cup of Champagne

Potato Chip Cookies

Pudding

Salad Dressing Cake (contains Miracle Whip salad dressing)

Small tubs of ice cream with wooden spoons for the children

Strawberry Pie

Tiger Tiger (or Tiger Tail) Ice Cream – orange ice cream striped with black licorice. Was made by Sani-Dairy

The Ultimate Dessert!

If you were a regular at the exquisite Ball Stores Department Store in downtown Muncie, you might have known Goldie "Mom" Farmer. Also known as Fancie Farmer, she joined Ball Stores in 1935 as a Pastry Cook in the cafeteria. She was the manager of the cafeteria downstairs for 34 of her 35 years there.

Goldie could produce a unique, unforgettable Chocolate Cake, among many other tempting desserts! In 1968, she compiled her favorite recipes into a cookbook to raise money for a church youth group trip to Europe.

The result was *Mom Farmer's Fancies for Finicky Folks*.

Sandra Minnick well remembers Goldie "Mom" Farmer. She describes this fascinating time in her life, "I have so many wonderful memories of eating at the Ball Stores Cafeteria when I was a student at Muncie Central High in the late 1940s to 1950.

The Heyday of Muncie, Indiana

As a young mother, I would take my children downtown to eat there. I was looking at some of my old cookbooks and came across one written by Fancie Farmer.".

Minnick loved all of Goldie's food. The secret ingredient in her heavenly chocolate cake, though, was quite the surprise! She asks an intriguing and obvious question, "Bacon in Chocolate Cake... who would get by with this today?"

Ball Stores Cake Recipe

```
CHOCOLATE CAKE

2 C white sugar          2/3 C bacon grease
2 eggs                   2½ C flour
½ C cocoa                ½ teaspoon salt
1 teaspoon vanilla       1 C sour milk
2 teaspoons soda

"If no sour milk, use 3/4 cup sweet milk and
1/4 cup vinegar.  Mix together."
Pour sour milk into bowl and add the 2 teaspoons soda.
Beat, then add other ingredients.  Mix well and add
1 scant-cup boiling water.  Mix well (Batter is very
thin.)  Bake in two 9" cake pans or one 10x12 pan.
Bake at 350 degrees about 40 minutes.
```

100 Sandra Minnick adoringly holds the book Goldie "Mom" Farmer gave her over 50 years ago

Fun Food Facts

Canned tomato juice was developed in Kokomo, Indiana, at the request of a doctor for nutritious baby food. In 1917, for the first time anywhere, tomato juice was served at the French Lick Resort and Spa in French Lick, Indiana.

Wonder Bread –obtained its name and colorful package design when the owner of the Taggart Baking Company (founded in Indianapolis) was amazed by the hundreds of colorful hot-air balloons released over the Indianapolis Speedway. Wonder Bread was made to feed troops in World War II and was the first sliced white bread.

Homemade Beer Bread with Gravy

Submitted by Donna Hunt of Farmland, Indiana

In 1992, Donna Hunt made a recipe book for her older children. Homemade Beer Bread with Gravy is one of the recipes she included. After each recipe, she wrote why the recipe was important to her or something about it. The following is what she transcribed:

"Dad brought this recipe home from somebody that worked at the foundry. It was around 1969, and I thought it was really neat because I could use the beer in it, and I was only 13!! It really does taste good, though, and it's easy!"

3 cups self-rising flour

3 tablespoons sugar

12 oz. beer

Mix all ingredients

Bake 45 to 50 minutes in greased loaf pan at 350 degrees

You can butter the top of the bread for the last 15 minutes of cooking time

For an added treat, make a package of white or homemade gravy, with or without sausage, and pour over the Homemade Beer Bread. Butter and jelly spread on the bread is tasty!

101 Donna Carol Hunt of Farmland, Indiana

Donna also makes a tasty, low-calorie chocolate cake. She simply adds a Diet Coke to a chocolate cake mix and bakes; it tastes like brownies.

Donna's family also enjoys it when she bakes a white cake mix, pokes holes in it with a wooden spoon, and pours JELL-O over it. It is delicious with whipped cream icing.

Fair-Style Lemon Shake-Ups (makes two drinks)

1/2 cup water

1/4 cup sugar

2 lemons

2 cups of ice cubes

1 cup of ice water

Bring the water and sugar to boil in a small saucepan. Boil for five minutes or until the sugar is completely dissolved.

Juice 1 1/2 lemons, reserving the fourth lemon half. Stir the lemon juice into the sugar syrup; you will have about 1 cup. Chill the lemon syrup in the fridge.

Blend the ice in a blender or food processor until crushed. Put half the crushed ice in a cocktail shaker, along with half the chilled lemon syrup (about 1/2 cup), along with 1/2 cup ice water.

Shake vigorously for a couple of minutes, then dump the whole mixture — including the ice, into a tall glass.

Repeat with the remaining ice, syrup, and ice water for the second shakeup. Cut the remaining lemon half into four slices and add two slices to each glass.

Black Cow - It uses root beer instead of seltzer.

Pour 3 oz. chocolate syrup in a large glass

Fill half full of root beer and stir well-heeled

Add 1 or 2 scoops of vanilla ice cream

Fill with more root beer

Green River Floats

Lime sherbet and 7-Up or Sprite

Purple Cow

Vanilla Ice Cream in purple grape soda (or grape juice)

Snow White

Vanilla Ice Cream and 7-Up or Sprite

White Cow or Vanilla Milk Shake

4 scoops vanilla ice cream

1 tablespoon Vanilla Extract (or 2 oz. Vanilla Syrup)

1 ½ cups milk into a blender, blend until smooth

Phosphate Drinks

Heydayers still talk about that Cherry or Lime Phosphate drink! Phosphates were carbonated beverages made from scratch by the "Soda Jerk" using carbonated soda water, flavored syrups, and phosphoric acid. Favorite flavors included cherry, lime, chocolate, and vanilla. Soda jerks kept it in a shaker bottle (like hot sauce or Worcestershire) and added just a few drops to each drink. The trick today is to find the Phosphoric Acid.

Snow Ice Cream

4 cups fresh snow (white snow only)

1 cup milk

¼ cup of sugar

1 teaspoon. vanilla

Mix to desired consistency

Despite the massive meat, potato and gravy meals, calories not often considered, questionable Cholesterol numbers, and the way many of us loved to devour food, people in the heyday still were inclined to let their taste buds lead the way. Well, until a wake-up call was received. If a teen started to gain weight, her guy might have teased her that she had a "midriff bulge." It was crushing.

Simple cooking tips

For super juicy burgers, add Evaporated Milk to hamburger mixture that is about to be barbecued on the grill.

Dip sausages in fresh pancake batter and fry

Good cooks basted their ham with 7-Up. The soda makes a great meat tenderizer. The drink also enhances cakes, frosting, pie crusts, and gelatin with its sweet and acidic properties.

Food portions were much smaller in the heyday. Mothers would purchase a little over a pound of meat to feed a family of five. The portion was the size of a "deck of cards," recommended today.

1960's Prices

Imagine shopping today with these general, 1960s prices...

Apples 3 pounds, 49 cents

Asparagus, 19 cents per pound

Baby Food, 8 cents a jar

Bacon- sliced, 39 cents per pound

Bananas, 2 pounds, 19 cents

Beef Chuck Roast, 49 cents a pound

Beef Ravioli, 30 cents a can

Beer 6-pack, 99 cents

Bologna, 28 cents a pound

Bread one loaf, 20 cents

Broiler Chickens, 29 cents per pound

Butter– Sweet Cream, 80 cents a pound

Cake Mixes, 25 cents

California Grapes, 14 cents per pound

Campbells Soup, 6 cans, 89 cents

Carrots 4 pounds, 29 cents

Joy Charlene Henley

Cat Food - cans of Puss 'n' Boots, 15 oz. can/2 for 25 cents or 8 oz. can/3 for 25 cents

Celery 2 stalks, 19 cents

Cereal, 28 cents a box

If a youngster lived in the home, you would usually see cereal in the grocery cart. Small-sized (one serving) variety packs of 6 and 9 boxes were popular.

There were so many kinds of cereal! It could take a heyday kid awhile to decide.

Alpha-Bits

Apple Jacks (48% sugar by weight)

Cap 'n Crunch

Cheerios

Chex (corn, rice, wheat)

Circus Fun

Cocoa Krispies

Cocoa Puffs

Corn Flakes

Corn Flakes with Instant Bananas

Crispy Numbers

Froot Loops

Frosty O's

Honeycomb

Joker Jacks

Kaboom

Kix

Life

Lucky Charms

Maypo

Oks

Puffa Rice

Quake

Quisp

Raisin Bran

Rice Krispies

Sugar Chex

Sugar Coated Crisp Rice

Sugar Frosted Flakes ("Sugar" omitted from the name in 1983)

Sugar Jets

Sugar Pops

Sugar Rice Krinkles

Sugar Smacks (contained initially 56% sugar by weight)

Sugar Stars

Total

Trix

Twinkles

Wackies

Wheat and Rice Honeys

Wheaties!

Chicken, 29 cents per pound

Chicken TV Dinner, 39 cents

Chocolate Milk, 10 cents a quart

Chuck Roast, 49 cents a pound

Coffee, 38 cents, 1 pound can. Chase and Sanborn, Folgers, Hills Brothers, Lyons, Maxwell House, Nescafe, and Sanka were popular.

Colby Cheese, 39 cents per pound

Cookies, 50 cents a package

Corn on the Cob, 12 ears, $1.00

Cottage Cheese, 2-pound carton, 39 cents

Crest Toothpaste, 50 cents

Crisco, 67 cents

Del Monte Peaches, 29 cents per can

102 Dog Bone

Dog Food, 5 pounds for 59 cents

Burgerbits	Gravy Train
Friskies Mix	Ken-L-Ration
Gaines Burgers	Purina Dog Chow

Egg Nog, 69 cents per quart

Eggs, 39 cents per dozen

Flour 79 cents, a 10-pound bag

Fresh Carrots, 9 cents per bunch

Frozen Cod Fillets, 33 cents per pound

Frozen French Fries, 10 cents for 8 ounces

Frozen Pot Pies, 29 cents

Frozen TV Dinners, 39 cents each

Gerber's Baby Food, 25 cents for 3

Grapefruit, 5 cents each

Grapes, 14 cents a pound

Green Peppers, 5 cents each

Ground Beef, 45 cents per pound - often 3 lbs. for $1.00 on sale

Gum, 5 cents a pack

Ham, 49 cents per pound

Heinz Ketchup, 22 cents

Ice Cream, 49 cents a half-gallon

JELL-O, 4 packages for 35 cents. Be sure to have an adequate supply of ripe bananas on hand. Sliced bananas in JELL-O was an old stand-by that was in style!

Keen Drink Mix, Moo Juice, P. D.Q., Funny Face Drink Mix Packs - 5 cents a pack. Made 2 quarts. The "Funny Face" drink flavor "Choo Choo Cherry Pie" - sweetened without sugar was popular! So was "Goofy Grape!"

Kielbasa, 59 cents per pound

Kleenex Tissue, 19 cents

Kool-Aid, 3 cents a pack

Kraft Deluxe Dinner, 39 cents

Kraft Miracle Whip, 51 cents

Kraft Processed Cheese, 39 cents for 8 ounces

Lamb Chops, 89 cents per pound

Land O' Lakes Butter, 67 cents per pound

Lettuce-Iceberg, 25 cents per head

Liver – Calf, 79 cents per pound

Luncheon Meat, 29 cents

Macaroni and Cheese, 39 cents a box

Margarine, 31 cents per pound

Mazola Vegetable Oil, 69 cents

The Heyday of Muncie, Indiana

Milk, 20 cents a quart/53 cents a gallon

Miracle Whip, 49 cents a quart jar

Onions, 29 cents for 2 pounds

Orange Juice, 19 cents a quart

Oranges, 2 dozen, 89 cents

Pepsi, 6 pack 59 cents

Pork and Beans, 8 cents

Pork Chops, 59 cents per pound

Pork Roast, 39 cents a pound

Porterhouse Steak, $1.19 per pound

Potatoes, 10 pounds for 39 cents

Prime Rib, 35 cents a pound

Rump Steak, $1.49 per pound

Salad Oil, 29 cents

Sirloin Steaks, 89 cents per pound

Skippy Peanut Butter, 79 cents

Soup, 6 cans 89 cents

Spam, 39 cents a tin

Spareribs (Country Style), 49 cents per pound

Starkist Tuna, 19 cents

Sugar 5 pounds, 9 cents

Sugared Donuts, 49 cents per dozen

Sweet Corn, 5 cents each

Sweet Potatoes, 3 pounds, for 29 cents

T-Bone Steak, 98 cents a pound

Tangerines, 29 cents a dozen

Toilet Paper 4 rolls, 29 cents/12 rolls 99 cents

Tomato Juice, large 46 oz. can 18 cents

Toothpaste (Crest), 50 cents

Joy Charlene Henley

Tuna Fish, 4 cans 88 cents

Turkeys, 39 cents per pound

Veal Cutlets, 68 cents per pound

Velveeta Cheese, 68 cents a one-pound loaf

Watermelon, 2.5 cents per pound

Wieners, 59 cents

Cost of Random Items:

Alarm Clock, $1.99

Aspirin 37 cents, 500 count

Automatic Electric Blanket, $9.94

Ball Stores Children's shoes, $4.88

Bedspreads, $5.00

Car (new), $2,600.00 in 1960; $3,270.00 in 1969

Charcoal, 97 cents a 20-pound bag

Children's Car Seats, $5.95

Christmas Tree Lights, $3.49

Cleaners, 12 cents

Ajax	Galaxy
Comet	Lestoil
Flash	Spic and Span

Dishwashing Liquids, 41 cents

Chiffon	Palmolive
Dove	Swan
Gentle Fels	Thrill
Ivory	Trend
Joy	Vel
Lux	

Dresses ("Better" dresses), $5.00

Electric Can Opener, $7.77

Flash Cubes (3-G.E. cubes- 4 flashes from one cube), $1.59

Gas, 25 cents a gallon in 1960 and 35 cents by 1969

Girl's dresses, 2 for $1.00

Haircuts, $1.50 to $3.00 in 1960s

Halo Hairspray, 59 cents

Jumper Cables, $1.00

Laundry soap, 59 cents a box

Ajax	Fab
All	Fairy Snow
Bonus	Ivory Snow
Breeze	Lux
Cheer	Oxydol
Cold Power	Persil
Cold Power XE	Rinso
Dash	Salvo
Dreft	Super-Suds
Duz	Tide

It was common to receive gifts in boxes of laundry soap such as a dishcloth, a glass, and other surprises. In the 1960s, stain removers and pre-treatments became popular.

Lawn Chairs, (webbed) $1.88

Levi Jeans, $5.00

Nylon Hose, 59 cents

McDonald's Hamburgers, 15 cents

    Cheeseburgers, 20 cents   Shakes, 22 cents

    Fries, 12 cents

Men's Cuff Link sets, gift-boxed, $1.00

Men's Dress Shirts, $2.98

Men's Plaid Jacket, $12.70

Men's Sport Shirts, $1.69

Men's T-Shirts, 3 for $1.00

Mink Stoles were sold in 1960 in Muncie at Roth's Smart Apparel on Fridays and Saturdays for $199.00.

Parakeets, 98 cents

Plastic Hanger Sets, 43 cents

Radios- Transistor Pocket (6 Transistor with carrying case and 9-volt battery) $2.99

Refrigerator (12 cubic feet) Yellow or Turquoise, $178.00

Rose Bushes, 49 cents

Sandbox, $7.77

Shower Curtains, 66 cents

Sinus, congestion, hay fever tablets Coricidin "D," 24 tabs for $1.23

Slacks (Misses), $1.88

Sports Shirts, $1.69

Spring Hats, $1.98

Stamps, 4 cents each

Swing Sets, $14.99 - $24.88

Teflon Fry Pan, $1.88

Incomes (Annual) $5,315 in 1960, $7,143 in 1967 and $8,540 by 1969

In 1967, the minimum wage was $1.40 an hour.

A new home ranged in price from $12,700 in 1960 to $24,600 in 1969.

A typical rent was approximately $98.

The Heyday of Muncie, Indiana

Classic Candy, how many do you remember?

It was common knowledge that kids needed the energy provided by candy.

Airheads
Almond Joy
Animal Crackers
Atomic Fireballs
BB Bats Taffy Suckers
Bazooka Gum
Beeman's Gum
Bit-O-Honey
Black Jack gum
Boston Baked Beans
Bubble Gum Cigarettes
Bun
Candy Buttons

103 Feeling so grownup with Candy Cigarettes

Candy Lipsticks
Candy Necklace
Caravelle
Charleston Chew
Charms – Sweet and sour pops and assorted candies

Cherry Sours
Chick-O-Sticks
Chiclets
Chocolate Gold Coins
Chuckles
Chunky
Circus Peanuts
Clark Bar
Clove gum
Dentyne gum
Dots
Double Bubble Gum
Doublemint gum
Fifth Avenue
Fizzie's Drink Tablets
Fruit Stripe gum
Goo Goo Cluster
Good and Plenty
Gumballs – grape ones were popular
Hershey's Almond Marshmallow Cup
Hershey's Kisses
Hershey's Milk Chocolate Bar (also with almonds)
Hot Tamales

Jaw Breakers

Jolly Rancher

Juicy Fruit gum

Jujubes

Kits Old Fashioned Taffy Squares/Chews

Lemonhead

Licorice

Lifesavers – did you ever taste Musk Lifesavers?

M & M's

Mallo Cup

Mike and Ike

Milk Duds

Milkshake

Moon Pies

Mounds

Necco Wafers

Nestle Crunch

Nik L Nips (miniature wax soda bottles with syrup)

Now and Later

Nut Goodie

Oh Henry!

One Hundred Grand

Peppermint Bullseye

Pez

Pixy Stix

Razzles

Red Hots

Red Vines Licorice Twists

Rocky Road

Root Beer Barrels

Scooter Pie

Sky Bar

Slo Poke

Starburst Fruit Chews

Sugar Daddy

Swedish Fish

Sweethearts

Teaberry Gum

Tootsie Rolls

Turkish Taffy

Twizzlers

Walnettos

Wax Lips

Zagnut

Zero

Zotz

At the local lunch counter, a tasty, toasted triple-decker ham salad sandwich for 60 cents and a banana split for 39 cents would sure hit the spot! Just take me back to 1967, please!

Chapter 18

It is About More Than Cornfields

Albany Shoe Tree in Albany started as a quirky tradition for local teenagers but grew to be embraced by the entire community. A shoe tree begins with one dreamer, tossing his or her footwear high into the sky, to catch on an out-of-reach branch. Many people inscribe messages on the shoes with a permanent marker, and it is quite a sight! Other Shoe Trees exist throughout the country. Take Highway 28 to Strong Road, then pass Strong Cemetery and turn right on to Edgewater Road. The tree is visible from the road.

Cindy's Diner is at 230 West Berry Street Fort Wayne. Small, no-frills diner with an old-fashioned jukebox!

Colonel Harland Sander's birthplace and childhood home in Clark County. Location: On SR 160 just east of I-65, on the right when traveling east, in Henryville.

The Elkhart Tooth Brick in Elkhart. A concrete block embedded with thousands of pulled teeth was created by a local dentist to memorialize his dog. Dr. Joseph Stamp practiced dentistry in Elkhart for 60 years, until he died at the age of 88 in 1978. He preserved them with chemicals in a barrel in the basement of his office. The brick is in the fenced-in exterior of the Time Was Museum in Elkhart, Indiana, just north of the intersection of North Main Street and Jackson Boulevard (directly across the street from the McDonald's).

Frances Farmer's Final Resting Place is at Oaklawn Memorial Gardens (Mausoleum), 9700 Allisonville, in Indianapolis. Legendary actress from Seattle, Washington, who hosted *Frances Farmer Presents* on WFBM TV 6, in Indianapolis, Monday – Friday, from 1959-1964.

"Hold On" is a breathtaking 5-figure, life-size, bronze sculpture located on the South Wing of the IU Health Hospital (formerly Ball Memorial Hospital) in Muncie. A creation by late Artist, Steven Clark. The sculpture was gifted to the hospital by way of the Hamer D. & Phyllis C. Shafer Foundation.

John Dillinger's Grave is at Crown Hill Funeral Home and Cemetery, 700 38th Street in Indianapolis.

Kissing Bridges in Brown and Parke Counties. Some 21 of these covered bridges are still in use across Indiana's Parke County, with many of them now covered in romantic notes that have been left by visitors. The covered bridges are known as kissing bridges as they were one of the few places courting couples could find some privacy hundreds of years ago. An annual festival dedicated to the structures is held in Parke County each October.

Modoc's Market at 205 South Miami Street in Wabash. This shop acquired its name from a runaway elephant that smashed through its doors, stole some peanuts, and spent five days on the lam. Google it for the history; this is one, humorous story!

Movies with an Indiana Connection include *Breaking Away*, *Close Encounters of The Third Kind*, *The Fault in Our Stars*, *Hoosiers*, *The Hudsucker Proxy*, *Public Enemies*, *Rudy*, and others. *Close Encounters of the Third Kind* took place in Muncie although not filmed there. The production department needed sets and scenery that were not available in Muncie. The movie set was furnished with a Muncie badge, a Ball State pennant, and uniforms to add authenticity. A member of the production company listened to police dispatch transmissions, and they may have taken a few shots of Prairie Creek. Actor Richard Dreyfuss wore a "Ball U" t-shirt, and reference to Cornbread Road is in the movie. If you are a movie buff, you cannot drive by Cornbread Road without thinking of *Close Encounters of the Third Kind*.

The Popcorn Festival is in the downtown Valparaiso area, 3 hours northwest of Muncie. It began in 1979 as a way to salute native Orville Redenbacher and popcorn. Scheduled annually on the first Saturday after Labor Day, the Valparaiso Popcorn Festival is an all-day event held in the downtown area. Included in the festivities are a 5-mile run (the Popcorn Panic), a block-long kiddie run (the Lit'l Kernel Puff), a 5-mile walk, live entertainment, hundreds of food and craft vendors and the nation's 2nd oldest Popcorn Parade. Free popcorn to every attendee! A popcorn festival also happens in Brazil, ndiana, which is the birthplace of Orville Redenbacher.

104 Wooden Coca-Cola Crate

Rock-Cola '50s Cafe is at 5730 Brookville Road Indianapolis. Cute and retro!

"Roseanne Conner's House" is located in Evansville. Who can forget the Conner house at the beginning of the show? The home used for outside shots of the Conner house in fictional Lanford, Illinois, sits on the southside of this Ohio River city at 619 South Runnymeade Avenue. The creator of the original *Roseanne*, TV producer Matt Williams, is an Evansville native.

Outdoor Evansville locations were shot for fictional scenes on the TV show *Roseanne*. Roseanne's hangout, the Lobo Lounge, is really located at 1200 Edgar Street and is Talk of the Town Pizza. The Third & Delaware street sign on the show is at the intersection of 900 West Delaware Street and 700 3rd Avenue. The church used in transition photos on the show is the St. Boniface Catholic Church at 418 North Wabash Avenue.

Ryan White Final Resting Place is at Cicero Cemetery in Cicero. It is approximately an hour west of Muncie. Born on December 6, 1971, in Russiaville, he was a 13-year-old who contracted AIDS in 1982 through a blood transfusion. White was living in Kokomo at the time of diagnosis and given six months to live. He died on April 8, 1990, one month before his high school graduation and only months before Congress passed the legislation bearing his name in August 1990: The Ryan White Comprehensive AIDS Resources Emergency (CARE) Act.

Seymour, Indiana, is the hometown of music legend John Mellencamp! It is located approximately two hours from Muncie in Southern Indiana. It is small with friendly folks!

Southside Soda Shop and Diner is at 1122 South Main Street in Goshen. You may have seen it featured on the *Food Network*.

Ready Set Go!

Abraham Lincoln's Indiana Boyhood Home is in Southern Indiana- 5 miles from Santa Claus, Indiana, in Spencer County. The site is located about ten minutes off the Interstate 64/ U.S. 231 junction and near the new U.S. 231 Route, named the Abraham Lincoln Memorial Parkway in his honor. Lincoln spent 14 childhood years in Southern Indiana- from 1816 to 1830. He grew from a 7-year-old to a 21-year-old during this time.

The Lincoln Boyhood Home was named a National Historic Landmark in 1960. Visitors will also discover the Lincoln Boyhood National Memorial, the Living Historical Farm, Lincoln State Park, the Lincoln Amphitheater, and the Lincoln Pioneer Village and Museum. Today, the visitor center is in the Memorial Building. The staff of the Lincoln Living Historical Farm dresses in period clothing. Lots to see and do!

105 Muncie's Grand Attraction

Appeal to the Great Spirit is a monument in a mini-park setting at the triangle intersection of North Walnut Street, North Granville Avenue, and East McCulloch Boulevard in Muncie. The monument was sculpted in 1929, by the distinguished artist, Cyrus E. Dallin. This memorial statue was presented to the City of Muncie by Mrs. Bertha C. Ball in tribute to her husband, Edmund Burke Ball, who died in 1925.

106 City of Muncie's symbolic landmark

Auburn Cord Duesenberg Automobile Museum is one of the "Top Ten Gearhead Destinations in the United States." Over 120 cars ranging from 1894 to 1999 and automotive displays on three floors. The museum has the most exceptional and extensive collection of Auburn, Cord, and Duesenberg automobiles in the world. Located in Auburn, the museum is approximately 100 miles north of Muncie.

The Heyday of Muncie, Indiana

Bankers Life Fieldhouse is at 125 South Pennsylvania Street in the heart of downtown Indianapolis. Bankers Life Fieldhouse offers more than 18,000 seats in a sports setting, more than 15,000 seats in concert configurations, and approximately 6,600 seats in a theater setup. It was formerly named Conseco Fieldhouse.

Bloomington, Indiana Rail Trail features a gravel surface suitable for walking, running, and most bicycles.

Bobby Helm's Grave in Hilldale Cemetery is at 1396 East Columbus Street in Martinsville. Approximately 2 hours southwest of Muncie. It is inconspicuous, located toward the back near the fence. People walked by, oblivious that it is the final resting place of the legendary singer of "Jingle Bell Rock."

Brown County State Park is the largest State Park in Indiana, attracting over one million people every year. It is approximately 120 miles southwest of Muncie.

It gets its name from Commanding General of the United States Army, General Jacob Brown. It is often referred to by its nickname, the Little Smokies, due to its resemblance to the Great Smoky Mountains.

107 Bring the Family!

Cammack Station is adorable, and the food is out of this world! It is located at 9200 West Jackson Street in the Muncie/Yorktown area. A retro atmosphere with sodas, ice cream, and sandwiches! Tasty food!

Cardinal Greenway is a rail-trail that encompasses 61 miles (97 km) of abandoned CSX road corridor in East Central Indiana. It runs through Muncie. Bring bikes for the family! Cardinal Greenway is a private, not-for-profit organization that encompasses the Cardinal Greenway, White River Greenway, Historic Wysor Street Depot, and Cardinal

Equestrian Trail. The Cardinal Greenway, the longest rail-trail in Indiana, stretches from Marion to Richmond, Indiana. As a public resource, Cardinal Greenway offers education, wellness programs, environmental awareness, and recreation for a wide range of audiences.

The Children's Museum of Indianapolis is at 3000 North Meridian Street in Indianapolis. With 472,900 square feet, more than 120,000 artifacts, and over one million visitors each year, it is the largest Children's Museum in the world. Its collection of over 120,000 artifacts and exhibit items is comprised of three domains: the American Collection, the Cultural World Collection, and the Natural World Collection. Among the exhibits are a simulated Cretaceous dinosaur habitat, a carousel, and a steam locomotive. Most displays are interactive, allowing children to actively participate.

Cole Porter's Final Resting Place is in Peru at Mount Hope Cemetery. It is approximately 70 miles northwest of Muncie. He left a legacy of over 1,400 songs. Born in Peru, the home where he resided as a child is now the Cole Porter Inn. Stay here, where it is kid-friendly, and you can see the room where Cole Porter was born and where he spent the first ten years of his life.

Conner Prairie is in Fishers. It is an Interactive History Park and Museum that preserves the William Conner home, listed on the National Register of Historic Places. It recreates part of life in Indiana in the 19th century on the White River. Have kids? They will love Prairie Town!

Dairy Dream on State Road 67 is in Albany at 805 West Walnut Street. Now, this is an old fashioned; ice cream drive-in...it is a genuine taste of Americana! It is worth the drive to have an ice cream cone that tastes like it is outta yesteryear! Family-owned since 1953 and the winner of several awards (for ice cream, food, drinks, and "Best of Show"), the tasty treats include smoothies, shakes, specialty sundaes, soft serve, and hand-dipped cones, homemade toppings, and Hawaiian Shaved Ice flavors. Be sure to order a Secret Recipe Sloppy Joe sandwich! Just what *really* is in that recipe?

Dunes State Park is 45 miles east of Chicago, Illinois, in Chesterton, Indiana. Dip your toes in Lake Michigan!

French Lick, Indiana is the home of the French Lick Springs Hotel and the West Baden Springs Hotel. These are two hotels that will make you feel like you have entered another world! You have not seen "grand" until you have been here! The hotels sit approximately one mile apart, 170 miles southwest of Muncie. Also, while in French Lick, stop by 33 Brick Street. Named after #33 Larry Bird – American NBA basketball player and coach, the Restaurant/Sports Pub has showcases of autographed sports memorabilia and a one-of-a-kind personal collection of awards owned by Larry Bird.

The Heyday of Muncie, Indiana

Heekin Park and the Walk of Fame in Muncie have a picnic shelter, playgrounds, sports courts, memorials- including a WWII Memorial and time capsule, a Vietnam Veterans Memorial and the Five Points Fountain, cabin rentals and a dog park.

Historic Hoosier Gym is just off of Highway 40 at 335 North Washington Street in Knightstown. You will find an authentic shrine to high school basketball. Built-in 1921, it has been home to generations of local basketball players. The movie *Hoosiers* was filmed in the gym, and it is said to be the most excellent sports movie of all time. You can believe it. In the film, the gym was the home court of the Hickory Huskers. It is a part of Indiana history, and a tourist destination for thousands of sports enthusiasts every year. Sit on the same bench as Coach Norman or shoot some hoops in the gym, then visit the museum. The Hoosier Gym is available for rent. It is a non-profit organization. If you have seen the movie, *Hoosiers*, a visit here should be emotional.

Indiana Beach Amusement and Waterpark at 5224 E Indiana Beach Rd on Lake Shafer, Monticello, is an approximate two-hour drive from Muncie. Head here via IN-26 West. It is located almost half-way between Indianapolis and Chicago, in north-central Indiana. Over 40 rides and attractions, six roller coasters, six water pool slides, kiddie rides, and arcade games will keep you busy. You will find a KOA campground, and the Boardwalk Resort will "wow" you!

Indiana Railroad Museum is in beautiful French Lick. The entire family will enjoy a ride on the French Lick Scenic Railway! There are several exciting train trips such as The Polar Express in November and December of each year and other seasonal themed rides.

Indianapolis Motor Speedway is five miles northwest of downtown Indianapolis. The Indianapolis Motor Speedway is the world's largest spectator sporting facility, home to the Indianapolis 500, NASCAR Cup Series and MotoGP World Championship.

Indianapolis Motor Speedway Museum, located on the grounds of the famous Indianapolis Motor Speedway, is recognized as one of the most highly visible museums in the world devoted to automobiles and auto racing. In 1987, the museum and speedway grounds received the designation of the National Historic Landmark.

Indianapolis Museum of Art has a collection of over 50,000 works of art from a variety of cultures and periods of art history. The Museum also features national and international traveling exhibitions throughout the year. The Virginia B. Fairbanks Art & Nature Park is adjacent to the museum. 4000 Michigan Road in Indianapolis is the address.

Indianapolis Zoo at 1200 West Washington Street is a hands-on, friendly place! Fun for the entire family!

108 I recognize that bright lipstick to the left, among the others! It was an honor to plant a kiss...Be still my heart!

James Dean Festival, the last weekend of September in Fairmount, includes the Fairmount Historical Museum, annual James Dean Run, Car Show, amusement rides, a parade, and you are bound to run into people who went to school with James Dean. You will hear lots of James Dean stories! Visit the grave of the Hollywood 1950s rebel, then drive into town for the festivities. Directions to Park Cemetery: take exit 55 off of I-69. Drive west into town, then turn right (north) on to Main Street Drive a half of a mile to the cemetery. Turn left at the second main entrance, just past a creek, and then take the second road to the right. The grave is at the top of a small hill.

Lake Monroe (also known as Monroe Reservoir) is the largest human-made body of water in Indiana. Located in South Central Indiana, the reservoir is about 10 miles southeast of Bloomington. It has a full-service marina. Swimming, biking, hiking, fishing, and camping

Lucas Oil Raceway is 10 miles west of Indianapolis in Brownsburg. 10267 East, US-136, Indianapolis. It has a 0.686-mile (1.104 km) oval, 2.5-mile (4.0 km) road course, and 4,400-foot (1,300 m) drag strip.

Lucas Oil Stadium is a multi-purpose sports stadium at 500 South Capitol Avenue in downtown Indianapolis. The stadium hosted Super Bowl XLVI on February 5, 2012, when the Giants defeated the Patriots by a score of 21–17. It was the first time the Super Bowl played in Indiana.

The Heyday of Muncie, Indiana

McCulloch Park is the largest community park in Muncie. Head to the southwest corner of the Whitely neighborhood at Broadway and Centennial Avenues.

Heydayers remember the Soapbox Derby races, riding the miniature train, the kid-powered hand cars, the playground, the bear pit, and refreshments. The park has a Disc Golf Course. The White River flows near-by.

Minnetrista Cultural Center is a Museum and Cultural Center in Muncie. 1200 North Minnetrista Parkway. George Alexander Ball's house, known as Oakhurst, was built in 1895, which sits near-by. The first-floor furnishings appear as they did in the 1920s.

Monument Circle at Christmas. The Circle of Lights, in the center of downtown Indianapolis, is the traditional lighting of the Soldiers and Sailors Monument. It is referred to by some as the world's tallest Christmas "tree."

It is common for 100,000 spectators to attend the ceremony, which in the past, has had horse-drawn carriages and live reindeer. Christmas fun for the entire family! The Colonel Eli Lilly Civil War Museum is housed in the lower level.

Mrs. Wick's Pies is your destination for authentic Sugar Cream Pie, also known as Hoosier Pie. It is the official Indiana State Pie. Head to 100 Cherry Street in Winchester.

Nashville, Indiana Delightful, charming town that comes alive during the holiday season! Visit a day or two before Christmas and feel the serenity in the air. Pick up some homemade fudge in one of the small shops or have a pizza at Harvest Moon Pizzeria. Autumn is gorgeous in Brown County. Approximately 120 miles southwest of Muncie.

Prairie Creek Reservoir and Campground Five miles southeast of Muncie. Playground, Picnic Shelters, Restrooms, Basketball, Boating, Fishing, Volleyball, Horseshoes, Swimming, Rental Facility

Santa Claus, Indiana, and Holiday World (an amusement park) and Splashin' Safari (a water park). This town is known as "America's Christmas Hometown." Holiday World features three of the top-rated wooden roller coasters and the world's longest water coaster! Free drinks, sunscreen, and parking. Frosty's Fun Center is a Christmas-themed 18-hole miniature golf course and arcade. It is also the home of the giant, melting snowman and Santa Claus Museum.

The world-famous Santa Claus Post Office at 45 North Kringle Place, Santa Claus, Indiana- with the 47579 zip code, is located here. The only Post Office in the world with the Santa Claus name, guests can mail postcards to family and friends. There is nothing like delighting a child with that famous Santa Claus postmark during the Christmas season! There is also a Santa Claus Christmas Store and lodging near-by. Year-round family fun! Approximately 230 miles southwest of Muncie.

Shipshewana is Amish Country in Northern Indiana. It is home to the Trading Place of America, the Midwest's largest Flea Market. You can also shop at over 100 stores, many of which carry excellent Amish products. Shipshewana shops are open year-round, six days a week. Be a courteous, safe driver, and due to carriages on the road, please drive slowly.

Starlite Drive-In 7630 South Old State Road 37 in Bloomington. Approximately 120 miles southwest of Muncie. One of the few remaining vintage picture shows! It is romantic, and you can do some serious hand holding, snuggling, and making out with your sweetie. Most movies are family-friendly should you bring the children. There are over 400 spaces for your viewing pleasure.

There are no highway lights, and it is not a high traffic area. The drive-in sits off the road. It is easy to see how some folks out for a drive, could just stumble upon it. You cannot miss the sign on the main road. Back in the day, ice cream was 10 cents, burgers 15 cents, and malts 20 cents. During struggling times, people used to go to the drive-in. Do not be surprised if drive-ins make a comeback!

In Indiana:

Neighbors used to invite you over for supper and still do!

A neighbor will jump start your car and refuse to accept your money for the kindness.

A neighbor will affix the snowplow attachment to their truck and surprise you by making sure your street and driveway are free of snow.

People will strike up a conversation in the small, downtown Post Office. Joy, who I met at the downtown Muncie Post Office when I first returned to Muncie, was friendly. I always enjoyed it when, while waiting in line, she would say from behind the counter, "Hi Joy," and I would reciprocate, "Hi Joy." We received some amusing stares!

Cars still pull over for funerals to show respect.

Neighbors give a big hi on walking trails.

People refer to you as "Hon" or "Sweet Pea" when you pay for your gas.

A beauty school in Muncie has provided free wigs for Cancer patients – a partnership between PJ's Beauty College and the American Cancer Society.

Some people can remember the names of every teacher, from elementary through high school – the rest of their lives.

The Heyday of Muncie, Indiana

The community spirit is so strong that onlookers had tears when the smokestack of the General Motors/Chevrolet Plant in Muncie – the last remnant of the razed factory, fell to the ground.

People are quite friendly in Muncie, anywhere and anytime! I had only been in Muncie a few weeks when a near-by shopper approached me as I was purchasing a case of bottled water. Out of the blue, she smiled and asked, "If The Lord came tomorrow, would you be ready?" I did not blink an eye and answered, "Yes." She looked surprised. We then began a brief conversation about God and the church, which was followed by an invitation to attend her church. I can certainly say this was the first time I had received an invitation to a church in a department store aisle. Expect the unexpected!

When country singer Rhonda Clemmons was diagnosed with a health issue, citizens and musicians turned out to lend their support. Held at a downtown Muncie establishment, musicians gave freely of their time and energy. Band members had commitments that evening yet loaded up their equipment that morning and traveled the distance to play at the fundraiser. Indiana musicians Souled Out Band, Carl Storie (Yes, "the" Carl Storie of "Dancin' Shoes" fame), and mega guitarist Chic Brown (sensational teen musician from the heyday) graced the stage!

Tell people you are from Indiana, and they respond with, "There's nothing there but cornfields." What is wrong with cornfields? Perhaps they have never had buttered mouth-watering roastin' ears (corn on the cob). The Indiana kind…nothing like it!

109 Muncie at Night

Chapter 19

50 Things to Love and Do in Muncie

1. **The Neely House** is an upscale restaurant in the 1850s Neely Homestead, at 617 East Adams Street.

2. **Concannon's Bakery** will delight you with an authentic Indiana Sugar Cream Pie. There is more! You will see a menu of sandwiches, house-baked sweets, bread, gourmet popcorn, and chocolate.

3. **McDonald's** on Madison is supposed to display the oldest McDonald's sign in the country. At one time, the sign continuously flashed how many burgers had sold. Children were fascinated by the blinking numbers.

4. Make it a family day and picnic at the **Prairie Creek Reservoir and Campground**!

5. When breaded tenderloin sandwiches are on the menu, just get them!

6. **Pizza King** awaits you! There is no pizza like a Royal Feast! Dine-in or out, get a Take-and-Bake pizza, or have some shipped on ice to your out of state location.

7. The **Muncie Children's Museum** is a happening place. At 515 South High Street, in the Horizon Convention Center, it houses creative, extraordinary exhibits, hands-on activities, and is an excellent place for a child's birthday party!

8. The **Elm Street Brewery** at 519 North Elm Street is a friendly place, visit and see why!

9. The **Minnetrista Cultural Center** at 1200 North Minnetrista Parkway is the home of exhibits, programs that focus on nature, local history, gardens, concerts, art, there is a Farmer's Market, a gift shop, and it is a place of community spirit! Think Ball Jars! Ask to tour the grounds and stately Ball Mansions. By the way, the name "Minnetrista" means "a gathering place by the water."

110 Near Downtown Muncie

10. A balloon release at the **Fallen Heroes Memorial Bridge** - in memory of a loved one, can be the ultimate tribute.

11. **The Fickle Peach**, 117 East Charles Street offers a large selection of vintage beer, located in a former historic bank.

12. See the downtown **Carnegie Library** has extensive History and Genealogy

13. **Autumn country pumpkins** are uniquely beautiful in Indiana, so take the youngins to select their future jack-o-lanterns!

14. There are magnificent, unobstructed, outlying areas to stargaze in the night sky. I saw the skies out by Matthews, Indiana (about a half-hour northwest of Muncie) lit-up. Those were some eye-catching, twinkling stars! If you're headed to Matthews, try to go in September to the **Cumberland Covered Bridge Festival**. You will find pony and horse

rides, live entertainment, scrumptious food, and the inflatable slide. The Bridge Festival is located northeast of Matthews, adjacent to the Mississinewa River, next to the historic 1877 Cumberland Covered Bridge.

15. **Ball State University**! There is nothing like the community spirit of Ball State University on game day! Some employees at grocery stores and other businesses, dress in Ball State colors. The bakery departments sell goods with "cardinal" red and white school colors. If you are a football fan, you will want to be at Scheumann Stadium to root for the Ball State Cardinals!

16. The Ball State University campus is a busy place! You will want to learn more about the **David Letterman Communication and Media Building,** the **David Owsley Museum of Art**, the **Planetarium and Observatory**, and **Worthington Arena**. The Asian American Student Association (AASA) hosts **Asian Awareness month** and a week of events, a fashion show, a street festival, tea time and meditation, and many other cultural events and programs! The duck pond is where heydayers used to ice skate. Who could forget the white skates with the pom-poms?

17. Attend a concert at the renowned **Emens Auditorium** on campus, a classy venue for the finest, top names in entertainment!

18. Head to **"The Village"** near the south end of the Ball State campus, where there are retail shops and restaurants to explore.

19. Teens love **Rock 'n Roll Summer and Winter Camps**! What a great gift (and investment) in your teen's talent, learning, and future. Cornerstone Center for the Arts is always pleased to partner with the camps. Music-minded students as young as age 11 may participate. I hear students rave about Owner/CEO/Camp Leader, professional musician, music instructor, Ball State Alumnus, Chris Swinney. Now, *that's* a plug! Contact the Muncie Music Center.

20. The 4th of July fireworks light up the sky over the **White River**...what a sight!

21. **Tuhey Park in Muncie** is at White River Boulevard and North Wheeling Avenue and was a favorite place for heydayers. Swimming, picnic, concessions, and play! Super family-friendly!

22. Mark your calendar each summer for the **Delaware County Fair in Muncie!**

23. **The Heorot Pub and Draught House** is an award-winning bar, located at 219 South Walnut Street. Features a wide selection of craft beers, plus classic pub grub and live bands. A popular downtown venue!

The Heyday of Muncie, Indiana

24. Book your reservations at the **Courtyard by Marriott Muncie**. Located downtown, it is a first-of-its-kind, fully functioning teaching hotel designed to provide job training and employment for people with disabilities. From day one, at least 20 percent of the hotel's 129-person workforce was comprised of people with developmental and other types of disabilities. The Arc of Indiana was instrumental in creating the project.

25. The historic **Wysor Street Depot**, at 700 East Wysor Street, has something for everyone. Built in 1901 and restored and reopened in 2004, it is now the headquarters for the Cardinal Greenway and houses a gift shop, historical memorabilia, programs, and special events.

26. Relax at The Island Muncie **"Muncie's Tropical Paradise,"** 400 West McGalliard, behind the Olive Garden. Park at the Trailhead next to Olive Garden and cross the bridge. Smoothies, entertainment, rental for private events, beach weddings, etc. Open evenings. Jerk Chicken, fresh fruit, and smoothies are included on the top-notch menu!

27 Visit the **Water Bowl** recreational center at 6811 North Old State Road 3, for family fun, swimming, volleyball, camping, fishing, private party facility, and a live music venue!

28. **Hartmeyer Horseback Riding Center, Stable, and Saddlery** is exciting! They even host birthday parties and have apparel and accessories. 7111 West Bethel

29. **Lowery's Candies** at 6255 West Kilgore Avenue is a wise choice for homemade chocolates and elegant gifts for that special someone.

30. **Canan Commons** is Muncie's downtown urban park that hosts community and cultural events, movies, and music during warm weather, picnic tables, a stage, a community Christmas tree, and the city's New Year's Eve celebration - complete with the ball drop.

31. Visit the **National Model Aviation Museum** at 5151 East Memorial Drive. The purpose of the non-profit is to promote the development of model aviation as a sport and recreational activity. It is a must-see for any radio control or model aircraft enthusiast.

32. **Tonne Winery** at 101 West Royerton Road is your destination for that over-the-top event.

33. The **Whisper Wall** is a half-circle brick wall, standing about four feet tall, said to have "hidden powers." You will find it between Bracken Library and the business building on the Ball State campus. If you stand on one side with a friend on the other, you can have a whispered conversation through the wall. It is a mystery how it works – but many claims it does.

34. **Mulligan's Bar and Grill** will serve you a handmade tenderloin sandwich that is out of this world! It is open to the public and located at 3325 South Walnut Street at the Crestview Golf Club.

35. Free downtown parking!

36. Head out to the **Muncie Visitor's Bureau** at 3700 South Madison Street in Muncie. Check-in with the folks there to learn more about Muncie- they know it all!

37. **The Erwin Davis Memorial Park** in the Morningside area of Muncie pays tribute to a great man. The park is an excellent example of how Muncie cherishes and remembers its own.

111 Famous place!   *112 Write Dave!*

38. If you are a David Letterman fan, "**Dave's Alley**" is the place to deposit a letter to the former late-night host in the "Letters to Dave" red mailbox downtown.

39. **Hurley Goodall** was the honoree of a bronze statue sculpted in his likeness in a ceremony outside of **Fire Station No.1.** The festivities were held on his 92nd birthday on Thursday, May 23, 2019. Goodall was born in the Whitely area of Muncie, is a Muncie Central grad, WWII veteran, and served as a State Representative as well as one of Muncie's first black firefighters. See the statue at 421 East Jackson Street in Muncie.

40. **The Muncie Civic Theatre** at 216 East Main Street, with its talented casts, is a happening place! Catch a production!

41. See the 25 foot tall **Paul Bunyan Statue** at 2770 West Kilgore Avenue outside Timbers Lounge. The statue dates back to the mid-1960s.

42 How long has it been since you went roller skating? Since the 1960s? Muncie's only roller skating rink, **Gibson Arena** is at 2610 South Mock Avenue. Even if roller

skating is not for you these days, take the youngsters in your life. Bask in the retro atmosphere! The skaters may get you out there yet!

43 The **Grand Masonic Temple is** on the National Register of Historic Places. It is now home for the Cornerstone Center for the Arts. You cannot miss its presence at 520 East Main Street.

44. Make it an annual family tradition to attend the Christmas sing at the **Muncie Fieldhouse** and support downtown businesses. If it is Christmas and you are in Muncie, you will feel that "something in the air."

45. The popular, **Mark III Tap Room** is Muncie's oldest gay bar, located at 306 South Walnut Street. It has been a fixture in Muncie since 1968.

46. First Thursday Gallery Walk. **The Artist Within** is a paint-your-own-pottery studio downtown. Make your selection, which includes everything from magnets to coaster sets to plate sets. There are drawing, painting, and pottery classes, and there is a birthday party room for your child's upcoming celebration!

47. **High Street Methodist Church**, downtown at High and Adams Streets, is over 150 years old.

48. **Escapades Family Fun Center** is an indoor playground at 4241 West Williamsburg Boulevard in Muncie! Teens may like to gather some friends and head to **Escape Muncie** at 300 North Pauline Avenue, where they can find the clues, solve the puzzles and open the locks!

49. Remember Fluffer Nutters? The **Caffeinery** downtown at 401 South Walnut Street has Fluffer Nutter lattes, among many other signature drinks! Or perhaps you prefer coffees, teas, bagels, muffins, or cookies.

50. **The Passing of the Buffalo** at the South Walnut Street roundabout is a tribute to Muncie's Native American settlers.

There are so many more than 50 Things to Love and Do in Muncie! Explore and find them!

Muncie is a Work In Progress

When many factories suffer such a long, industrial decline and must close, as occurred in Muncie and other cities, poverty can rear its ugly head. It was always there but lurked more in the shadows. Bouncing back can take many years or decades. With community food giveaways and local Social Services agencies attempting to meet the demands, it has not been easy.

Most Mom and pop stores have vanished. I recently went through a check-out line and was asked to give $1.00 to a charity. Have you been asked if you want to round up to the next dollar and give it to the local food bank? A dollar may not seem like much, but if others give too, the money will grow. The power of mere dollars and cents can be enormous. This philosophy is a good one with the world in such a need. Any sudden circumstance- including loss of work, lack of jobs, serious illness, divorce, tragedy, or the unthinkable can happen and delve any of us into extreme poverty or need. It is easy to think it will not happen to us, yet we are so vulnerable, and life is so unpredictable that our lives can change in a split second. In this respect, we are not so different. Whether giving money, rolling up our sleeves and volunteering time and energy, increasing awareness of social service agencies, or saying prayers, there are many ways to be involved. Volunteers are angels on this earth!

Charitable Organizations

Muncie has Social Service organizations that are ready to help and can use support. Here are a few:

A Better Way Services, Inc.

Action for Animals

Animal Rescue Fund

Beyond I Can

Big Brothers Big Sisters

Boys and Girls Club of Muncie

Bridges Community Services

Children's Clothing Center of Delaware County

Christian Ministries of Delaware County

First Choice for Women

Future Choices, Inc.

Greater Muncie Habitat for Humanity

Hillcroft Services

Inside Out Muncie

Little Red Door Cancer Agency

Meridian Health Services

Muncie Mission Ministries, Inc.

Muncie OUTreach

Muncie Salvation Army

Ross Community Center, Inc.

Second Harvest Food Bank

Soup Kitchen of Muncie

United Way of Delaware County

Whitely Community Council, Inc.

Wounded Veterans Foundation

Youth Opportunity Center

In Muncie's historic district, signs welcome people to the area, and slowly but surely, many of the homes have acquired fresh paint. The homes are beautifully ancient, boast history and character. Some have sold for bargain-basement prices. Muncie also has some elegant mansion-type homes. There was always a heritage and charm to the city, characteristics that grand spanking new buildings cannot usually reflect. "New" is not wrapped in layers of history and is not always necessary. Apartments for seniors and disabled people now stand on former school, business, and vacant land lots. I love the transformation of the old, historic Roberts Hotel into The Lofts at Roberts- a community of one and two-bedroom apartment homes for adults 55 and over. Perhaps we need to see more of this!

At Christmas, firemen, wives, and families have been known to volunteer at Muncie Fire Station 1, gathering donations, distributing gifts with Santa, making hot chocolate, holding bicycle raffles, and other festivities. Roger Overbey was on hand filming one Christmas Eve day as Santa made his way along downtown streets to the fire station. The crowd went wild, and of course, the children loved to pose for the camera. While volunteering at the event, I will never forget a precious child who appeared to be approximately age five, who stepped down from Santa's lap. I handed her a doll, and she wandered away. A few minutes later, she gently tugged on my arm and said she wanted to ask me something. She hesitated. We stepped out of the crowd, and she whispered, "I want another doll that I saw over there...can I have her?" We went to take a look. She quickly rummaged through a container of toys until she saw the doll, she grabbed it, and her face sparkled brighter than any Christmas tree. I told her to take her baby home and love her. The little things will always be the big things.

    I happened to be waiting in line in the check-out of a department store in Southern Indiana when I saw a child gazing at the Giving Tree. She carefully examined each gift tag and then dropped to her knees. Oblivious to people coming and going in the near-by entrance, she bowed her head, clasped her hands, and prayed. Then, she would stand up, look at another gift tag, drop to her knees, and pray again. She repeated this process for several minutes. The unshakeable faith of a child... we should all be so rich.

Chapter 20

50 Ways to Help "Create" a Heyday for the Child(ren) You Love

The heyday is all about wonder and can encompass a flurry of emotions. Looking back at your heyday, what do you wish to instill from that time, in the children you love? What is important to you? Is the ability to stop and smell the roses necessary for a good life? Are you setting an example to live life to the fullest? Do you believe we need to have big belly laughs because it is healthy? When your grandchildren think of you, do you want them to remember how you would suddenly start dancing around the living room with no music? Or for your granddaughter to feel especially loved because grandpa gave up his Saturday mornings to teach her guitar? In 25 years, will your grandson be craving your fluffy blueberry pancakes, or will he be baking them for his children on a leisurely Saturday morning? The children in your life will undoubtedly reap what you sow. The smallest thing you do today can leave an impression for a lifetime. It helps to simply be more aware that the actions we display today are "teaching" and leaving a heyday legacy. Understandably, most of us do not think of life this way. There are times when life is so stressful, we can barely make it through today, let alone think of life decades from now. Granted, life is not always happy. A day of simplicity and silliness, though, really can be good for the soul!

1. Talk and giggle about the heyday, share some pictures from back in the day and enlist your child's "help" putting them in an album. It provides an excellent opportunity to discuss family history and explore Genealogy. It can be especially fun if your child learns he or she resembles someone in a family picture!

2. Encourage children and adults in your life to keep and preserve possessions from the heyday. Discarding that Les Paul guitar, amplifier, Chevy Impala, or autographed picture is a common regret people have in later years. These can have tremendous sentimental and monetary value.

3. Create traditions such as opening one gift on Christmas Eve, attending a Christmas Eve Candlelight Service, sending holiday letters to troops, or watching *Holiday*

Inn, White Christmas, It's a Wonderful Life, Miracle On 34th Street, Babes in Toyland, The Nutcracker and other holiday spectaculars.

4. Wiggle your toes in the sand on a hot day while eating a popsicle and let 'er drip! In case you haven't heard, it is a groovy grandma and grandpa who do this!

5. Have a game night with the kiddos and make popcorn! Let them show you how to play Jacks and Pick-Up Sticks. If children are preschool or kindergarten age, play classic board games such as Candy Land or Chutes and Ladders. You can praise their skill.

6. Teach your children to trust their intuition. If something does not feel right, it probably is not right. The child in your life will embrace this and carry this wisdom throughout their life.

7. When children especially enjoy something you cook, be sure to later make it especially for them. If you want to leave a lasting impression, share the "secret" ingredient(s) and "pinky swear" to never tell! The child will feel extra special! When your child is old enough, give a cooking lesson, and teach him or her how to make it. Or...perhaps you prefer the intrigue of "mum's the word" for now, and you are not telling!

8. Spend a rainy afternoon coloring a picture in a book selected by your child or grandchild. Some still remember their Lennon Sisters coloring book. It is easy to feel like an artist with a coloring book and a fat box of Crayolas. Be sure to put the masterpiece on your refrigerator for the world to see.

9. Teach your child to follow their dreams. Healthy doses of inspiration and self-esteem, encouraging a child to dwell in possibility and an "if you can dream it, you can live it" attitude can carry a child far in life. They will remember who instilled this in them and, hopefully, pass it on to their children and grandchildren.

10. Bake cookies at Christmas...in various shapes with decorations and remember the sprinkles! Some families use this annual tradition as a Prayer Time and encourage children and grandchildren to pray for those less fortunate.

113 They will be scrumptious!

11. Teach the children in your life to be humble at Christmas and the reason for the season. Gather some donations for the local food bank or other charities. Feed others at a Thanksgiving meal for the homeless or open your home to a person who would otherwise spend Christmas

alone. Verbally emphasizing that giving is more important than receiving is one thing, but when you demonstrate it, the message is loud and clear.

12. Share the wise, old sayings (and their meanings) you learned from your parents and grandparents so they will be passed down to the next and subsequent generations. Examples: Don't count your chickens before they hatch, Pretty is as pretty does, You'll catch more flies with honey than vinegar, A penny saved is a penny earned, Don't judge a book by its cover, The early bird catches the worm, Strike while the iron is hot, Any job worth doing is worth doing well, Where there's a will there's a way, In a pickle and Not my cup of tea. Then, there are the nonsensical sayings such as: See You Soon, Baboon! What's The Plan, Stan? Give a hug, Ladybug…Maybe Two, Kangaroo! Chow Chow, Brown Cow! In An Hour, Sunflower! Bye Bye, Butterfly! Be sweet, Parakeet! Know What I Mean, Jelly Bean? Hit the Road Happy Toad! Take care, Polar Bear! You do not always have to speak their language, once in awhile teach the young people in your life to speak yours!

13. Make snowmen, snowwomen, or snow angels. You can thaw out later. Let child teach you how to make the snow characters as you watch in awe. It will be remembered that Grandma and Grandpa stood out in the cold, freezing their behinds off. Oh, what we do for love!

14. Take the child in your life to Sunday School and Vacation Bible School, where both of you can volunteer.

15. Go on an old-fashioned picnic in nature – like back in the day. You know the kind…with a real deal picnic basket, tablecloth, and blanket, and be sure to tote your child's favorite sandwiches. Or pack some cold chicken like we used to do!

114 Swing from a Tree

16. Go to the playground or park- be sure to swing and go down the slide, if possible. If you cannot participate, remember your presence is enough. Always.

17. Help with homework- no calculators allowed. Make an effort to do it the old-fashioned way. Do not be surprised if you have a problem with the new math. Your child will probably teach you. Emphasize that merely getting the correct answer is not enough. It is also essential to understand the process of how the answer is derived. Know the date of your child's feared, upcoming test, and be the biggest cheerleader on the planet!

18. Generously support school sports, fundraisers, and events with your time, energy, and money.

19. Take your child or grandchild with you to vote. Or, if you do not vote in person, discuss voting day and patriotism. Flaunt your civic pride! Depending on the age of the child, some current city issues or current events may be worth a discussion. Teach children that most public servants deserve a thank-you for their dedication and commitment. You can plant a seed that one day your child or grandchild could become the President! We just never know.

20. Hop on the bike and ride through the neighborhood after supper. Or, if the old body is getting a little creaky, walk alongside the bike rider. It is a win-win situation. Both of you get fresh air and exercise!

21. Be a doer. If the neighborhood needs spruced up, the yard needs some nurturing or a project is long overdue, grab the kiddos and get busy! Lend a helping hand to a neighbor! Referring to this or other tasks as "chores" is not exactly motivating. The word itself implies an unpleasant task. Remember, sometimes it is all about the presentation! Recognize this as an opportunity, and remember you are "teaching" initiative.

22. Remember that prayer and mealtime often go together. Rituals can be a memorable part of the heyday. Bring back the traditional family Sunday dinner!

23. Share often- whether it be something as simple as refreshments in your backyard or the giving of your compassion to help a neighbor through a challenging time. Discuss how kindness is contagious!

24. Go to the airport and watch the planes arrive and depart. Discuss where you would go if you were boarding the plane and what you would do there.

25. Ride the city bus downtown and back home

26. Watch and listen to your child practice for a recital and plan to attend. Sure, you may have heard the same notes of the song 42 times but keep listening. You can emphasize later how hard work and perseverance paid off

27. Help a child handwrite thank-you cards after their birthday party and address valentines

28. Permit children to express themselves within reason (art, dance steps, fashions, etc.). Their "new look" could be something to chuckle about in later years. All of us have "those" pictures!

29. Play "High-Waters" or "High Jump" in the hose. A leader (can be a parent or grandparent) makes a narrow, steady stream of water flow from the hose by putting their thumb over part of the spray opening. Hold the hose low as children jump over the stream. After each player has a turn, the leader raises the hose to make the stream a bit higher. Players repeat jumping over the stream as it rises. When a player gets wet, they exit the game. Play continues until the winner remains.

30. Get dirty in the sandbox and make mud pies.

31. Get a Hula Hoop for your child and yourself. FYI... Adults may do better with a lightly weighted hoop that is available at a sports store.

32. It is said most children today only know how to tell time by a Digital clock. Teach the child in your life how to tell time using an Analog clock that has moving hands and hours, usually marked from 1 to 12. It may be easier to teach this at a younger age. Older children say they do not need to learn it because they will not use it. Besides, in this digital age, it can be considered somewhat "square." Remember that "square" can be dandy if approached, right!

33. If you have a record player, get out those 45s and 78s, to introduce and play music from your generation. If the oldies seem to be a hit, maybe you can attend an Oldies Show. When Davy Jones of The Monkees gave a concert, there was a younger generation that knew every lyric.

34. Patronize small, local businesses or just browse... recreate the heyday trend of "window shopping."

35. Stop and smell the roses, literally.

36. Help your child save money-whether it be in a savings account or a piggy bank. Watch that money g-r-o-w together!

37. If possible, make sure the teenager in your life can drive both a manual and a stick-shift. The day could come when it will be necessary to drive a stick.

38. Read to your children and grandchildren regularly. The quiet and calm of a bedtime story provides precious moments.

39. Dress up and have a tea party or go to a kiddie matinee

40. Have a weekly date to get an ice cream cone

41. Watch sunrises and sunsets of many colors

42. Pray with one another in the quietness and stillness before bedtime

43. Go for a country drive to nowhere in the car and stop for a frosty root beer

44. Watch episodes of *The Lawrence Welk Show*, *The Andy Griffith Show*, and *I Love Lucy*

45. With your child, create a "Blessings List" of the things you are thankful to have…those of family, home, health, and heart and discuss how to pass these blessings on to others. Update the list as needed.

46. Share your feelings about five things that made you happy as a child! Then ask your child to do the same. Discuss the vast differences in your childhood lives.

47. Demonstrate that consideration of others, manners, and courtesy never go out of style.

48. Teach age-appropriate life skills starting at an early age, from better managing one's own emotions to picking up after one's self to getting the hang of good study habits. Hopefully, these life skills will be handed down to future generations.

49. Whether it be prayer, the belief in miracles or positive vibes, impress upon your child the importance and ability to have hope. It can sometimes sustain us and depending on the dire circumstance, it could one day be as essential as the air we breathe.

50. Teach that the small things are the big things. When the children are adults, they will get it!

Five and Dime Stores

If you are feeling especially adventurous, plan a trip to a Five and Dime store! Woolworths and Ben Franklin may be gone; however, a few of the gems are still around. They are the real deal. Because a Five and Dime can be a rare find, it is worth the drive. The kids will learn their money can go a long way, and there is just so much to see!

A.L. Stickle's Variety Store 13 East Market Street, Rhinebeck, NY. You will find retro tea towels, timeless toys, and surprises!

The Heyday of Muncie, Indiana

A. Schwab 163 Beale St, Memphis, TN. It opened in 1876. Visit the old-fashioned soda counter! The store sells upper class, regional merchandise, and memorabilia.

115 Berdine's Five and Dime

Berdine's Five and Dime 106 North Court Street, Harrisville, WV. "One Giant Leap Back in Time." Old fashioned health remedies, bins of novelties, candy counter, plenty of good cheer! Karen at the store says it is the oldest in the nation! She has been there for nearly 40 years. There is something for everyone. Only have a dollar or less to spend? There are little animals and even adorable finger puppets for 25 or 50 cents. There are old fashioned wind-up toys. They do business the old-fashioned way, so have your cash when you visit. Karen shells out old-fashioned hospitality too when overheard asking a customer approaching the cash register, "Are you ready, young lady?"

Bonnesen's 5 & 10 Store 408 Chestnut Street Atlantic, IA. A good, old fashioned candy store, lots to see!

Dick's 5 & 10 103 West Main Street Branson, MO. Elaine at the store says the store has been a landmark for more than 50 years. Trains run overhead, nostalgic and novelty candies, historical collections of offerings, and an ever-changing "fun aisle."

Dooley's 5-10-25 Store, Inc. 131 East Main Street Fredericksburg, TX. Tim Dooley's family has been in business since 1923, and he is the third generation. He says there is a "good mix" of customers who visit their 6,000 square foot store - estimating 60% older people and 40% younger (under age 30).

Some just happen to stumble upon the store. Dooley promises there is "something for everybody!" In keeping with the good old days, the store does not accept credit or debit cards. He warns, "We trust people to take their check; however, should a check bounce, I'm going to go after you like it's a million bucks!"

He often hears the comments about how the store "takes me back to my childhood." He shared a story of five young customers who came into the store- approximate ages 18-24. Between all five, they purchased $1.39 in merchandise and could not come up with the cash. Dooley sadly chalks it up to "a sign of the times."

Five and Dime General Stores 58 East San Francisco Street, Santa Fe, NM. It is the first Five & Dime General Store that opened in May 1998 in the location of the original Woolworths in Santa Fe. There are also locations in San Antonio, TX, Monterey CA, Branson, MO, San Diego, CA, Savannah, GA, Charleston, SC, Kansas City, KS, and St. Augustine, FL.

Guerneville 5 and 10 6252 Main Street, Guerneville, CA- a resort town. Been in business since 1949. There is something for everyone with a variety of candies, games, puzzles, books, toys, balloons, pet supplies, jewelry, incense and candles, cards, and notions. The folks here say people with little pocket money to those who are very rich will enjoy stopping by.

Sine's 5 & 10 236 West Broad Street Suite 240, Quakertown, PA. Family owned and operated since 1912. Old-fashioned 5 & 10 complete with a soda fountain/lunch counter. Over ten varieties of bulk candy, novelty, and penny candies. Breakfast and lunch await patrons at the soda fountain that boasts an original root beer barrel. Milkshakes, ice cream sodas, and sundaes made with Edy's Ice Cream are available all day.

116 Sine's Five & 10

Over 200 model airplanes are suspended from the ceiling, including a 10-foot long airship, the U. S. S. Akron. A standard-gauge train runs along 200 feet of track crossing two 50-foot Suspension Bridges.

The Heyday of Muncie, Indiana

A Christmas room is open year 'round for holiday shopping. Services include key and shade cutting. Linda Fox at the store says the most popular items from the soda fountain are the Hamburger BBQ (a Sloppy Joe type burger) and potato salad. All items are homemade!

Vidler's 676-694 Main Street East Aurora, NY, 20 minutes from Buffalo. One of the largest five-and-dimes in the world! 75,000 items, across four buildings on two levels. They will tell you, "We haven't found anyone bigger than us yet!"

Where is **Wall Drug**? It is the question on one of several 15-cent bumper stickers sold at Wall Drug and spotted on vehicles throughout the country. Although Wall Drug is not indicative of the typical Five and Dime store back in the day, it is worth a mention. A combination drug store, gift shops, and eatery (seats 500), it is a tourist attraction that

117 Wall Drug Sticker

is difficult to miss. It is not unusual to see whimsical signs as far as 200 miles away from the Wall, South Dakota location, advertising the free ice water, and a five-cent cup of coffee.

Hundreds of signs line the east-west approaches along Interstate 90 in South Dakota. At its peak in the 1960s, Wall Drug had over 3,000 highway signs. Located at 510 Main Street in the tiny Midwestern town, (population 882 as of 2014), you will find souvenirs, postcards, coffee cups, toys, jewelry- including Black Hills Gold, belts, buckles, state collectible items and much more. Wall Drug can attract up to 22,000 visitors a day from May to August—mostly tourists en route to the Badlands or the Black Hills to see Mount Rushmore or Crazy Horse. Fun, quirky place!

Probably the essential factor in helping create a heyday is that it costs little. It is about the simple things: flying kites and dropping in at the local Martial Arts school with grandmother, to "just watch." These times will be cherished more than any toy buried at the bottom of a box.

Chapter 21

God Gave Us Memory So That We Might Have Roses in December

Have you discovered that growing up in the 1960s was much more fun than being in your 60s?

Do you remember the first time you…

Logged on to a computer?

Logged on to the Internet?

Played Pac Man?

Obtained and used a Debit Card at the ATM?

Rented a movie?

Recorded a video on your VCR?

Used a TIVO?

Used a variety of social media and had the world at your fingertips?

Learned to send and receive an email?

Instant Messaged?

Used a laptop?

Shopped online?

Took an online class?

Purchased or read a book online?

Used a cordless phone?

Answered a phone with Caller ID?

Used a cell phone?

Sent or received a text?

The Heyday of Muncie, Indiana

Said good-bye to your answering machine?

Canceled your Landline service so your cell phone would be your only phone?

Discovered YouTube?

Used a Video Cam?

Used a CD player?

Used a Walkman?

Used an iPad?

Used an iPod?

Saw your groceries scanned?

Went to the doctor/dentist and was handed a tablet to complete your "paperwork?"

Checked your medical records online?

Renewed your prescription from your cell phone?

Compared store-to-store prices from your cell phone?

Saw a digital camera and the pictures you took seconds ago?

Paid for gas at the pump?

Used GPS?

No longer needed a key to start your car?

It is a different world that some staunch heydayers, at first, attempted to resist. They would tell you they did not need the Internet, believed being online was for the younger crowd, they did not know how to type, it would be too difficult to learn, and life had been lived well without computers. Then, they learned about the convenience and what they could do online.

Social Networking plays a significant role in planning Alumni Reunions and events. There are various pages for school alumni on the Internet. Wanda Clark Resler of Muncie is the Administrator of the "Classmates of Muncie Central High School" Facebook page. She does an excellent job of keeping Muncie Central High School alumni in touch and planning activities. Whether it is an informal Pizza King get-together or a posh 50-year reunion, Wanda has it covered! A real gem is the "Lost Muncie" Facebook page, that is approaching 30,000 members! Larry Broadwater and Jeff Koenker created the perfect place for Muncie alumni to re-connect, post memories and pictures.

There are several Muncie pages on Facebook and probably for your hometown. Explore and connect!

With the world now at your fingertips, how do you feel about growing up without the Internet? Do you feel pleased or deprived that high-tech was not a part of your life?

Progress and high-tech can be incredible; however, the good old days are here to stay! Well, for many of us, anyway.

Is it any wonder we love the heyday?

We felt safe.

We were rooted in innocence.

Family time was a priority.

Children were encouraged to occupy themselves, and sometimes they were bored.

Respect was imperative.

The culture was influential.

A sense of right and wrong prevailed.

People had a backbone and took a stand for their beliefs. We did not have to wonder where someone stood on an issue. Not everyone went along with the program, and people understood this.

Routine and the structure of time provided a healthy balance for a quality life.

Education was a priority with an emphasis on hard work, homework, achievements, and goals.

The lack of high-tech brought people closer. We felt hugs with every fiber of our being; people heard the pain and need for compassion in our voices; they saw our smiles and wiped our tears. We had to make an effort to see one another...it was not as easy as clicking a mouse or texting. The energy that went into communicating and spending time with one another was priceless. I still correspond with a friend across the country via letters. I also hand write personal, thank-you notes and have received them. It can be seen these days as classy.

The Heyday of Muncie, Indiana

Anticipation honed our patience. We looked forward to saving allowance for an item or checking the mailbox each day for a promised letter. Just because we wanted it, we did not get it, and we certainly did not always get it now. The adage that states good things are worth waiting for was taught.

Freedom reigned– a child could wander off the beaten path and gaze at the daffodils, play outside until dusk and then run home. The world was not such a scary place.

The community spirit was one of a slower, gentler pace.

You may be retro if you cherish…

A hand-dipped, chocolate Malted shake at a nostalgic ice cream shop – instead of a milkshake from a fast-food restaurant

Classic cars that are built solid

Furniture made of real wood and not cheap contents

Products made in the U.S.A.

Old fashioned romance, being "courted" and leaving some of the "sultry" stuff to the imagination

Buying a basket on the spur of the moment and planning a picnic by the pond

Eating outside on the old-style picnic table (with attached benches)

Marriage and the trust that accompanies a commitment

Stay-at-home mothers

Hanging your clean clothes in the backyard on the line to dry

Family-friendly television programs and music with no cuss words and vulgar content

Vinyl records

Pressure cookers

Home-cooked meals

A tasty, grilled cheese sandwich and tomato soup (especially fixed by mom or dad when not feeling well)

Sitting in a place where the retro décor is much better than the food itself

Joy Charlene Henley

Saying "God Bless America" and "Merry Christmas"

Decorating with Christmas displays and lights no earlier than December

A Big Boy sandwich. Big Boy restaurants are not a thing of the past. Currently, there are eight locations in Indiana, 30 locations in Kentucky, and 82 locations in Ohio! I have visited Big Boy restaurants in Anderson, Indiana, and Louisville, Kentucky, and the sandwiches are as tasty as ever!

118 Window Shopping!

The precious memory of being a kid and spotting a bottle of Royal Crown Cola. As a friend recently shared, "I really thought it was made for royalty, and I remember asking for it so I could turn into a princess!"

Hugs and other physical forms of affection instead of virtual ones

A visit or phone call instead of a text or email

Hearing "I love you" as the person looks into your eyes instead of seeing it on your cell phone screen

The good old days when the phone was attached to the wall since you often misplace your phone

Shopping in a store and not ordering online

Browsing or buying the old catalogs and wishing you could order, just one more time, from Alden's, J.C. Penney, Montgomery Ward, the Sears Wish Book, and Spiegel Catalogs

Quality customer service with a human being in the U.S.A.

Scoring an unused tube of Yardley of London Slicker lipstick and paying upwards of $100.00

Manners

Dressing in the style of days gone by

Reading the newspaper with your cup of coffee each day

Smoking a pipe

Listening to the ball game on the radio

The Big Band Sound

The Heyday of Muncie, Indiana

Playing cards

Pink bathrooms

Landline telephones with more reliable reception

Family vacations and reunions

Making anything and everything from scratch… food, clothes, etc.

Knowing your neighbor's name

A ceramic white or green Christmas Tree with lights, like grandma's

The gas station giving full-service

Your hometown phone book from 1966 and guard it with your life

119 Telephone Directory for Muncie, Indiana from 1966

A full set of encyclopedias

Pulling a road map out of the glove box in the car to find directions

Seeing a youngster riding a bike with small plastic streamers hanging from the handlebars

The fun of watching retro TV instead of modern programming

Knowing every line from each *Leave it to Beaver* episode

The dream of going to a Dog 'n Suds once more! The iconic drive-in is still going strong. Begin by checking locations in Arkansas, Colorado, Illinois, Indiana, Michigan, Missouri, Ohio, and Wisconsin, then GO!

Going topless and heading to Mount Airy, North Carolina, to the annual Mayberry Days! That's right... put the top down on the convertible and mark this off your Bucket List! The city is the real-life hometown of actor Andy Griffith and where the fictional town of Mayberry on *The Andy Griffith Show* was based. It is the ideal place to sit a spell. Go to the Mayberry Motor Inn at 501 Andy Griffith Parkway North and stay in the "Aunt Bee" room. You will see actress Frances Bavier's real-life possessions! The motor inn owner attended the estate auction of the legendary actress. Or how about a stroll over to Wally's Service Station? You can visit the Andy Griffith Museum and see the Andy Griffith Playhouse. Take the family to the parade! You will not be bored here.

A slice of pineapple upside-down cake or ice cream cake roll

Putting the cell phone away while out for dinner or attending unique events…no texting, taking pictures and posting them on social media while in the company of others

Items from yesteryear in your home and realizing their value and comfort

Volunteering for Christmas events and giving the surroundings and games an "old fashioned" theme

A traditional Santa who was jolly and round with rosy cheeks

Flocking your Christmas tree with spray snow

Awakening to realize you had a happy dream about back in the day

Embracing memories and those familiar emotions and feelings that surface when you least expect it

Falling in love under a starry sky

The Heyday of Muncie, Indiana

Standing in the same spot you did 50+ years ago because it somehow validates that you genuinely are that same child who was there once upon a time. No matter where you have gone or how badly life has beaten you up, you are still you. Perhaps as we get older, we need that validation, for whatever reason. The reason is probably different for each of us.

Going for a drive to nowhere

A good game of horseshoes and you still own a set

Mashed potatoes as your comfort food

The days of listening to the late Morry Mannies. He served as the radio play-by-play announcer for Ball State athletics for 56 years and covered high school sports for many decades. He was a member of the Ball State Athletics Hall of Fame, Delaware County Athletic Hall of Fame, Indiana Basketball Hall of Fame, and more!

Knick-knacks

Polka dots

120 Coca-Cola Vending Machine

Walking to the corner pop machine on the back porch of an old house

Attending the annual "Happy Together Tour" and other Oldies shows

Attending a Leonid and Friends concert – A Russian cover/tribute band that keeps the heyday music alive by touring the U.S. and playing the music of "Chicago" and other bands.

After Returning to my Hometown, I was Surprised to Learn

That day when I made the emotional turn on to Walnut Street, more was at play than just seeing my hometown. The impact of the passing of decades hit hard. I felt old and out of sorts. I expected happy, positive emotions. I may not know exactly all that I missed after leaving my hometown, but I grieved it. If this makes sense.

The childhood home can seem unusually stark, cold, and lonely with the passing of those we love. It will never have the same warmth and glow. One of the most challenging scenarios can occur when you drive by your childhood home, see many people in the window, and feel the emptiness. It is a moment that can cut like a knife. For probably the first time, the house can seem like a mere structure. What truly made it home was the family and love inside it.

The house in the historic district where I resided before age six, was about to be razed when I arrived in Muncie. In its place, a home was built by Habitat for Humanity. It was Habitat's first home built in a local historic district.

When you arrive in Muncie, try-hard, and you may smell the aroma of Pizza King in the air! It will entice you to one of the many Pizza King locations in town. Go for the "Royal Feast" pizza, and the first familiar bite will taste like the last one you had decades ago.

The WLBC towers on the south side of Muncie are now gone. They were a landmark that, especially when lit at night, told returning Muncie folks they were "home." You will see and feel the void.

121 Because sometimes a girl needs a Royal Feast!

WERK-FM at 104.9 is still spinning the hits! To this day, while heading north on I-69 to Muncie, I experience the anticipation of waiting for the WERK reception to kick in on my car radio. Sounding great, WERK!

Burkie's – home of delicious burgers and tenderloin sandwiches, closed. Cannot fathom Muncie without it.

The Heyday of Muncie, Indiana

Emerald Lake – in the Gaston area of Indiana, is no longer there, but I was glad to drive the 15 miles- on the snowy back roads to see where it once stood. I believe a mobile home park now stands in its place and gone are the children's squeals, the curvy slide, and the refreshment stand. It represented the best of summers. Sometimes, I can still smell the Sea & Ski and Tanya Suntan Lotions and hear "Ride, Captain Ride" blasting from the transistor radio.

Muncie Central High School is at 801 North Walnut Street. Many heydayers attended the "old" Muncie Central High School over on South High Street. It does not matter which location you attended, just as long as you are still a Bearcat! Or a Rebel if you attended Southside High School at 1601 East 26th Street. Southside closed on June 13, 2014, and consolidated with Muncie Central High School. Or perhaps you attended Burris School, on the west side of Muncie, home of the "Owls." Muncie had great public and private schools back in the day!

It is essential to understand that just because we travel 2,200+ miles to our hometown, people there are busy and may not drop everything to see us. A friend warned me about this when I left Seattle. It does not mean they do not care. So, respect that life gets hectic. Maybe we will connect by phone, text, or social media. We do what works! Many of these friends are the ones who call, and despite distance and time, we just start talking where we left off years ago.

It is ok to feel a bit sad when we see people from long ago. Not because we do not share a strong bond, but due to the "newness" of re-establishing contact after many years. The friend from yesteryear can now have adult children, grandchildren, and others in their life whom we do not know. Sadly, we see that life carried on for both of us, and we missed some best parts of the lives of one another. On the flip side, with so many new faces, this is an opportunity to meet new people.

If you have been away from your hometown for decades, you may tend to remember things through child-like eyes. When I saw the "big hill" behind my house where I used to sled on Christmas day, it was actually a small incline. Once upon a time, small things from childhood appeared so large.

All of us do not share the same common values and beliefs instilled during the heyday, despite growing up together in the same place. Our individual heyday stories would also be quite different. Isn't this neat?

122 You're in Muncie Central High School country now!

Two years after the historic Muncie Fieldhouse was damaged in a storm, the grand re-opening of the gymnasium occurred in December 2019! The gymnasium initially opened in 1928 and is one of the largest in the country.

I still have a fascination with Ball Jars.

I love Cammack Station! Give me one of those cheeseburgers, please!

Change is good, and it is easy to become emotional – whether the scenery is familiar or not as we remember. You could have tears and not know why. A reason is not required.

We have a powerful bond to our heyday through our senses and our hearts. A sentimental woman can grab a Kleenex and crank up the 1960s tunes, "What Becomes of the Broken Hearted" or "Blue Velvet" and still weep and swoon...her girlfriends will understand. We touch base again with an Oldie we once loved and may repeatedly play it until we are convinced, we never want to hear it again. Well, until next week.

People may say they do not understand driving across the country to the hometown where they remained their entire lives. Or some have no desire to return to their hometown or heyday. So, not everyone will share your passion. A very few may suggest you wear "rose-colored glasses," do not remember things the way they were, or even tell you

The Heyday of Muncie, Indiana

nostalgia is "a disorder." They do not understand that you are not living in the past; you remember it for the positives it brought to your life. If you share with curious people why you made the journey, it may encourage them to embrace their heyday. It also helps them to know you better.

We can see ourselves in every child who runs to get money and then darts for the ice cream truck! These days, the ice cream van covered in stickers does not have the same intrigue. It just cannot compare with our large, white "Mr. Softee" truck or the light green "Mr. Freezer Fresh" that cruised the neighborhoods.

My hometown and I have something significant in common. We are older and showing some wear and tear. It is supposed to be this way.

It gave me goosebumps to lay eyes on my junior high/sophomore sweetheart when he walked through the door after nearly 40 years! Suddenly, I did not have visible eye lines created by the passage of time. I was again, the girl with the smooth complexion who twirled her blonde locks while riding in his car. I looked at him through the same, sweet spirit and familiar baby blue eyes he gazed into a lifetime ago. I could have sworn I heard the Blood Sweat and Tears song, "I Love You More Than You'll Ever Know," playing in the background, and was that fireworks in the sky?

If you recall, in the Preface, Jerry Burger, Ph.D., concluded from his survey that people who make the journey home are not necessarily interested in seeing the people from their past. Instead, they visit the houses, apartments, playgrounds, schools, neighborhoods, parks, and other places that once made up the landscape of their childhood. The vast majority of people who make a trip to see a former home select a place they lived in during their elementary school years (approximately 5 to 12 years old). Although I visited family and friends, it was my quiet, alone time that spoke volumes. My contentment in my hometown occurred most of the time when I was alone in a familiar spot, such as my elementary school, near my former family home, etc. I could not help but wonder what my life would have been like had I stayed. I found myself slightly envious of those who did and built their lives there.

123 Joy Henley, Class of 1972

Joy Charlene Henley

Remembering the Heyday and Incorporating it into Everyday Life

Celebrate old fashioned romance in your marriage, relationship, or dating! Some folks are having another whirl at love, especially after age 50! I know a couple who fell in love at nearly 80 years of age and were married! Give her a single rose, surprise him with his favorite dinner or pie and dance impromptu under the moonlight. Sing to her. What? There is no music? Who needs music?

Do you have a Bucket List of goals you want to achieve, dreams you want to fulfill, and life experiences you hope to live before you grow much older? Want to get your kicks on Route 66? Just do it! Although your Bucket List may consist of significant goals like vacations and extravagances, remember the simple goals can be just as important.

Look up old friends on Social Media. Worried, they may not remember you? Odds are they will have some recollection of you. If, by chance, the person is not the one you seek, people are usually eager to make new friends! While searching for a heyday friend, I may not have found him, but I connected with someone who has the same name!

Purchase a subscription to the Archives of your local newspaper and browse. They are inexpensive, and some publications have one-month subscriptions. You might feel old if you read something about yourself or see a picture that you cannot recall. It happened with a few friends. Since it was 50+ years ago, let's cut ourselves some slack. Some newspapers back then would print the addresses of people in pictures. When children were featured, and captions told the names of the parents and address, it spoke to the trust we had in our communities. Today, if a newspaper showed a picture of children and gave the address where they lived, it would invite danger. Not to mention outrage, parents. Some divorce announcements in the newspaper announced which parent was awarded custody of the children and the amount of child support that was court-ordered.

Today, some states still teach Cursive Writing. However, an education in High-Technology- mainly computers is considered more beneficial by some. The Declaration of Independence and The Constitution of the United States of America are in Cursive. So are grandpa's and great-grandma's letters. Are we possibly being too trendy or progressive? Is it vital to "change with the times" and be innovative? What happens to students who do not learn best by sitting at the computer, who have difficulty focusing, whose wrists hurt, and who do not have strong manual dexterity? The omission of Cursive Writing in school curriculums presents many challenges. Cursive Writing was something important to be mastered back in the day. Know what the children in your life are taught and not taught, and if you have something to say, make your voice heard.

The Heyday of Muncie, Indiana

I used to sit by the picture window and watch the snow glisten below the streetlight. The revolving color wheel turned the aluminum Christmas tree an array of colors. Some stores will try to sell you trees that are dull replicas of the aluminum ones back in the day. Most in today's stores have an off silver or gray tint, so beware. One Christmas, I traveled nearly an hour (one way) from home to purchase a super shiny, tinsel-type tree that catches colors. Why would I want what some scoff at and call a "space-age" tree, many decades later? Because it was my childhood, family Christmas tree in my living room, and this my friend, gives me comfort. Especially since parents who shared that Christmas tree in the living room are no longer with us.

On Christmas Eve, I used to lie in bed and convince myself there had to be a way that Santa was real. The more my friends attempted to instill doubt in my mind, the stronger my belief. I usually have a popsicle or some kind of ice cream in the freezer. I feel ten years old when I see Christmas lights, and I don mittens and run outside when the snow starts to fall. I make delicious meatloaf like my mom. The heyday affects each of us in different ways. Look back at yesterday, and if you compare then with now, you just may find remnants of the heyday in your current routine and daily life. They are there!

Hopefully, we can look back and chuckle at ourselves! Those silly bangs, lip-synching, stuffing Kleenex in bras, holding on to the corner of the wall and dancing to the music (for lack of a partner) in junior high, getting a hickey in the movie balcony and making prank phone calls…we like to think all young people did that. Whew, thank goodness there were no cell phones with cameras or Caller ID!

A high school friend recently laughed and asked me if I remember when we thought local radio DJs were "celebrities." Of course, they were not really superstars, or were they? Well, Larry McCabe and Bill Shirk in their WERK days could be the exception! I had a crush on Lar-on-the-Air, you know!

You could say being a retro person has paid off. If I were to tally up the money and prizes I have won through the years, it would be a bundle! I never imagined such a thing. Years ago, I was a "regular" at Oldies Nights that were hosted by various radio stations. The events happened at upscale venues such as lounges in exquisite hotels. From Oldies Trivia to guessing an Oldies song in three notes, to naming that TV theme from the 1960s upon the stage, I was fierce and played to win. Let's just say I have had my share of Gift Certificates and some lavish dinners in the most luxurious hotels!

Once, a snippet of a song played so quickly that the woman next to me said she did not know how I could name the title when she did not even hear the music! Another night, there was a high stakes contest, and my toughest competitor sat far across the room from me. We knew each other well since we often ended up like this. Usually, we stood in front of people to give our answers. For some reason, we were to write our answers that one time. We heard a few seconds of a song (or was that two music notes?) and had to give the three-syllable name of who recorded it. He stretched his neck to flash a serious look across the room at me. I reciprocated. There was some intense eye contact darting back and forth. I knew he knew...he knew I knew. We sat there, fixated on one another. Each of us that night walked off with prizes!

Then, there was the feature presentation- The Twist Contest, and I had a preferred partner each time I entered. I believe we may have had a reputation! I remember once, my partner rose from his chair, and as we headed toward the dance floor for the contest, a couple snarled and said they were leaving. They dropped out and walked off! The lounge could get pretty loud as my partner, and I twisted down to the floor. My partner gyrated (even on his back) like a squiggly snake, twisting across the floor with Chubby Checker blasting and people cheering on the sidelines. I assure you Chubby never saw anything like this! My partner and I often walked off with $50.00, which was standard. Even split, not bad for about two and a half minutes of dancing! It has been years since I competitively did The Twist in the big leagues. I usually still draw a crowd when I dance the "Mashed Potatoes" though. Hey, I have been doing it since I was 12. I drew a crowd then, too.

The Pogo Stick contest generated much hype! Kudos to those who could jump and stay on it so long! After a guy friend won the competition and a very generous all-expense-paid trip for two to Sun Valley, I regretted not entering. It was one of the few contests that got away.

So, I made it back to my land of enchantment! It was a well-planned journey, and some of it went nothing as anticipated. Am I surprised? Not really. First, because I know God is in charge and second because I have learned life often requires going with the flow. To think, I planned to only stay in Muncie from Aug. 2009 until spring 2010! Here I am, a decade later, still in my beloved Indiana! I often think of my friend Ruthie's prediction before Justin and I departed on our cross-country road trip, that God would not have us go on this journey without having something wonderful waiting on the other end. After we arrived in Muncie, Justin never imagined the love of his life was living a day trip away. He left Seattle a bachelor and soon became engaged!

The Heyday of Muncie, Indiana

My story is not all-inconclusive. It is simply designed to pique your curiosity and encourage you to further explore the heyday. I hope you share your experiences with others and introduce your loved ones to a time that helped make you… you! The music greats are more than a list of names. Listening to their music may take you back or introduce you to new talent! If you are too young to have lived in the 1960s and my story has sent you to the brink of culture shock…hold on while I tell the rest. It is possible your grandpa rode a motorcycle, bent the rules, and was known as a bad boy! While grandma may have had super long eyelashes, danced in a cage, and was a shameless flirt!

As for this grandma, I am a retro girl for life! I keep the heyday alive as others do every day. I promote my hometown in prospect for companies, new jobs, and families. I hope you visit it. These days, I hope Muncie shines a bit brighter on the map. Heck, I hope it *lights up* the map!

If you see me on I-69 heading toward Muncie, be sure to nod, wave, or if we happen to be tuned in to the same radio station, sing along with me at the stoplight! You will recognize me by the Oldies license frame on my car!

At sunset and with summer winding down, I recently went to my elementary school building to sit on the playground and embrace the child in me. I always knew no matter where I ventured in life, I would one day sit in this spot again. It is the closest feeling I can achieve to traveling in a time machine. On this day, as I turned to leave, a Pixy Stix was not on the ground as during a previous visit. A large brown leaf magically appeared in front of my parked car. I looked up to see trees. There were none. I searched for other leaves that had fallen on or near trucks and cars. Again, there were none. Well, wasn't I special for Mother Nature to give me the only leaf that landed out of nowhere? I glanced at the giggling group that sped by on bikes. Yesterday, that was me. I thought, *ah to be that young again*, as I glanced at a couple of small, budding age spots on my arm. The rambunctious children did not know they were making memories; they just thought they were having fun. A boy waved and whizzed by as he made an exaggerated silly face. I smiled. Yes, indeed, it was a great heyday! My Magic 8 Ball tells me another is on the way.

All WERK pictures courtesy of Larry McCabe. All content pertaining to WERK-AM 990 refers only to WERK AM Radio, operated by Robert Poorman, his Management and employees at that time.

Picture Credits

Index	Picture	Credit	Page
1	White River	Joy Charlene Henley	xi
2	Des Moines Marina	Joy Charlene Henley	5
3	Montana	Joy Charlene Henley	8
4	Mount Rushmore	Joy Charlene Henley	9
5	Native American Heritage	Joy Charlene Henley	11
6	Mississippi Rapids	Joy Charlene Henley	12
7	Indiana	Joy Charlene Henley	12
8	Sister Belle	Joy Charlene Henley	15
9	The Rivoli Theatre	John Disher	19
10	Joy holding Dennis the Menace Doll at Fence	Relative of Author	21
11	Justin's feet at the top of Willis Tower	Justin Willhight	22
12	Indiana Sunset	Joy Charlene Henley	23
13	Wrapped Christmas Presents	Public Domain	24
14	Jacks	Public Domain	26
15	Marbles	Public Domain	26
16	Slinky	Public Domain	26
17	A Kid's Favorite Ride	Public Domain	27
18	Wagon	Public Domain	27
19	Lego Building Set	Public Domain	28
20	Little Golden Books	Joy Charlene Henley	30
21	Boys will be boys!	Brad Holt- 2.0 Generic 60 Guns	37
22	Viewmaster Slides	Public Domain	40
23	Icicles	Public Domain	41
24	Alphabet Blocks	Public Domain	42
25	Bird Drawing	Public Domain	43
26	Ballerina	Skitterphoto from Pexels CC0 License	46
27	Greyhound Bus	Public Domain	48
28	Ice Tray	Public Domain	49
29	Exercise Belt	Public Domain	50
30	Thermos Bottles	Public Domain	53

Index	Picture	Credit	Page
31	Tube Testing Machine	Public Domain	54
32	Television	Public Domain	54
33	Clock	Public Domain	55
34	Amusement Park Ride	Public Domain	56
35	Bel Air	Public Domain	57
36	Chevrolet Impala	Public Domain	59
37	Anthony Elementary School	Joy Charlene Henley	60
38	Boy and Girl singing	Public Domain	64
39	Pencils	Public Domain	67
40	Sister Belle hangin' out	Joy Charlene Henley	69
41	Basketball going in the hoop	Public Domain	74
42	Baby in the back window of a car	Public Domain	84
43	Woodbury Cold Cream	Public Domain	89
44	Hairstyles	Public Domain	91
45	Hair Curlers	Public Domain	91
46	Brylcreem	Public Domain	93
47	Record Player	Photo By Andrea Turner from Pexels	96
48	Girl typing in Hot Pants and Go-Go Boots	Public Domain	97
49	The Archies 45 Record	Public Domain	99
50	The Beatles	Public Domain	100
51	Bob Dylan and Joan Baez	Public Domain	101
52	Elvis Jukebox	Public Domain	103
53	Jefferson Airplane record	Public Domain	106
54	Johnny Mathis	Public Domain	106
55	45 Record Adaptor	Public Domain	109
56	Peace Sign	Public Domain	110
57	Jukebox	Sam Howzit CCBY2.0	114
58	VW Vans	Public Domain	119
59	Midi Dress in Go-Go Boots	Public Domain	120
60	Tie-Dye Shirt	Public Domain	121
61	Go-Go Dancer in Cage	Public Domain	125
62	Larry Carmichael	Larry Carmichael	126

Index	Picture	Credit	Page
63	Rod McClure	Rod McClure	128
64	Randy Henzlik	Nancy Henzlik	130
65	Wayne Cochran and Larry McCabe	Larry McCabe	133
66	Kade Puckett	Lee Terrell and Timberly Ferree	137
67	Cynda Williams and Roger Overbey	Roger Overbey	138
68	Roger Overbey, Jack, and Ozzy Osbourne	Roger Overbey	139
69	Dr. Gregory H. Williams and Roger Overbey	Roger Overbey	139
70	Erik Estrada and Roger Overbey	Roger Overbey	140
71	Kim Ousley	Kim Ousley	141
72	Kim Ousley	Kim Ousley	142
73	Agnes Moorehead as "Endora"	Public Domain	154
74	Marilyn Monroe	Public Domain	157
75	President John F. Kennedy and First Lady Jacqueline Kennedy	This work is in the public domain in the United States because it is a work prepared by an officer or employee of the United States Government as part of that person's official duties under the terms of Title 17, Chapter 1, Section 105 of the United States Code. Author: Cecil (Cecil William) Stoughton, 1920-2008, Photographer (NARA Record: 4538278)	161
76	The Kennedy Children, Caroline and "John- John," play in the White House	"Hypeskin_Kennedycollection-046" By Urcameras Is Licensed Under CC PDM 1.0	162
77	Mercury Space Capsule	Public Domain	162
78	Moon Landing	Public Domain	164
79	Ron Bonham	Roger Overbey	168
80	Kathy Garver	Kathy Garver	173
81	A & W	Public Domain	175
82	Ball State University Entrance	Joy Charlene Henley	176
83	Freezer-Fresh Ice Cream Truck	Tony's Freezer Fresh	179
84	Masonic Temple	Public Domain	181
85	Fire Station #1	Public Domain	182
86	Muncie Public Library	Public Domain	183
87	Muncie YWCA	Public Domain	186
88	Le Anne Richardson Parsons	Le Anne Richardson Parsons	187
89	Jack Dudley	Norval Jack Dudley	189
90	Microphone	Public Domain	192

Joy Charlene Henley

Index	Picture	Credit	Page
91	Larry McCabe	Larry McCabe	194
92	WERK Sheet	Larry McCabe	197
93	Larry McCabe	Larry McCabe	200
94	James Brown and Larry McCabe	Larry McCabe	202
95	Dick Clark and Larry McCabe	Larry McCabe	203
96	WERK DJs and Union 76 Girls Gather Around Shirk's Jaguar	Larry McCabe	205
97	Betty Harris in Newspaper Office	Courtesy of Margaret Scott	208
98	Betty Harris	Courtesy of Margaret Scott	212
99	Olive Loaf	Public Domain	215
100	Sandra Minnick Holding Book	Sandra Minnick	219
101	Donna Hunt with Two Recipe/Cookbooks	Donna Carol Hunt	220
102	Clip-Art Dog Bone with a Bow	Public Domain	225
103	Children Smoking Candy Cigarettes	Public Domain	231
104	Wooden Coca-Cola Crate	Public Domain	234
105	Appeal to the Great Spirit	Joy Charlene Henley	236
106	Appeal to the Great Spirit	Joy Charlene Henley	236
107	Cammack Station	Joy Charlene Henley	237
108	James Dean Grave	Joy Charlene Henley	240
109	Muncie At Night	Joy Charlene Henley	244
110	Fallen Heroes Memorial Bridge	Joy Charlene Henley	245
111	Dave's Alley	Joy Charlene Henley	248
112	Dave's Alley	Joy Charlene Henley	248
113	Cookies on Tray	Public Domain	254
114	Swing from a tree	Public Domain	255
115	Berdine's Five and Dime	Berdine's Five and Dime	259
116	Sine's Five & 10	Sine's Five & 10	260
117	Wall Drug	Wall Drug	261
118	Window Shopping	Public Domain	266
119	Muncie Telephone Directory	Joy Charlene Henley	267
120	Coca-Cola Vending Machine	Public Domain	269
121	Royal Feast Pizza	Rod McClure	270
122	Bearcat Way Sign	Joy Charlene Henley	272
123	Joy Henley Class of 1972	High School Portrait	273

Made in the USA
Middletown, DE
21 June 2023

33093037R00166